L-1 INTRACOMPANY TRANSFEREE VISA APPLICATION

Attorney Brian D. Lerner

Law Offices of Brian D. Lerner, A Professional Corporation

Attorney Brian D. Lerner

L-1 Intracompany Transferee Visa Application

L-1 Intracompany Transferee Visa Application

Written by Attorney Brian D. Lerner

Print ISBN: 978-1-948774-92-5
Ebook ISBN: 978-1-948774-91-8

INTRODUCTION

There are a multitude of different immigration petitions and applications. They are complex and full of requirements. Obviously it would be best to hire and immigration attorney to best prepare the petitions and application. However, this can certainly cost thousands of dollars.

The next best option is to get a sample of the petition written by an experienced immigration attorney. The samples cost a fraction what would be charged by an immigration attorney. However, while the reader has to alter, amend and change the parts of the sample petition to reflect their actual situation, it is a fantastic roadmap for them to use. If the reader has purchased the entire petition or application, they will have real live samples of cover letters, forms, declarations, affidavits and the necessary exhibits to use. The samples come from real cases and the names of those clients have been redacted to protect the privacy of that person or corporation.

These are petitions and applications that have been drafted by an experienced immigration attorney with over 25 years of experience. Get the benefits of that experience without the costs.

About the Law Offices of Brian D. Lerner

Brian D. Lerner has been a licensed attorney since 1992 and started the Law Offices of Brian D. Lerner, APC. The law practice consists of Immigration and Nationality Law and everything involved with and regarding immigration which includes citizenship, investment visas, family and employment visas, removal and deportation hearings, appeals, waivers, adjustment, consulate processing and all types of immigration and citizenship matters. Thousands of families have been reunited and/or permitted to stay in the U.S. and/or return to the U.S. because of the successful work of Immigration Attorney Brian D. Lerner.

This law offices handles all types of immigration cases including family based and employment based. Immigration issues range from immigration court proceedings to trying to fix what paralegals may have done that was neither correct nor proper. Foreign nationals must have experience lawyers admitted to practice law.

The Law Offices of Brian D. Lerner, APC, handles cases arising from business visas, work permits, Green Cards, non-immigrant visas, deportation, citizenship, appeals and all areas of immigration. The Law Offices of Brian D. Lerner, APC does EB-5 Investor Visas, H-1B Specialty Occupation, L-1 Intracompany Transferee, E-2 Treaty Investor, E-1 Treaty Trader, O-1 Extraordinary Ability among others. Regarding immigrant visas for the Green Card, the firm does PERM and advanced degree PERM, Family Petitions, and Extraordinary Alien Petitions. In addition to affirmative petitions, the Law Firm represents people in deportation and removal hearings, including political asylum, withholding of removal, and convention against torture cases.

Brian D. Lerner has been certified as an expert in Immigration & Nationality Law by the California State Bar, Board of Legal Specialization sicne 2000 and has been re-certified three times. He now passes on his decades of experience by allowing the Reader, Law Schools, Professors and other Immigration Attorneys to purchase sample petitions on every facet of Immigration Law.

TABLE OF CONTENTS

About the L-1 Application

Are you an entrepreneur that has your own business in your home country? Want to come to the United States to start a branch office of your current business? Alternatively, do you want to buy a new business and keep your current business in your home country running? Don't have the $1,000,000 required for the EB-5? Don't come from an E-2 country? Don't worry! The L-1 Intracompany Transferee Visa will require only about $25,000 investment and you can come to the U.S. to pursue your dreams. This sample L-1 Intracompany Transferee Visa Petition gives you everything you need to get the best chance of approval. It includes all relevant exhibits, forms, cover letter, business plan and supporting evidence. It has been prepared by an expert Immigration Attorney. Thus, this book will allow you to see a guide of how it is done, prepared and submitted.

SECTION 1
Attorney Cover Letter

Law Offices of Brian D. Lerner
A PROFESSIONAL CORPORATION
CERTIFIED SPECIALIST IN IMMIGRATION AND NATIONALITY LAW
ADMITTED TO THE U.S. SUPREME COURT
LONG BEACH, CALIFORNIA (562) 495-0554
CARSON, CALIFORNIA (310) 684-5420

December 8, 2017

U.S. Citizenship and Immigration Services
California Service Center
Attn: I-129 (L-1)
24000 Avila Road, 2nd Floor, Room 2312
Laguna Niguel, CA 92677

Re: Petition: I-129, Petition for Nonimmigrant Worker (L-1A)
Petitioner: Consorcio Integrador Sonora 80M US, LLC
Beneficiary: [redacted]

Dear Officer:

Consorcio Integrador Sonora 80M US, LLC, a solar farms development and consulting company located in Los Angels, California, through undersigned counsel, hereby seeks to classify Mr. [redacted] as an intra-company transferee pursuant to section 101(a)(15)(L) of the Immigration and Nationality Act (hereinafter "INA" or "Act").

We enclose the following forms and fees with this petition:

- G-28, Notice of Entry of Appearance as Attorney or Accredited Representative;
- I-129, Petition for Nonimmigrant Worker, and $460 Filing Fee and $500 Fraud Prevention and Detection Fee;
- L Classification Supplement to Form I-129; and
- I-907, Request for Premium Processing Service, and $1,225 Filing Fee.

We submit copies of the following exhibits with this petition:

TABLE OF EXHIBITS

Exhibits:	**Description:**
1	Supporting Letter from Foreign Company;
	About Foreign Company
2	Record of Registration;
3	Articles of Incorporation/By-Laws;
4	Tax Identification Card;
5	Certificate of Tax Status;
6	Federal Taxpayer Registry;

8	Amended and Restated Shares Purchase Agreement;
9	Organizational Chart;
10	Photographs;

About Petitioner/U.S. Company

11	Articles of Organization;
12	Operating Agreement;
13	Membership Certificate;
14	Lease/Membership Agreement;
15	Photographs;
16	Proposed Organizational Chart;
17	Business Plan;

About Beneficiary

18	Passport (Spain);
19	I-94 and Travel History;
20	Permanent Resident Card (Mexico); and
21	Resume/Curriculum Vitae.

I.
INTRODUCTION.

Section 101(a)(15)(L) of the Act defines a nonimmigrant intra-company transferee is as:

> An alien who, within 3 years preceding the time of his application for admission into the United States, has been employed continuously for one year by a firm or corporation or other legal entity or an affiliate or subsidiary thereof and who seeks to enter the United States temporarily in order to continue to render his services to the same employer or a subsidiary or affiliate thereof in a capacity that is managerial, executive, or involves specialized knowledge, and the alien spouse and minor children of any such alien if accompanying him or following to join him.

See also 8 C.F.R. § 214.2(l).

II.
CONSORCIO INTEGRADOR SONORA 80M US, LLC AND CONSORCIO INTEGRADOR SONORA 80M S.A. DE C.V. ARE QUALIFYING ORGANIZATIONS.

Pursuant to 8 C.F.R. § 214.2(l)(3)(i), an individual petition filed on Form I-129 shall be accompanied by:

> Evidence that the petitioner and the organization which employed or will employ the alien are qualifying organizations as defined in paragraph (l)(1)(ii)(G) of this section.

Pursuant to section 214.2(l)(1)(ii)(G), the term "qualifying organization" means a United States or

(1) Meets exactly one of the qualifying relationships specified in the definitions of a parent, branch, affiliate or subsidiary specified in paragraph (l)(1)(ii) of this section;

(2) Is or will be doing business (engaging in international trade is not required) as an employer in the United States and in at least one other country directly or through a parent, branch, affiliate, or subsidiary for the duration of the alien's stay in the United States as an intracompany transferee; and

(3) Otherwise meets the requirements of section 101(a)(15)(L) of the Act."

Pursuant to 8 C.F.R. § 214.2(l)(1)(ii)(K), the term "subsidiary" includes:

> a firm, corporation, or other legal entity of which a parent owns, directly or indirectly, more than half of the entity and controls the entity; or owns, directly or indirectly, half of the entity and controls the entity; or owns, directly or indirectly, 50 percent of a 50-50 joint venture and has equal control and veto power over the entity; or owns, directly or indirectly, less than half of the entity, but in fact controls the entity.

In the present case, Consorcio Integrador Sonora 80M US, LLC is owned in whole by Consorcio Integrador Sonora 80M S.A. de C.V. As such, Consorcio Integrador Sonora 80M US, LLC is a subsidiary of Consorcio Integrador Sonora 80M S.A. de C.V. Please see **Exhibits 1, 11-13 and 17.**

III.
MR. [redacted] WILL BE EMPLOYED IN AN EXECUTIVE CAPACITY IN THE UNITED STATES.

Pursuant to 8 C.F.R. § 214.2(l)(3)(ii), an individual petition filed on Form I - 129 shall be accompanied by:

> Evidence that the alien will be employed in an executive, managerial, or specialized knowledge capacity, including a detailed description of the services to be performed."

Pursuant to 8 C.F.R. § 214.2(l)(1)(ii)(C), the term "executive capacity" means an assignment within an organization in which the employee primarily:

(1) Directs the management of the organization or a major component or function of the organization;

(2) Establishes the goals and policies of the organization, component, or function;

(3) Exercises wide latitude in discretionary decision-making; and

executives, the board of directors, or stockholders of the organization.

As the Chief Executive Officer (hereinafter "CEO") of Consorcio Integrador Sonora 80M US, LLC, Mr. [redacted] will be responsible for the overall structure and operation of the company. He will hold the top executive position in the company and therefore, will have complete control and responsibility for both long-term strategy and day-to-day operations of the business. Mr. [redacted] has been extremely valuable to Consorcio Integrador Sonora 80M S.A. de C.V. and is needed for Consorcio Integrador Sonora 80M US, LLC to have success in the United States. Without him, there is little chance of that happening. Please see **Exhibit 1;** *Matter of* ____, EAC 99 120 52239 (AAU Jan. 22, 2002); *Matter of* ____, EAC 98 090 54650 (AAU Feb. 26, 1999); *Matter of* ____, EAC 97 214 52947 (AAU Sept. 23, 1998).

IV.
MR. [redacted] HAS AT LEAST ONE CONTINUOUS YEAR OF FULL-TIME EMPLOYMENT WITH CONSORCIO INTEGRADOR SONORA 80M S.A. DE C.V. IN MEXICO IN A POSITION THAT IS EXECUTIVE IN NATURE.

Pursuant to 8 C.F.R. § 214.2(l)(3)(iii), an individual petition filed on Form I-129 shall be accompanied by:

> Evidence that the alien has at least one continuous year of full-time employment abroad with a qualifying organization within the three years preceding the filing of the petition.

In addition, pursuant to 8 C.F.R. § 214.2(l)(3)(iv), an individual petition filed on Form I-129 shall be accompanied by:

> Evidence that the alien's prior year of employment abroad was in a position that was managerial, executive, or involved specialized knowledge and that the alien's prior education, training, and employment qualifies him/her to perform the intended services in the United States; however, the work in the United States need not be the same work which the alien performed abroad.

In the present case, Mr. [redacted] has been the CEO of Consorcio Integrador Sonora 80M S.A. de C.V. in Mexico since May 2012. He has demonstrated his abilities at Consorcio Integrador Sonora 80M S.A. de C.V. as shown by its growth and success. Please see **Exhibits 1-10, 17 and 21.**

V.
CONSORCIO INTEGRADOR SONORA 80M US, LLC IS A NEW OFFICE.

Pursuant to 8 C.F.R. § 214.2(l)(3)(v), when a beneficiary is coming to the United States as a manager or executive to open or to be employed in a new office in the United States, the petitioner shall submit evidence that:

> (A) Sufficient physical premises to house the new office have been secured;

> the three year period preceding the filing of the petition in an executive or managerial capacity and that the proposed employment involved executive or managerial authority over the new operation; and
>
> (C) The intended United States operation, within one year of the approval of the petition, will support an executive or managerial position as defined in paragraphs (l)(1)(ii)(B) or (C) of this section, supported by information regarding:
>
> (1) The proposed nature of the office describing the scope of the entity, its organizational structure, and its financial goals;
>
> (2) The size of the United States investment and the financial ability of the foreign entity to remunerate the beneficiary and to commence doing business in the United States; and
>
> (3) The organizational structure of the foreign entity.

Pursuant to 8 C.F.R. § 214.2(l)(1)(ii)(F), the term "new office" means:

> An organization which has been doing business in the United States through a parent, branch, affiliate, or subsidiary for less than one year.

In the present case, Consorcio Integrador Sonora 80M US, LLC is a solar farms development and consulting company located in Santa Monica, California. Consorcio Integrador Sonora 80M US, LLC, was recently incorporated in the State of California to carry out this function under the direction of its parent company, Consorcio Integrador Sonora 80M S.A. de C.V., which has been doing business in Mexico with Mr. ████████ as its CEO since May 2012. With its success abroad, Consorcio Integrador Sonora 80M S.A. de C.V. has now decided to commence operations in the U.S. market by establishing Consorcio Integrador Sonora 80M US, LLC.

In addition to the supporting letter from Consorcio Integrador Sonora 80M S.A. de C.V, enclosed, among other things, please find documents for both companies, showing among other things, the organizational structures, financial statements to demonstrate the financial capability of Consorcio Integrador Sonora 80M S.A. de C.V to support and establish Consorcio Integrador Sonora 80M US, LLC, in the United States, and a copy of Consorcio Integrador Sonora 80M US, LLC's lease agreement, photographs and business plan. Please see **Exhibits 1-17.**

VI.

THE SERVICES OF MR. ████████ WILL BE USED FOR A TEMPORARY PERIOD AND HE WILL BE TRANSFERRED ABROAD UPON COMPLETION OF HIS TEMPORARY SERVICES IN THE UNITED STATES.

Pursuant to 8 C.F.R. § 214.2(l)(3)(vii), if the beneficiary is an owner or major stockholder of the company, the petition must be accompanied by evidence that:

> "the beneficiary's services are to be used for a temporary period and evidence that the beneficiary will be transferred to an assignment

States."

In the present case, the services of Mr. [redacted] will be used for a temporary period. Once the operations of Consorcio Integrador Sonora 80M US, LLC are fully established in the United States and the company has proven successful in the U.S. market, it is planned to have Mr. [redacted] return to Consorcio Integrador Sonora 80M S.A. de C.V in Mexico. Please see **Exhibit 1.**

VII.
WHETHER AN L-1 APPLICANT IS COMING TO THE U.S. FOR A TEMPORARY PERIOD OF TIME IS NO LONGAR AN ISSUE WITH CONCERN TO USCIS OR DOS.

Pursuant to section 214(h) of the Act, an L-1 applicant's separate application for permanent residency shall not constitute evidence of intention to abandon foreign residence:

> The fact that an alien is the beneficiary of an application for a preference status filed under section 1154 of this title or has otherwise sought permanent residence in the United States shall not constitute evidence of an intention to abandon a foreign residence for purposes of obtaining a visa as a nonimmigrant described in subparagraph (H)(i)(b) or (c), (L), or (V) of section 1101(a)(15) of this title.

Prior section 214(h) of the Act and the amendments to section 214(b) of the Act, temporariness was a substantial concern in L-1 adjudications. Now, section 214(h) eliminates the issue of whether an L-1 applicant is actually being transferred on a temporary basis. Additionally, the Foreign Affairs Manual specifically prescribes that when evaluating an L-1 visa applicant's eligibility, consulates "shall not focus on the issue of temporariness of stay or immigrant intent." 9 FAM 41.54 N4 *Issue of Temporariness of Stay*.

VIII.
CONCLUSION

Based upon the foregoing, we respectfully request that USCIS approve the instant petition. If you should have any questions, please feel free to contact our office at (562) 495-0554.

Sincerely,

Christopher A. Reed
Attorney at Law

SECTION 2
Forms

Notice of Entry of Appearance as Attorney or Accredited Representative

Department of Homeland Security

DHS
Form G-28
OMB No. 1615-0105
Expires 03/31/2018

Part 1. Information About Attorney or Accredited Representative

1. USCIS ELIS Account Number (*if any*) ►

Name and Address of Attorney or Accredited Representative

2.a. Family Name (*Last Name*): Reed
2.b. Given Name (*First Name*): Christopher
2.c. Middle Name: Allan
3.a. Street Number and Name: 3233 E Broadway
3.b. Apt. ☐ Ste. ☐ Flr. ☐
3.c. City or Town: Long Beach
3.d. State: CA 3.e. ZIP Code: 90803
3.f. Province:
3.g. Postal Code:
3.h. Country: USA
4. Daytime Telephone Number: 5624950554
5. Fax Number: 5626088672
6. E-Mail Address (*if any*): creed@eimmigration.org
7. Mobile Telephone Number (*if any*):

Part 2. Notice of Appearance as Attorney or Accredited Representative

This appearance relates to immigration matters before (*Select only one box*):

1.a. [X] USCIS
1.b. List the form numbers: I-129 / I-129L
2.a. ☐ ICE
2.b. List the specific matter in which appearance is entered:
3.a. ☐ CBP
3.b. List the specific matter in which appearance is entered:

I enter my appearance as attorney or accredited representative at the request of:

4. Select **only one** box:
☐ Applicant [X] Petitioner ☐ Requestor
☐ Respondent (ICE, CBP)

Information About Applicant, Petitioner, Requestor, or Respondent

5.a. Family Name (*Last Name*):
5.b. Given Name (*First Name*):
5.c. Middle Name:
6. Name of Company or Organization (*if applicable*): See Part 6

Part 2. Notice of Appearance as Attorney or Accredited Representative *(continued)*

Information About Applicant, Petitioner, Requestor, or Respondent (continued)

7. USCIS ELIS Account Number *(if any)*

▶

8. Alien Registration Number (A-Number) or Receipt Number

9. Daytime Telephone Number

4242388249

10. Mobile Telephone Number *(if any)*

11. E-Mail Address *(if any)*

info@sonora80m.com

Mailing Address of Applicant, Petitioner, Requestor, or Respondent

NOTE: Provide the mailing address of the applicant, petitioner, requestor, or respondent. Do **not** provide the business mailing address of the attorney or accredited representative **unless** it serves as the safe mailing address on the application, petition, or request being filed with this Form G-28.

12.a. Street Number and Name: 520 Broadway

12.b. Apt. ☐ Ste. ☐ Flr. ☐

12.c. City or Town: Santa Monica

12.d. State: CA 12.e. ZIP Code: 90401

12.f. Province

12.g. Postal Code

12.h. Country

USA

Part 3. Eligibility Information for Attorney or Accredited Representative

Select **all** applicable items.

1.a. ☒ I am an attorney eligible to practice law in, and a member in good standing of, the bar of the highest courts of the following states, possessions, territories, commonwealths, or the District of Columbia. *(If you need additional space, use Part 6.)*

Licensing Authority

California Supreme Court

1.b. Bar Number *(if applicable)*

235438

1.c. Name of Law Firm

Law Offices of Brian D. Lerner

1.d. I *(choose one)* ☒ ***am not*** ☐ ***am***

subject to any order of any court or administrative agency disbarring, suspending, enjoining, restraining, or otherwise restricting me in the practice of law. If you are subject to any orders, explain in the space below. *(If you need additional space, use Part 6.)*

2.a. ☐ I am an accredited representative of the following qualified nonprofit religious, charitable, social service, or similar organization established in the United States, so recognized by the Department of Justice, Board of Immigration Appeals, in accordance with 8 CFR 292.2. Provide the name of the organization and the expiration date of accreditation.

2.b. Name of Recognized Organization

2.c. Date accreditation expires

(mm/dd/yyyy) ▶

Part 3. Eligibility Information for Attorney or Accredited Representative *(continued)*

3. [ ] I am associated with

[ ]

the attorney or accredited representative of record who previously filed Form G-28 in this case, and my appearance as an attorney or accredited representative is at his or her request.

NOTE: If you select this item, also complete Item Numbers 1.a. - 1.b. or Item Numbers 2.a. - 2.c. in Part 3. *(whichever is appropriate).*

4.a. [ ] I am a law student or law graduate working under the direct supervision of the attorney or accredited representative of record on this form in accordance with the requirements in 8 CFR 292.1(a)(2)(iv).

4.b. Name of Law Student or Law Graduate

[ ]

Part 4. Applicant, Petitioner, Requestor, or Respondent Consent to Representation, Contact Information, and Signature

Consent to Representation and Release of Information

1. I have requested the representation of and consented to being represented by the attorney or accredited representative named in **Part 1.** of this form. According to the Privacy Act of 1974 and DHS policy, I also consent to the disclosure to the named attorney or accredited representative of any record pertaining to me that appears in any system of records of USCIS, ICE or CBP.

When you (the applicant, petitioner, requestor, or respondent) are represented, DHS will send notices to both you and your attorney or accredited representative either through mail or electronic delivery.

DHS will also send the Form I-94, Arrival Departure Record, to you **unless** you select **Item Number 2.a.** in **Part 4.** All secure identity documents and Travel Documents will be sent to you (the applicant, petitioner, requestor, or respondent) at your U.S. mailing address **unless** you ask us to send your secure identity documents to your attorney of record or accredited representative.

If you do not want to receive original notices or secure identity documents directly, but would rather have such notices and documents sent to your attorney of record or accredited representative, please select **all applicable** boxes below:

2.a. [X] I request DHS send any notice (including Form I-94) on an application, petition, or request to the U.S. business address of my attorney of record or accredited representative as listed in this form. I understand that I may change this election at any future date through written notice to DHS.

2.b. [ ] I request that DHS send any secure identity document, such as a Permanent Resident Card, Employment Authorization Document, or Travel Document, that I am approved to receive and authorized to possess, to the U.S. business address of my attorney of record or accredited representative as listed in this form or to a designated military or diplomatic address for pickup in a foreign country (if permitted). I consent to having my secure identity document sent to my attorney of record or accredited representative's U.S. business address and understand that I may request, at any future date and through written notice to DHS, that DHS send any secure identity document to me directly.

3.a. Signature of Applicant, Petitioner, Requestor, or Respondent

➡ [x (signature)]

3.b. Date of Signature *(mm/dd/yyyy)* ► 12/04/2017

Part 5. Signature of Attorney or Accredited Representative

I have read and understand the regulations and conditions contained in 8 CFR 103.2 and 292 governing appearances and representation before the Department of Homeland Security. I declare under penalty of perjury under the laws of the United States that the information I have provided on this form is true and correct.

1. Signature of Attorney or Accredited Representative

[(signature)]

2. Signature of Law Student or Law Graduate

[ ]

3. Date of Signature *(mm/dd/yyyy)* ► 12/8/17

Part 6. Additional Information

Use the space provided below to provide additional information pertaining to **Part 3., Item Numbers 1.a. - 1.d.** or to provide your U.S. business address for purposes of receiving secure identity documents for your client (if your client has consented to your receipt of such documents under **Part 4.**)

Part 2, Number 6: Consorcio Integrador Sonora 80M US LLC

Petition for a Nonimmigrant Worker

Department of Homeland Security
U.S. Citizenship and Immigration Services

USCIS
Form I-129
OMB No. 1615-0009
Expires 12/31/2018

For USCIS Use Only	Receipt	Partial Approval (explain)	Action Block

Class:
No. of Workers:
Job Code:
Validity Dates:
From:
To:

☐ **Classification Approved**
☐ Consulate/POE/PFI Notified
At:
☐ Extension Granted
☐ COS/Extension Granted

▶ **START HERE - Type or print in black ink.**

Part 1. Petitioner Information

If you are an individual filing this petition, complete **Item Number 1.** **If you are a company or an organization filing this petition,** complete **Item Number 2.**

1. **Legal Name of Individual Petitioner**

Family Name (Last Name) | Given Name (First Name) | Middle Name

2. **Company or Organization Name**

Consorcio Integrador Sonora 80M US, LLC

3. **Mailing Address of Individual, Company or Organization**

In Care Of Name

Street Number and Name: 520 Broadway
Apt. Ste. Flr. Number: ☐ ☐ ☐

City or Town: Santa Monica
State: CA
ZIP Code: 90401

Province | Postal Code | Country: USA

4. **Contact Information**

Daytime Telephone Number | Mobile Telephone Number | Email Address (if any)

5. **Other Information**

Federal Employer Identification Number (FEIN) ▶
Individual IRS Tax Number ▶
U.S. Social Security Number (if any) ▶

Part 2. Information About This Petition (See instructions for fee information)

1. **Requested Nonimmigrant Classification** (Write classification symbol): L-1A

2. **Basis for Classification** (select **only one** box):
   - [X] a. New employment.
   - [ ] b. Continuation of previously approved employment without change with the same employer.
   - [ ] c. Change in previously approved employment.
   - [ ] d. New concurrent employment.
   - [ ] e. Change of employer.
   - [ ] f. Amended petition.

3. **Provide the most recent petition/application receipt number for the beneficiary. If none exists, indicate "None."** ▶

4. **Requested Action** (select **only one** box):
   - [X] a. Notify the office in **Part 4.** so each beneficiary can obtain a visa or be admitted. (**NOTE:** A petition is **not** required for E-1, E-2, E-3, H-1B1 Chile/Singapore, or TN visa beneficiaries.)
   - [ ] b. Change the status and extend the stay of each beneficiary because the beneficiary(ies) is/are now in the United States in another status (see instructions for limita tions). This is a va ila blanly when you check "New Employment" in **Item Number 2.**, above.
   - [ ] c. Extend the sta yof ea chbeneficiary because the beneficiary(ies) now hold(s) this status.
   - [ ] d. Amend the stay of each beneficiary because the beneficiary(ies) now hold(s) this status.
   - [ ] e. Extend the status of a nonimmigrant classification based on a free trade agreement. (See Trade Agreement Supplement to Form I-129 for TN and H-1B1.)
   - [ ] f. Change status to a nonimmigrant classification based on a free trade agreement. (See Trade Agreement Supplement to Form I-129 for TN and H-1B1.)

5. **Total number of workers included in this petition.** (See instructions relating to when more than one worker can be included.) ▶ 1

Part 3. Beneficiary Information (Information about the beneficiary/beneficiaries you are filing for. Complete the blocks below. Use the Attachment-1 sheet to name each beneficiary included in this petition.)

1. **If an Entertainment Group, Provide the Group Name**

2. **Provide Name of Beneficiary**

Fa milyName (Last Name)	Given Name (First Name)	Middle Name

3. **Provide all other names the beneficiary has used. Inclu**[redacted] **knames, aliases, maiden name, and names from all previous marriages.**

Family Name (Last Name)	Given Name (Fir stName)	Middle Name

4. **Other Information**

Date of birth (mm/dd/yyyy) 03/31/1976

Gender [X] Male [ ] Female

U.S. Social Security Number (if any) ▶

Part 3. Beneficiary Information (Information about the beneficiary/beneficiaries you are filing for. Complete the blocks below. Use the Attachment-1 sheet to name each beneficiary included in this petition.) (continued)

Alien Registration Number (A-Number) ► A-

Country of Birth: Spain

Province of Birth:

Country of Citizenship or Nationality:

[redacted] is in the United States, complete the following:

Date of Last Arrival (mm/dd/yyyy): 12/07/2017

I-94 Arrival-Departure Record Number ►

Passport or Travel Document Number:

Date Passport or Travel Document Issued (mm/dd/yyyy):

Date Passport or Travel Document Expires (mm/dd/yyyy): 08/18/2018

Passport or Travel Document Country of Issuance:

Current Nonimmigrant Status: B-2

Date Status Expires or D/S (mm/dd/yyyy): 02/20/2018

Student and Exchange Visitor Information System (SEVIS) Number (if any):

Employment Authorization Document (EAD) Number (if any):

6. **Current Residential U.S. Address** (if applicable) (do not list a P.O. Box)

Street Number and Name:

Apt. ☒ Ste. ☐ Flr. ☐ Number: 502

City or Town: Santa Monica

State: CA

ZIP Code: 90401

Part 4. Processing Information

1. If a beneficiary or beneficiaries named in **Part 3.** is/are outside the United States, or a requested extension of stay or change of status cannot be granted, state the U.S. Consulate or inspection facility you want notified if this petition is approved.

a. **Type of Office** (select only one box): ☒ Consulate ☐ Pre-flight inspection ☐ Port of Entry

b. **Office Address (City)**

c. **U.S. State or Foreign Country**: Mexico

d. **Beneficiary's Foreign Address**

Street Number and Name:

Apt. ☒ Ste. ☐ Flr. ☐ Number: 208

City or Town:

State: Mexico

Province:

Postal Code: 0090

Country: Mexico

2. Does each person in this petition have a valid passport? ☒ Yes ☐ No. If no, go to **Part 9.** and type or print your explanation.

Part 4. Processing Information (continued)

3. Are you filing any other petitions with this one?
☐ Yes. If yes, how many? ▶ ☒ No

4. Are you filing any applications for replacement/initial I-94, Arrival-Departure Records with this petition? Note that if the beneficiary was issued an electronic Form I-94 by CBP when he/she was admitted to the United States at an air or sea port, he/she may be able to obtain the Form I-94 from the CBP Website at www.cbp.gov/i94 instead of filing an application for a replacement/initial I-94.
☐ Yes. If yes, how many? ▶ ☒ No

5. Are you filing any applications for dependents with this petition?
☐ Yes. If yes, how many? ▶ ☒ No

6. Is any beneficiary in this petition in removal proceedings?
☐ Yes. If yes, proceed to **Part 9.** and list the beneficiary's(ies) name(s). ☒ No

7. Have you ever filed an immigrant petition for any beneficiary in this petition?
☐ Yes. If yes, how many? ▶ ☒ No

8. Did you indicate you were filing a new petition in **Part 2.**?
☐ Yes. If yes, answer the questions below. ☒ No. If no, proceed to **Item Number 9.**

a. Has any beneficiary in this petition ever been given the classification you are now requesting within the last seven years?
☐ Yes. If yes, proceed to **Part 9.** and type or print your explanation. ☐ No

b. Has any beneficiary in this petition ever been denied the classification you are now requesting within the last seven years?
☐ Yes. If yes, proceed to **Part 9.** and type or print your explanation. ☐ No

9. Have you ever previously filed a nonimmigrant petition for this beneficiary?
☐ Yes. If yes, proceed to **Part 9.** and type or print your explanation. ☒ No

10. If you are filing for an entertainment group, has any beneficiary in this petition not been with the group for at least one year?
☐ Yes. If yes, proceed to **Part 9.** and type or print your explanation. ☒ No

11.a. Has any beneficiary in this petition ever been a J-1 exchange visitor or J-2 dependent of a J-1 exchange visitor?
☐ Yes. If yes, proceed to **Item Number 11.b.** ☒ No

11.b. If you checked yes in **Item Number 11.a.**, provide the dates the beneficiary maintained status as a J-1 exchange visitor or J-2 dependent. Also, provide evidence of this status by attaching a copy of either a DS-2019, Certificate of Eligibility for Exchange Visitor (J-1) Status, a Form IAP-66, or a copy of the passport that includes the J visa stamp.

Part 5. Basic Information About the Proposed Employment and Employer

Attach the Form I-129 supplement relevant to the classification of the worker(s) you are requesting.

1. Job Title: Chief Executive Officer (CEO)
2. LCA or ETA Case Number:

Part 5. Basic Information About the Proposed Employment and Employer (continued)

3. Address where the beneficiary(ies) will work if different from address in **Part 1.**

Street Number and Name	Apt. Ste. Flr.	Number
	☐ ☐ ☐	

City or Town	State	ZIP Code

4. Did you include an itinerary with the petition? ☐ Yes ☒ No
5. Will the beneficiary(ies) work for you off-site at another company or organization's location? ☐ Yes ☒ No
6. Will the beneficiary(ies) work exclusively in the Commonwealth of the Northern Mariana Islands (CNMI)? ☐ Yes ☒ No
7. Is this a full-time position? ☒ Yes ☐ No
8. If the answer to **Item Number 7.** is no, how many hours per week for the position? ►
9. Wages: $ 250,000 per (Specify hour, week, month, or year) ► Year
10. Other Compensation (Explain)

    Normal Corporate Benefits

11. Dates of intended employment From: (mm/dd/yyyy) 02/01/2018 To: (mm/dd/yyyy) 01/31/2019
12. Type of Business
13. Year Established 2017
14. Current Number of Employees in the United States: New Company
15. Gross Annual Income: New Company
16. Net Annual Income: New Company

Part 6. Certification Regarding the Release of Controlled Technology or Technical Data to Foreign Persons in the United States

(This section of the form is required only for H-1B, H-1B1 Chile/Singapore, L-1, and O-1A petitions. It is not required for any other classifications. Please review the Form I-129 General Filing Instructions before completing this section.)

Select Item Number 1. or Item Number 2. as appropriate. DO NOT select both boxes.

With respect to the technology or technical data the petitioner will release or otherwise provide access to the beneficiary, the petitioner certifies that it has reviewed the Export Administration Regulations (EAR) and the International Traffic in Arms Regulations (ITAR) and has determined that:

1. ☒ A license is not required from either the U.S. Department of Commerce or the U.S. Department of State to release such technology or technical data to the foreign person; or
2. ☐ A license is required from the U.S. Department of Commerce and/or the U.S. Department of State to release such technology or technical data to the beneficiary and the petitioner will prevent access to the controlled technology or technical data by the beneficiary until and unless the petitioner has received the required license or other authorization to release it to the beneficiary.

Part 7. Declaration, Signature, and Contact Information of Petitioner or Authorized Signatory (Read the information on penalties in the instructions before completing this section.)

Copies of any documents submitted are exact photocopies of unaltered, original documents, and I understand that, as the petitioner, I may be required to submit original documents to U.S. Citizenship and Immigration Services (USCIS) at a later date.

I authorize the release of any information from my records, or from the petitioning organization's records that USCIS needs to determine eligibility for the immigration benefit sought. I recognize the authority of USCIS to conduct audits of this petition using publicly available open source information. I also recognize that any supporting evidence submitted in support of this petition may be verified by USCIS through any means determined appropriate by USCIS, including but not limited to, on-site compliance reviews.

If filing this petition on behalf of an organization, I certify that I am authorized to do so by the organization.

I certify, under penalty of perjury, that I have reviewed this petition and that all of the information contained in the petition, including all responses to specific questions, and in the supporting documents, is complete, true, and correct.

1. **Name and Title of Authorized Signatory**

Family Name (Last Name) | Given Name (First Name)

Title: Owner/Director

2. **Signature and Date**

Signature of Authorized Signatory

Date of Signature (mm/dd/yyyy) 12/04/2017

3. **Signatory's Contact Information**

Daytime Telephone Number

NOTE: If you do not fully complete this form or fail to submit the required documents listed in the instructions, a final decision on your petition may be delayed or the petition may be denied.

Part 8. Declaration, Signature, and Contact Information of Person Preparing Form, If Other Than Petitioner

Provide the following information concerning the preparer:

1. **Name of Preparer**

Family Name (Last Name): Reed | Given Name (First Name): Christopher

2. **Preparer's Business or Organization Name** (if any)

(If applicable, provide the name of your accredited organization recognized by the Board of Immigration Appeals (BIA).)

Law Offices of Brian D. Lerner, APC

Part 8. Declaration, Signature, and Contact Information of Person Preparing Form, If Other Than Petitioner (continued)

3. **Preparer's Mailing Address**

Street Number and Name	Apt. Ste. Flr. Number
3233 E. Broadway	☐ ☐ ☐

City or Town	State	ZIP Code
Long Beac h	CA	90803

Province	Postal Code	Country
		USA

4. **Preparer's Contact Information**

Daytime Telephone Number	Fax Number	Email Address (if any)
(58) 49 5-0 554	[redacted]	creed@eimmigration.org

Preparer's Declaration

By my signature, I certify, swear, or affirm, under penalty of perjury, that I prepared this petition on behalf of, at the request of, and with the express consent of the petitioner or authorized signatory. The petitioner has reviewed this completed petition as prepared by me and informed me that all of the information in the form and in the supporting documents, is complete, true, and correct.

5. **Signature and Date**

Signature of Preparer	Date of Signature (mm/dd/yyyy)
[signature]	12/8/17

Part 9. Additional Information About Your Petition For Nonimmigrant Worker

If you require more space to provide any additional information within this petition, use the space below. If you require more space than what is provided to complete this petition, you may make a copy of **Part 9.** to complete and file with this petition. In order to assist us in reviewing your response, you must identify the **Page Number, Part Number and Item Number** corresponding to the additional information.

1. A-Number ▶ **A-**

2. **Page Number** **Part Number** **Item Number**

3. **Page Number** **Part Number** **Item Number**

4. **Page Number** **Part Number** **Item Number**

L Classification Supplement to Form I-129

Department of Homeland Security
U.S. Citizenship and Immigration Services

USCIS
Form I-129
OMB No. 1615-0009
Expires 12/31/2018

1. Name of the Petitioner
Consorcio Integrador Sonora 80M US, LLC

2. Name of the Beneficiary

3. This petition is (select **only one** box): ☒ **a.** An individual petition ☐ **b.** A blanket petition

4.a. Does the petitioner employ 50 or more individuals in the U.S.? ☐ Yes ☒ No

4.b. If yes, are more than 50 percent of those employee in H-1B, L-1A, or L-1B nonimmigrant status? ☐ Yes ☐ No

Section 1. Complete This Section If Filing For An Individual Petition

1. Classification sought (select **only one** box): ☒ **a.** L-1A manager or executive ☐ **b.** L-1B specialized knowledge

2. List the beneficiary's and any dependent family member's prior periods of stay in an H or L classification in the United States for the last seven years. Be sure to list only those periods in which the beneficiary and/or family members were physically present in the U.S. in an H or L classification. Do not include periods in which the beneficiary was in a dependent status, for example, H-4 or L-2 status. If more space is needed, go to **Part 9. of Form I-129**.

NOTE: Submit photocopies of Forms I-94, I-797, and/or other USCIS issued documents noting these periods of stay in the H or L classification. (If more space is needed, attach an additional sheet.)

Subject's Name	Period of Stay (mm/dd/yyyy) From	To

3. Name of Employer Abroad
Consorcio Integrador Sonora 80M S.A. de C.V.

4. Address of Employer Abroad

Street Number and Name	Apt. Ste. Flr. Number
	☐ ☐ ☐

City or Town	State	ZIP Code

Province	Postal Code	Country
	03810	Mexico

Section 1. Complete This Section If Filing For An Individual Petition (continued)

5. Dates of beneficiary's employment with this employer. Explain any interruptions in employment.

Dates of Employment (mm/dd/yyyy) From	To	Explanation of Interruptions
05/2012	Present	

6. Describe the beneficiary's duties abroad for the 3 years preceding the filing of the petition. (If the beneficiary is currently inside the United States, describe the beneficiary's duties abroad for the 3 years preceding the beneficiary's admission to the United States.)

Chief Executive Officer. See Attached.

7. Describe the beneficiary's proposed duties in the United States.

Chief Executive Officer. See Attached.

8. Summarize the beneficiary's education and work experience.

See Attached CV/Resume.

9. How is the U.S. company related to the company abroad? (select **only one** box)

☐ a. Parent ☐ b. Branch ☒ c. Subsidiary ☐ d. Affiliate ☐ e. Joint Venture

Section 1. Complete This Section If Filing For An Individual Petition (continued)

10. Describe the percentage of stock ownership and managerial control of each company that has a qualifying relationship. Provide the Federal Employer Identification Number for each U.S. company that has a qualifying relationship.

Percentage of company stock ownership and managerial control of each company that has a qualifying relationship.	Federal Employer Identification Number for each U.S. company that has a qualifying relationship
Consorcio Integrador Sonora 80M US, LLC - 100% owned by Foreign Parent Below	
Consorcio Integrador Sonora 80M S.A. de C.V.	

11. Do the companies currently have the same qualifying relationship as they did during the one-year period of the alien's employment with the company abroad?

☐ Yes ☒ No. If no, provide an explanation in **Part 9. of Form I-129** that the U.S. company has and will have a qualifying relationship with another foreign entity during the full period of the requested period of stay.

12. Is the beneficiary coming to the United States to open a new office?

☒ Yes ☐ No (attach explanation)

If you are seeking L-1B specialized knowledge status for an individual, answer the following question:

13.a. Will the beneficiary be stationed primarily offsite (at the worksite of an employer other than the petitioner or its affiliate, subsidiary, or parent)?

☐ Yes ☒ No

13.b. If you answered yes to the preceding question, describe how and by whom the beneficiary's work will be controlled and supervised. Include a description of the amount of time each supervisor is expected to control and supervise the work. If you need additional space to respond to this question, proceed to **Part 9.** of the Form I-129, and type or print your explanation.

13.c. If you answered yes to the preceding question, describe the reasons why placement at another worksite outside the petitioner, subsidiary, affiliate, or parent is needed. Include a description of how the beneficiary's duties at another worksite relate to the need for the specialized knowledge he or she possesses. If you need additional space to respond to this question, proceed to **Part 9.** of the Form I-129, and type or print your explanation.

Section 2. Complete This Section If Filing A Blanket Petition

List all U.S. and foreign parent, branches, subsidiaries, and affiliates included in this petition. (Attach separate sheets of paper if additional space is needed.)

Name and Address	Relationship

Section 3. Additional Fees

NOTE: A petitioner that seeks initial approval of L nonimmigrant status for a beneficiary, or seeks approval to employ an L nonimmigrant currently working for another employer, must submit an additional **$500** Fraud Prevention and Detection fee. For petitions filed on or after December 18, 2015, you must submit an additional fee of **$4,500** if you responded yes to both questions in **Item Numbers 4.a.** and **4.b.** on the first page of this L Classification Supplement. This **$4,500** fee is mandated by the provisions of Public Law 114-113.

These fees, when applicable, may not be waived. You must include payment of the fees with your submission of this form. Failure to submit the fees when required will result in rejection or denial of your submission. Each of these fees should be paid by separate checks or money orders.

Request for Premium Processing Service

Department of Homeland Security
U.S. Citizenship and Immigration Services

USCIS
Form I-907
OMB No. 1615-0048
Expires 01/31/2018

For USCIS Use Only	Request Physically Received by USCIS	Returned	Resubmitted	Receipt
	Date	Date	Date	
	Date	Date	Date	Action Block
	Remarks			

To be completed by an attorney or accredited representative (if any).	☒ Select this box if Form G-28 is attached.	Attorney State Bar Number (if applicable)	Attorney or Accredited Representative USCIS ELIS Account Number (if any)
		235438	

►**START HERE - Type or print in black ink.**

Part 1. Information About the Person Filing This Request

1. **Alien Registration Number (A-Number)** (if any)
► A-

2. **Family Name (Last Name)** **Given Name (First Name)** **Middle Name**

3. **Company or Organ** **Named in the Related Case:** If filed on behalf of a company or organization
Consocio Integrador Sonora 80M US, LLC

4. **Mailing Address**
In Care Of Name

Street Number and Name or PO Box Number: 520 Broadway
Apt. ☐ Ste. ☐ Flr. ☐ Number

City or Town: Santa Monica
State: CA
ZIP Code: 90401

Province
Postal Code
Country: USA

5. Is your current mailing address the same as your physical address? ☒ Yes ☐ No

If you answered "No," provide your physical address in **Item Number 6.**

Part 1. Information About the Person Filing This Request *(continued)*

6. **Physical Address**

Street Number and Name:

Apt. ☐ Ste. ☐ Flr. ☐ Number:

City or Town:

State:

ZIP Code:

Province:

Postal Code:

Country:

7. **Request for Premium Processing Service:** (select **only one** box)

☒ I am the **petitioner** who is filing or has filed a petition eligible for Premium Processing Service.

☐ I am the attorney or accredited representative **for the petitioner** who is filing or has filed a petition eligible for Premium Processing Service. (Complete and submit Form G-28, if Form G-28 has not been submitted with the petition.)

☐ I am the **applicant** who is filing or has filed an application eligible for Premium Processing Service.

☐ I am the attorney or accredited representative **for the applicant** who is filing or has filed an application eligible for Premium Processing Service. (Complete and submit Form G-28, if Form G-28 has not been submitted with the application.)

Part 2. Information About the Request

1. **Form Number of Related Petition or Application**: I-129

2. **Receipt Number of Related Petition or Application**:

3. **Classification or Eligibility Requested**: L-1A

4. **Petitioner or Applicant in the Related Case**

Family Name (Last Name): Consocio Integrador Sonora 80M US, LLC

Given Name (First Name):

Middle Name:

5. **Beneficiary in the Related Case**

Family Name (Last Name): [redacted]

Middle Name:

6. **Name of Point of Contact for the Company or Organization**

Family Name (Last Name): [redacted]

...me (First Name):

Middle Name:

Position Title: Chief Executive Officer (CEO)

7. **Company or Organization IRS Tax Number (if any)**:

Part 2. Information About the Request *(continued)*

8. **Address of Petitioner, Applicant, Company or Organization Named in Related Case**

Street Number and Name	Apt. Ste. Flr.	Number
520 Broadway	☐ ☐ ☐	

City or Town	State	ZIP Code
Santa Monica	CA	90401

Province	Postal Code	Country
		USA

Part 3. Requestor's Statement, Certification, Signature, and Contact Information

I understand that U.S. Citizenship and Immigration Services (USCIS) will refund the Premium Processing Service fee to the person listed in **Part 1.** of this request if USCIS does not take an action on the related case within 15 calendar days after the appropriate USCIS office physically receives this request. I understand that case actions include a referral for investigation of suspected fraud or misrepresentation, or the issuance of:

1. An approval notice;
2. A request for evidence;
3. A notice of intent to deny; or
4. A denial notice.

Requestor's Statement

NOTE: Select the box for either **Item A.** or **B.** in **Item Number 1.** If applicable, select the box for **Item Number 2.**

1. **Requestor's Statement Regarding the Interpreter**

   A. ☒ I can read and understand English, and have read and understand each and every question and instruction on this request, as well as my answer to each question.

   B. ☐ The interpreter named in **Part 4.** has read to me each and every question and instruction on this request, as well as my answer to each question, in ________, a language in which I am fluent. I understand each and every question and instruction on this request as translated to me by my interpreter, and have provided true and correct responses in the language indicated above.

2. **Requestor's Statement Regarding the Preparer**

   ☒ I have requested the services of and consented to Christopher A. Reed, ☒ who is ☐ is not an attorney or accredited representative, preparing this request for me.

Requestor's Certification

I certify, under penalty of perjury under the laws of the United States of America, that the information in my request and any document submitted with my request is complete, true and correct.

Copies of any documents I have submitted are exact photocopies of unaltered, original documents, and I understand that USCIS may require that I submit original documents to USCIS at a later date. Furthermore, I authorize the release of any information from my records that USCIS may need to determine my eligibility for the immigration benefit that I seek.

I furthermore authorize release of information contained in this request and in supporting documents, and in my USCIS records, to other entities and persons where necessary for the administration of U.S. immigration laws.

Part 3. Requestor's Statement, Certification, Signature, and Contact Information *(continued)*

Requestor's Signature

3. Requestor's Signature

Date of Signature (mm/dd/yyyy) ► 12/04/2017

Requestor's Contact Information

4. Requestor's Daytime Telephone Number

5. Requestor's Mobile Telephone Number (if any)

6. Requestor's Email Address (if any)

7. Requestor's Fax Number (if any)

Part 4. Interpreter's Contact Information, Certification, and Signature

Provide the following information about the interpreter:

Interpreter's Full Name

1. Interpreter's Family Name (Last Name)

Interpreter's Given Name (First Name)

2. Interpreter's Business or Organization Name (if any)

Interpreter's Mailing Address

3. Street Number and Name

Apt. Ste. Flr. Number

City or Town

State

ZIP Code

Province

Postal Code

Country

Interpreter's Contact Information

4. Interpreter's Daytime Telephone Number

5. Interpreter's Email Address (if any)

Interpreter's Certification

I certify that:

I am fluent in English and ____, which is the same language provided in **Part 3., Item B.** in **Item Number 1.**;

I have read to this requestor each and every question and instruction on this request, as well as the answer to each question, in the language provided in **Part 3., Item B.** in **Item Number 1.**; and

The requestor has informed me that they understand each and every instruction and question on the request, as well as their answer to each question.

Part 4. Interpreter's Contact Information, Certification, and Signature *(continued)*

Interpreter's Signature

6. **Interpreter's Signature** | **Date of Signature** (mm/dd/yyyy) ►

Part 5. Name, Contact Information, Declaration, and Signature of the Person Preparing this Request, If Other Than the Requestor

Provide the following information about the preparer:

Preparer's Full Name

1. **Preparer's Family Name (Last Name)**: Red
   Preparer's Given Name (First Name): Christopher
2. **Preparer's Business or Organization Name (if any)**: Law Offices of Brian D. Lerner, APC

Preparer's Mailing Address

3. **Street Number and Name**: 3233 E. Boadway
   Apt. ☐ Ste. ☐ Flr. ☐ **Number**
   City or Town: bng Beach
   State: CA
   ZIP Code: 90803
   Province
   Postal Code
   Country: USA

Preparer's Contact information

4. **Preparer's Telephone Number**: (562) 495-0554
5. **Preparer's Fax Number**: [redacted]
6. **Preparer's Email Address (if any)**: creed@eimmigration.org

Preparer's Statement

7.A. ☐ I am not an attorney or accredited representative but have prepared this request on behalf of the requestor with the requestor's consent.

7.B. ☒ I am an attorney or accredited representative and my representation of the requestor in this case (choose one) ☒ extends ☐ does not extend beyond the preparation of this request.

Part 5. Name, Contact Information, Declaration, and Signature of the Person Preparing this Request, If Other Than the Requestor *(continued)*

Preparer's Declaration

By my signature, I certify, swear or affirm, under penalty of perjury, that I prepared this request on behalf of, at the request of, and with the express consent of, the requestor. I completed the request based only on responses the requestor provided to me. After completing the request, I reviewed it and all of the requestor's responses with the requestor, who agreed with each and every answer provided for each question on the request and, when required, supplied additional information to respond to a question on the request.

Preparer's Signature

8. **Preparer's Signature** [signature]

Date of Signature (mm/dd/yyyy) ► 12/8/17

Notice of Entry of Appearance as Attorney or Accredited Representative

Department of Homeland Security

DHS
Form G-28
OMB No. 1615-0105
Expires 03/31/2018

Part 1. Information About Attorney or Accredited Representative

1. USCIS ELIS Account Number *(if any)*
▶

Name and Address of Attorney or Accredited Representative

2.a. Family Name *(Last Name)*: Reed
2.b. Given Name *(First Name)*: Christopher
2.c. Middle Name: Allan
3.a. Street Number and Name: 3233 E Broadway
3.b. Apt. ☐ Ste. ☐ Flr. ☐
3.c. City or Town: Long Beach
3.d. State: CA 3.e. ZIP Code: 90803
3.f. Province:
3.g. Postal Code:
3.h. Country: USA
4. Daytime Telephone Number: 5624950554
5. Fax Number: [redacted]
6. E-Mail Address *(if any)*: creed@eimmigration.org
7. Mobile Telephone Number *(if any)*:

Part 2. Notice of Appearance as Attorney or Accredited Representative

This appearance relates to immigration matters before *(Select only one box)*:

1.a. ☒ USCIS
1.b. List the form numbers: I-129 / I-129L
2.a. ☐ ICE
2.b. List the specific matter in which appearance is entered:
3.a. ☐ CBP
3.b. List the specific matter in which appearance is entered:

I enter my appearance as attorney or accredited representative at the request of:

4. Select **only one** box:
☐ Applicant ☒ Petitioner ☐ Requestor
☐ Respondent (ICE, CBP)

Information About Applicant, Petitioner, Requestor, or Respondent

5.a. Family Name *(Last Name)*: [redacted]
5.b. Given Name *(First Name)*: [redacted]
5.c. Middle Name: [redacted]
6. Name of Company or Organization *(if applicable)*: See Part 6

SECTION 3
Exhibits

Exhibit 2

Translation from Spanish
26 May 2017

PUBLIC REGISTRY OF REAL PROPERTY AND COMMERCE
OF THE FEDERAL DISTRICT

RECORD OF REGISTRATION

THE INSTRUMENTS DESCRIBED IN THIS DOCUMENT WERE RECORDED ON THE ELECTRONIC COMMERCIAL FOLIO NUMBER 472638 - 1

NAME / BUSINESS NAME
CONSORCIO INTEGRADOR SONORA 80M, SOCIEDAD ANÓNIMA DE CAPITAL VARIABLE

Address MEXICO CITY, FED. DISTRICT

HOW RECEIVED

Internal Control	Date received	Time
101939	05-08-2012	14:47:24

INFORMATION REGARDING OFFICIAL OF THE PUBLIC FAITH/AUTHORITY
111057163
Address

BY MEANS OF DOCUMENT NUMBER: 5629

THE FOLLOWING INSTRUMENTS WERE RECORDED

Key FME	Precodified Form	Date recorded
M4 472638	INCORPORATION OF COMPANY	05-08-2012

Electronic signature authenticity characters:
44ed49d1932d13aff65ff955f22d6c19b8f101a9 Sequence No. 203552

REGISTRATION FEE

AMOUNT	DATE OF PAYMENT	PAYMENT VOUCHER
13,772.00 Pesos	05-04-2012	9390010444401XJQPP9Q
13,772.00 Pesos		

DIRECTOR: [redacted]

The electronic signature authenticity characters which appear below each instrument correspond to the electronic seal authorized by the Ministry of the Economy in accordance with the provisions of Article 21A, Section II, paragraphs c and d, and Article 30A of the Code of Commerce and Article 15 of the Regulation of the Public Registry of Commerce.

Public Registry
of Real Property
and Commerce of
the Federal District

ROSETTA STONE *ASSOCIATES IN TRANSLATION*
7375 N. Calle sin Celo, Tucson, AZ 85718 • (520) 575-9200 • rosettrans@aol.com • www.rosettrans.com
• ATA-Certified •

Certification

AT THE REQUEST OF THE INTERESTED PARTY, I hereby certify that I have translated the following document:

Public Registry of Commerce Registration of
CONSORCIO INTEGRADOR SONORA 80M, S.A. DE C.V.

from the Spanish into the English language on this 26th day of May 2017, and that the information contained in the translated document is a true, complete and correct reflection of the original text, to the best of my ability as a Professional Translator.

ROSETTA STONE ASSOCIATES IN TRANSLATION

Carola P. Myers

CAROLA P. MYERS
Member, A.C.I.A. - ATA-Certified

REGISTRO PÚBLICO DE LA PROPIEDAD Y DE COMERCIO DEL
DISTRITO FEDERAL

BOLETA DE INSCRIPCIÓN

LOS ACTOS DESCRITOS EN EL PRESENTE DOCUMENTO QUEDARON INSCRITOS EN EL FOLIO MERCANTIL ELECTRÓNICO NÚMERO: 472638 - 1

NOMBRE / DENOMINACION Ó RAZÓN SOCIAL

CONSORCIO INTEGRADOR SONORA 80M, SOCIEDAD ANÓNIMA DE CAPITAL VARIABLE

Domicilio MEXICO, DISTRITO FEDERAL

DATOS DE RECEPCIÓN:

Control Interno	Fecha de Ingreso	Hora
101939	08/05/2012	14:47:24

DATOS DEL FEDATARIO/AUTORIDAD:

111057163

Domicilio

MEDIANTE EL DOCUMENTO NÚMERO: 5629

SE INSCRIBIERON LOS SIGUIENTES ACTOS

Clave	FME	Forma Precodificada	Fecha Registro
M4	472638	CONSTITUCIÓN DE SOCIEDAD	08/05/2012

Caracteres de autenticidad de la Firma Electrónica: 44ed49d1932d13aff65ff955f22d6c19b8f101a9 Secuencia No. 203552

DERECHOS DE INSCRIPCIÓN

IMPORTE	FECHA DE PAGO	BOLETA DE PAGO
$ 13,772.00	04/05/2012	9390010444401XJQPP9Q
$ 13,772.00		

EL RESPONSABLE DE LA OFICINA: Alfredo Garcia Rosas

Los caracteres de autenticidad de la firma electrónica que aparecen en seguida de cada acto, corresponden al sello electrónico generado por la Secretaria de Economia, de acuerdo a lo previsto en los artículos 21 Bis, Fracción II, inciso c) y d) y 30 Bis del Código de Comercio y 15 del Reglamento del Registro Público de Comercio.

Exhibit
3

CERTIFIED COPY

BLVD. MANUEL AVILA CAMACHO No. 92, SUITE 1-A
COL. EL CONDE, NAUCALPAN, STATE OF MEXICO
TEL.: 24-87-35-77 55-76-27-47

INSTRUMENT NUMBER FIVE THOUSAND SIX HUNDRED AND TWENTY-NINE

VOLUME NUMBER NINETY-NINE

FOLIO NUMBER ONE HUNDRED AND FIFTEEN

In Naucalpan de Juárez, State of Mexico, on July twelve, two thousand eleven, I, **PATRICIA M. RUIZ DE CHÁVEZ RINCÓN GALLARDO, ESQ.**, Notary Public Number one hundred and sixty-three of the State of Mexico, residing in this City, acting within the ordinary protocol of my office, certify:

THE ORGANIZATION OF A CORPORATION UNDER THE NAME OF CONSORCIO INTEGRADOR SONORA 80M, SOCIEDAD ANÓNIMA DE CAPITAL VARIABLE, ESTABLISHED BY CONSULTORIA DE COMERCIO INTERNACIONAL DE ESPAÑA, SOCIEDAD ANÓNIMA DE CAPITAL VARIABLE, represented herein by Mr. *sic]* in his capacity of Legal Representative; **SERVICIOS ESPECIALIZADOS EN MONTAJES INDUSTRIALES**, represented herein by Mr. **ALFONSO AVELINO CRUZ SUÁREZ** in his capacity of the company's Sole Administrator; **AYETH PRICELLA FLORES ROSAS, CÉSAR ROMERO RODRÍGUEZ, A.A.C.F. MANIOBRAS Y CONSTRUCCIONES ELÉCTRICAS, SOCIEDAD ANÓNIMA DE CAPITAL VARIABLE**, represented herein by Mr. **WILBERTH JOSÉ JESÚS CAUICH PENICHE** in his capacity of the company's Sole Administrator, and **LETICIA IVETTE LAZCANO ESQUEDA**, in accordance with the following:

SWORN STATEMENT

For the purposes of Article seventy-nine, Section VIII, and Article one hundred and sixty of the Notarial Law of the State of Mexico, the parties appearing before me, having first been sworn to be truthful and cautioned as to the penalties for making false statements, declared that the representations made in this instrument are truthful.

PREAMBLE

SOLE PREAMBLE. PERMIT FROM THE MINISTRY OF FOREIGN AFFAIRS.

In order to execute this instrument, Permit number "0925784" (zero nine two five seven eight four), File number "20110907925" (two zero one one zero nine zero seven nine two five), Folio number "110708098001" (one one zero seven zero eight zero nine eight zero zero one) dated July eight, two thousand eleven was applied for and obtained from the Ministry of Foreign Affairs; [said permit] being issued in order to organize the company named **CONSORCIO INTEGRADOR SONORA 80M, SOCIEDAD ANÓNIMA DE CAPITAL VARIABLE,** and which document I am adding to the appendix under the letter "**A**".

By virtue of the foregoing, the parties execute this instrument in accordance with the following

ARTICLE

SOLE ARTICLE. The parties organize a Sociedad Anónima de Capital Variable (corporation) in accordance with current laws in the United Mexican States, in particular in accordance with chapters five, eight and related provisions of the General Corporation Law, the organization and operations of which shall be governed by the following:

CORPORATE BYLAWS

NAME, OBJECT, DURATION, CORPORATE OFFICES, AND NATIONALITY

ARTICLE ONE. The name of the corporation is **CONSORCIO INTEGRADOR SONORA 80M,** followed by the words "**SOCIEDAD ANÓNIMA DE CAPITAL VARIABLE**" or the abbreviation "**S.A. de C.V.**"

ARTICLE TWO. The object of the corporation is:

a. The promotion, marketing, investment, executing engineering projects, acquisition of equipment, construction, contracting, start-up and maintenance of power generating projects, and environmental projects.

b. To acquire, sell, subdivide and divide into lots all manner of urban and suburban land; to perform all types of urbanization and remediation work such as streets, pavements, sidewalks, architectural embellishments, canals, bridges, overpasses, electrical networks and lines, distribution and transmission substations, street lighting, drainage work and other similar services and facilities; to contract and work with engineers, architects, and builders; to consult and advise; [to execute] all types of projects and buildings on behalf of the company or third parties, with individuals or legal, civil, commercial or industrial entities, or with local and federal governments of the Republic.

c. To enter into any type of contracts for personal services with engineers, architects, project technicians, and builders; to acquire and install construction equipment, vehicles, storage facilities and offices for such objects; to buy, sell, import, export, and manufacture all types of construction materials and articles, whether of iron, aluminum, wood, granite, marble, plastic or of any other material; to obtain and grant any type of loans, whether or not secured by real or personal property, and generally to execute any type of contracts or agreements, and to perform any kind of operations of a civil or commercial nature directly or indirectly related with the aforementioned corporate objects, and all that which is useful to its smooth functioning and enhanced development.

d. [To perform] soil analysis and building control by lab tests; to supervise, coordinate, perform technical and administrative reviews; to inspect and render expert assessments on all types of works, buildings and projects; to acquire, sell, encumber, lease and operate any type of urban and suburban properties; to build, construct, execute, install, repair and conduct studies and projects, and to remodel all types of projects and buildings, such as homes, buildings, low-income housing, condominiums, schools, businesses, banks, offices, and industrial facilities.

e. To give or obtain loans with or without specific guarantees and to provide endorsements or guarantees in business transactions directly related to the company's objects and activities.

f. To market, construct, manufacture, buy and sell, lease, import, export, assemble, and distribute all manner of industrial and commercial activities, as well as to export and import machinery, equipment, tools, merchandise, and any other implements needed to develop the company.

g. To use, operate, acquire, sell and license patents, commercial name brands, and advertising.

h. In general, to undertake any activity related to the products, articles, services and rights described in the foregoing paragraphs, with any of these to be undertaken in the Mexican Republic or foreign countries, including activities performed by agents, commission merchants, representatives, intermediaries or distributors.

i. To carry out all necessary legal actions, be they civil, commercial, administrative, or of any other kind related to the object of the company.

j. To issue warrants, bonds, and all types of credit documents, certificates or similar documents with the participation of the institutions prescribed by law.

k. To establish, transact, or negotiate in any manner whatsoever with factories, plants, laboratories, warehouses, offices, stores and other establishments deemed fit to further the company's objects.

l. To provide and receive all types of technical, administrative or supervisory services.

m. To register, acquire, dispose of and deal in trademarks, brand names, patents, investments, and processes.

n. To partner with professionals or professional companies in other special fields in order to provide professional services in other areas, whether in the Mexican Republic or abroad, and to grant them the representation or the position of correspondent for the company, or for the latter to act as their representative or correspondent.

o. To manage and operate all types of commercial service establishments.

p. To enter into technical assistance, acquisition, transfer and operating contracts for any kind of domestic or foreign technology.

q. To issue, remit, endorse, accept, guarantee, discount, contract or sign any kinds of securities and credit transactions, without being in the hypothetical situation contemplated in Articles four of the Stock Market Law.

To this effect, the company may do the following, including but not limited to:

1. Lending and contracting for any type of additional professional or technical services, as well as rendering and contracting for support related to or desirable for the development of the corporate object, and for legal and accounting matters.

2. Acquiring shares, partnership interests, ownership interests, interest portions or bonds in all types of partnerships or companies, as well as becoming a part thereof, as may be necessary or desirable for the development of the corporate object.

3. Accepting or conferring all manner of merchant commissions or powers of attorney in its own behalf or that of a third party.

4. Establishing agencies or representations, and acting as a commission merchant, agent, representative, commercial middleman or distributor.

5. Participating in any public or private calls for bids and/or competitions, both in the Mexican Republic and abroad, as well as acquiring, obtaining, utilizing or disposing of any letters patent, makes, trademarks, brand names, franchises, options, preferential rights, copyrights, industrial and artistic rights, whether in the Mexican Republic or abroad, as well as concessions, permits and/or authorizations given by any authority, that are directly or indirectly related to the corporate object.

6. Acquiring or in any other way owning, leasing, managing, encumbering or selling or disposing of any furnishings, in rem rights and real property by themselves or through a third party, as may be necessary or desirable for the corporate object.

CHECKED *[Initials]*

7. Hiring all personnel necessary to meet the corporate object and delegating to one or several persons the completion of mandates, commissions, services and activities appropriate for its objects.

8. Granting or receiving any kind of loan or financing, as well as providing any kind of guarantee secured by real or personal property to collateralize such loans, including bank bonds or guarantees, and issuing, vouching for, granting, underwriting, and in general conducting transactions with all types of credit instruments related to the obligations of the company or of third parties, as may be necessary or desirable for the company.

9. In general, taking any actions and entering into any contracts and agreements, whether they are of a labor-related, civil, commercial, administrative or any other nature permitted under Mexican law, both with individuals and private or public legal entities that are directly or indirectly related to achieving the corporate object.

ARTICLE THREE. The **DURATION** of the company shall be **NINETY-NINE YEARS**, beginning on the date this instrument is signed.

ARTICLE FOUR. The company's headquarters are in **MEXICO CITY, FEDERAL DISTRICT**, but agencies, branch offices and official business locations can be established anywhere in the Mexican Republic or abroad, which shall not be understood to mean a change of the company's principal place of business.

ARTICLE FIVE. The **NATIONALITY** of the company is **MEXICAN**. The current or future foreign shareholders of the company formally agree vis-à-vis the Ministry of Foreign Affairs to consider themselves [Mexican] nationals with respect to any corporate shares they may acquire or own, and regarding any assets, rights, concessions, holdings or property interests owned by the company itself, or any rights and obligations deriving from contracts to which the company is a party with Mexican authorities, and not to invoke the protection of their government at the risk of losing any shares they may have acquired to the benefit of the Mexican nation.

By virtue of the foregoing, the pact contemplated in Section one of Article twenty-seven of the Constitution of the United [Mexican] States is deemed to have been concluded with the Ministry of Foreign Affairs.

CORPORATE CAPITAL AND SHARES

ARTICLE SIX. The corporate capital is variable. The fixed minimum capital is **THREE MILLION PESOS NATIONAL CURRENCY**, divided into **THREE THOUSAND** registered shares with a face value of **ONE THOUSAND PESOS NATIONAL CURRENCY** each, fully subscribed and paid in.

The variable capital is unlimited and is represented by shares of the series determined by the Shareholders Meeting that decides to issue them.

The corporate capital is subject to being increased by the partners' subsequent contributions or by admitting new partners, and may be reduced by the full or partial withdrawal of contributions, provided such withdrawal does not compromise the minimum established by the General Corporation Law.

ARTICLE SEVEN. The corporate shares shall be of equal value and confer equal rights and obligations on their owners.

ARTICLE EIGHT. The company shall keep a stock register in accordance with Articles one hundred and twenty-eight and one hundred and twenty-nine of the General Corporation Law.

The company shall consider those listed in the aforementioned register as owners.

ARTICLE NINE. Increases to the fixed minimum portion of the corporate capital shall be made by decision of the Extraordinary General Shareholders Meeting, followed by an amendment of these Bylaws. Increases to the variable portion of the corporate capital may be made by decision of the Extraordinary General Shareholders Meeting. When such decisions are made, the Shareholders Meeting that decides on the increase, or any later Shareholders Meeting, shall set the terms and guidelines by which such increase and the corresponding issue of shares should be made.

In the event of an increase in the corporate capital, shareholders shall have preferential rights in proportion to the number of shares already held to subscribe to the shares being issued. They must exercise such rights within fifteen days after the decision of the Shareholders Meeting regarding the increase of the corporate capital is published in the official newspaper where the company's corporate offices are located and/or in one of the major newspapers there.

If a shareholder fails to exercise the right to subscribe to a capital increase, the remaining shareholders, in proportion to their holdings of shares, can subscribe to the shares for which the relevant preferential right was not exercised.

If some shares remain unsubscribed after the period referred to in the preceding paragraphs has elapsed, they may be offered for subscription and payment on the terms and during the periods determined by the Shareholders Meeting that decided to increase the capital, or on the terms established by the Board of Directors or the Sole Administrator or the delegates designated by the Shareholders Meeting for this purpose, with the understanding that the price at which the shares are offered to third parties may not be lower than the price at which they were offered to the company's shareholders for subscription and payment.

No further capital increase may be decided unless the shares of the previously decreed increase are fully subscribed and paid in, nor may any reduction be decided that would result in reducing the agreed minimum capital.

ARTICLE TEN. Reductions of the minimum fixed capital require a resolution by the Extraordinary Shareholders Meeting, followed by an amendment to these Bylaws; in addition, the requirements of Article nine of the General Corporation Law must be met. Reductions of the variable capital, except for those arising from the exercise of the withdrawal right referred to in this Article, can be made by resolution of the Ordinary Shareholders Meeting.

In the event the corporate capital is reduced by reimbursing the shareholders, it shall be done on a proportional basis between all shares that represent the corporate capital, with the understanding that the redemption price may not be less than the book value of the shares in accordance with the most recent financial statement approved by the Extraordinary General Shareholders Meeting before the reduction was decided.

Any reduction of the corporate capital as a result of the exercise of the right of withdrawal by a shareholder owning representative shares of the variable portion of the corporate capital must comply with the requirements set forth in Articles two hundred and twenty and two hundred and twenty-one of the General Corporation Law.

Payment of the reimbursement may be demanded from the company beginning on the day following the Ordinary Shareholders Meeting approving the financial statement for the business year in which the withdrawal takes effect.

Any increase or reduction of the corporate capital shall be recorded in a registry book kept by the company for this purpose.

ARTICLE ELEVEN. The Extraordinary General Shareholders Meeting can decide to amortize shares with distributable profits without reducing the corporate capital, meeting the requirements of Article one hundred and thirty-six of the General Corporation Law. The amortization shall be made proportionately between all shareholders so that after the amortization they all hold the same percentages in the corporate capital and ownership interest as before.

The amortized shares and corresponding securities shall be canceled.

ARTICLE TWELVE. The permanent securities or provisional certificates representing the shares shall be registered and can cover one or more shares, and shall contain all information referred to in Article one hundred and twenty-five of the General Corporation Law.

SHAREHOLDERS MEETINGS

ARTICLE THIRTEEN. The General Shareholders Meeting is the supreme organ of the company. They can be ordinary or extraordinary. Extraordinary meetings shall be those convened in order to address: 1. Any business indicated in Article one hundred and eighty-two of the General Corporation Law; 2. The amortization of shares with distributable profits referred to in Article eleven of these Bylaws, and 3. Any business requiring a resolution by the shareholders relating to a bankruptcy procedure or suspension of payments by the company. Ordinary meetings shall be those convened to address any of the matters indicated in Article one hundred and eighty-one of the General Corporation Law, and to deal with any other business not reserved to Extraordinary Shareholders Meetings. Shareholders Meetings shall be held at the corporate headquarters and are invalid without this requirement, except for an Act of God or force majeure.

ARTICLE FOURTEEN. Meeting notices for Shareholders Meetings must be made by the Board of Directors or the Sole Administrator or by the Shareholders Representative, except where [otherwise] provided by Articles one hundred and sixty-eight, one hundred and eighty-four, and one hundred and eighty-five of the General Corporation Law.

Meeting notices for Shareholders Meetings shall be published at least fifteen days before the date scheduled for the meeting in the Official Gazette (to which the shareholders give the designation of official newspaper for the corporate place of business), and in one of the major papers at the corporate place of business.

Meeting notices shall list the agenda and must be signed by the person(s) calling the meeting.

Meetings may be held without any prior notice if the entire corporate capital is fully represented at the time votes are taken.

If all shareholders are gathered at a meeting, the meeting can decide business of any type, including those not listed on the relevant agenda.

ARTICLE FIFTEEN. Shareholders whose names are recorded one day before the meeting in the company's book of registered shares as owning one or more shares shall be admitted to the Shareholders Meeting; if not, they may prove their capacity of shareholder by any other legal means. They can be represented by a proxy designated by the shareholder by a power of attorney signed before two witnesses or by an agent or agents holding sufficient general or special power of attorney granted under the terms of applicable laws.

The Board of Directors or the Sole Administrator and the company's Shareholders Representative(s) cannot represent any shareholder at the Shareholders Meetings.

ARTICLE SIXTEEN. The meetings are presided by the Chairman of the Board of Directors or the Sole Administrator, and in his/her absence, by the individual appointed by majority vote of the shareholders in attendance.

The role of Secretary at the Shareholders Meetings is exercised by the individual holding the position of company secretary; in his/her absence, it is handled by the person designated by majority vote of the shareholders present. The Chairman shall appoint one or more scrutineers from among the shareholders present to conduct a count of the shares represented, to determine if a quorum is present, and to count the votes cast.

ARTICLE SEVENTEEN. The Minutes of the Shareholders Meetings shall be prepared by the Secretary, recorded in the corresponding book, and signed by the Chairman and the Secretary of the Shareholders Meeting, as well as by the Shareholders Representative(s) who may have attended. An attendance list and the documents attesting that the meeting notice was conducted according to law and these Bylaws shall be included with the Minutes.

If the Minutes of the Shareholders Meeting cannot be recorded in the corresponding book for some reason, the Minutes must be notarized.

All Minutes of Extraordinary Shareholders Meetings must be notarized and recorded with the Public Registry of Commerce.

ARTICLE EIGHTEEN. Ordinary Shareholders Meetings shall be held at least once a year within four months following the close of each business year, and whenever they are convened to address some business in their area of responsibility.

Extraordinary Shareholders Meetings shall be held when they are convened to address some business in their area of responsibility.

ARTICLE NINETEEN. In order for the Shareholders Meetings to be considered legally conducted and their decisions valid, the provisions of Articles one hundred and eighty-nine, one hundred and ninety, and one hundred and ninety-one of the General Corporation Law must be met.

Regardless of the foregoing, decisions taken outside of a shareholders meeting may be adopted by the unanimous vote of the shareholders who represented all of the shares into which the corporate capital is divided or of the special share category involved, if applicable, and these decisions shall have the same validity for all legal effects as if they had been adopted during a general or special Shareholders Meeting, respectively, provided however that they are confirmed in writing. The document containing the written confirmation shall be sent to the company's Secretary who shall record the respective decisions in the corresponding Minute book, with the annotation that these decisions were adopted in accordance with these Bylaws.

ARTICLE TWENTY. Decisions legally adopted by the Shareholders Meetings are binding, even for dissidents and those who did not attend, except for the right to challenge them under the General Corporation Law.

MANAGEMENT AND SUPERVISION OF THE CORPORATION

ARTICLE TWENTY-ONE. Management of the company, as decided by the Shareholders Meeting, can be handled by a Sole Administrator or a Board of Directors formed by the number of shareholding board members agreed to by the Shareholders Meeting that elects them. Deputies acting in the absence of a respective shareholder can also be elected.

ARTICLE TWENTY-TWO. The members of the Board of Directors or the Sole Administrator can be shareholders or not; they hold their office for one year, but shall remain in office until the individuals designated to take their place assume the position. They can be reelected and shall receive such remuneration as decided by the Ordinary Shareholders Meeting. If the corporate management is given to a Board of Directors, the minority shareholders reserve the right to designate a board member in accordance with Article one hundred and forty-four of the General Corporation Law.

ARTICLE TWENTY-THREE. The Board of Directors shall hold meetings when convened for this purpose by the Chairman, the Secretary, by the Shareholders' Representative(s), or by any board member.

The meetings of the Board of Directors shall be convened by means of a written notice sent by certified mail with return receipt; it shall list the agenda, place, date and time of the proposed meeting and must be received by all members of the Board of Directors at least fifteen days before the date scheduled for the meeting.

ARTICLE TWENTY-FOUR. The meetings of the company's Board of Directors for which the provisions concerning meeting notices set forth in Article twenty-three of these Bylaws have been met, shall be deemed to be legally in session upon the first meeting notice if the majority of all office-holding board members are present. In the event the required quorum is not reached upon the first meeting notice, a second or further meeting notice may be issued, and the meeting shall be deemed legally in session regardless of the number of board members in attendance, provided there are more than two, with the understanding, however, that each board member is notified of that second or further meeting notice not less than fifteen days prior to the date of the proposed meeting, and the agenda must be the same as the one for the first meeting notice.

Except when more voting is required in accordance with the General Corporation Law, the Board of Directors shall adopt its decisions by majority vote of those present. In case of a tie, the Chairman of the Board shall cast the deciding vote. Decisions may also be taken outside a board meeting by unanimous vote and shall for all legal effects have the same validity as if they had been adopted during a board meeting, provided they are confirmed in writing.

Regardless of the above, the decisions of the Board of Directors meeting upon a first, second or further meeting notice to address the following matters must have the unanimous vote of all its members:

1. Authorization to sell, encumber, transfer, assign or convey by any legal means any corporate shares or ownership interests that represent the corporate capital of companies in which the Company is a shareholder or partner, regardless of the amount or percentage of its shareholding.

2. Approval of changes to or deviations from the annual budget in amounts that exceed ten percent of the budget or the relevant budgetary column.

3. Granting powers of attorney to carry out acts of ownership on behalf of the Company.

4. Authorization to sell or encumber any of the company's assets (including intangibles) or those of any of its subsidiaries which individually or together represent more than five percent of the book value of all of the company's assets at a consolidated level, as per the company's most recent financial statements approved by the shareholders.

[Initials] CHECKED

ARTICLE TWENTY-FIVE. In the absence of an express appointment by the Shareholders Meeting which decides on his/her designation, the board members shall appoint the Chairman from among themselves during the first Board meeting immediately after the Shareholders Meeting in which they themselves were appointed. They shall also appoint a Secretary who may or may not be a board member, as well as the other individuals who will hold the positions to be created to better perform their duties. Permanent or temporary absences in the Board of Directors shall be covered by the respective alternates.

ARTICLE TWENTY-SIX. The Board of Directors or the Sole Administrator is the company's legal representative and will therefore be invested with and hold the most far-reaching powers to achieve the corporate objective and direct and manage the company, and shall therefore act with the following powers, including but not limited to:

I. ***GENERAL POWER OF ATTORNEY FOR LITIGATION AND COLLECTIONS*** with all general and even special powers that require a special clause according to law, pursuant to paragraph one of Article seven point seven hundred and seventy-one and Article seven point eight hundred and six of the Civil Code in effect in the State of Mexico and related articles in the states where he/she may practice.

These powers include, but are not limited to the following:

I. To drop any type of lawsuit, including judicial protection proceedings.

II. To reach settlements.

III. To be bound by arbitration rulings.

IV. To answer and formulate interrogatories.

V. To challenge judges.

VII. *[sic]* To receive payments.

VIII. To take other measures as expressly determined by law.

These may be exercised when dealing with individuals, all types of administrative or judicial authorities, including federal or local authorities, and conciliation and arbitration boards.

II. ***GENERAL POWER OF ATTORNEY FOR MANAGEMENT ACTS*** under the terms of the second paragraph of the aforementioned Article seven point seven hundred and seventy-one of the Civil Code of the State of Mexico and the related articles in the states where he/she may practice.

III. ***GENERAL POWER OF ATTORNEY FOR ACTS OF OWNERSHIP*** under the terms of the third paragraph of the aforementioned Article seven point seven hundred and seventy-one of the Civil Code of the State of Mexico and the related articles in the states where he/she may practice.

IV. ***GENERAL POWER OF ATTORNEY IN LABOR MATTERS***, with express powers to appear before any labor authority, federal and local conciliation board, federal and local conciliation and arbitration board, and in particular any hearings during the conciliation stage in labor-related proceedings; the power to make agreements that may result from such hearings, as well as in particular to answer and formulate interrogatories, to mediate, settle, formulate agreements, file police reports and complaints, drop any kind of lawsuit and appeal, including judicial protection proceedings, represent the company before all types of authorities, be they judicial, administrative or any other kind who hear labor conflict cases, under the terms of Articles eleven, eight hundred and seventy-eight, six hundred and ninety-two, sections one, two and three, seven hundred and eighty-six, and eight hundred and seventy-six of the Federal Labor Law.

V. ***POWER OF ATTORNEY TO GRANT, SIGN, GUARANTEE, AND ENDORSE LOAN DOCUMENTS*** under the General Law of Securities and Credit Transactions, as well as to verify all types of bank and commercial transactions, and to open or close revolving accounts at banks and other financial institutions.

VI. To delegate his/her powers to one or various board members to act separately or as a committee.

VII. Power to grant general or special powers of attorney and to revoke one or the other.

VIII. To freely appoint and remove a director general or general manager, managers, directors and other officers, technical consultants and employees of the company, to delegate all or part of these powers to one or more individuals, and to set their remuneration.

IX. Power to take part in any calls for bids, as well as to deal with the MINISTRY OF THE TREASURY AND PUBLIC CREDIT, THE MEXICAN INSTITUTE OF SOCIAL SECURITY (IMSS), and the INSTITUTE OF THE NATIONAL WORKERS HOUSING FUND (INFONAVIT).

X. Pursuant to Article seven point seven hundred and sixty-eight of the Civil Code for the State of Mexico, the powers set forth above for the Board of Directors or Sole Administrator, if applicable, shall be valid for ninety-nine years.

The powers listed above may be restricted by the General Shareholders Meeting, which reserves the right to delegate all or part thereof to one or more board members of the company or to an outsider.

ARTICLE TWENTY-SEVEN. Oversight over the company shall be exercised by one or more shareholders' representatives appointed by the Shareholders Meeting, and they can have their respective alternates. Shareholders owning shares representing at least twenty-five percent of the representative shares of the corporate capital shall at all times have the right to designate a shareholders' representative. The shareholders' representatives and, if applicable, their deputies need not be shareholders of the company; they are appointed annually, may be reelected one or more times, and remain in office until the Shareholders Meeting makes new appointments and the appointees assume their post.

The shareholders' representatives shall have the duties and obligations listed in Article one hundred and sixty-six of the General Corporation Law, as well as any others which the Shareholders Meeting may delegate, and their remuneration shall be set by the Shareholders Meeting on an annual basis.

THE FISCAL YEAR OF THE COMPANY AND FINANCIAL DATA

ARTICLE TWENTY-EIGHT. The fiscal year of the company shall coincide with the calendar year except for the first year which shall begin on the date this instrument is signed, and will end on December thirty-one of the same year.

ARTICLE TWENTY-NINE. Within four months from the end of each business year, the Board of Directors or the Sole Administrator shall prepare the following financial and any other information that may be necessary in accordance with Articles one hundred and seventy-two of the General Corporation Law. This report shall be prepared according to the provisions of Articles one hundred and seventy-three, one hundred and seventy-six, and one hundred and seventy-seven of the aforementioned law, and must be completed and made available to shareholders at least fifteen days before the date on which the Shareholders Meeting is held for its discussion.

PROFITS AND LOSSES

ARTICLE THIRTY. For earnings distributions, the provisions of Articles sixteen, seventeen, eighteen, nineteen, twenty and twenty-one of the General Corporation Law shall be observed, and distributions may only take place after the financial statements showing a profit have been duly approved by the Shareholders Meeting.

At least five percent of net profits shall be set aside each year to constitute, increase or, where applicable, replace the legal reserve fund until the fund equals twenty percent of the corporate capital.

The earnings obtained shall be distributed among all shareholders in proportion to the number of their shares or, if applicable, the amount paid for them.

Losses, if any, shall be borne in the same proportion up to the amount of their shares.

The founders reserve no special property interest of any kind, except to the extent that corresponds to the number of their shares.

DISSOLUTION AND LIQUIDATION

ARTICLE THIRTY-ONE. When dissolving or liquidating the company, the provisions of the General Corporation Law shall be observed. After the company is dissolved, it is placed in liquidation. The Extraordinary Shareholders Meeting shall designate one or more liquidators who shall have the powers provided by law or as determined by the Extraordinary Shareholders Meeting that appoints them.

The liquidator(s) shall conduct the liquidation in keeping with the guidelines which, if applicable, the Shareholders Meeting may establish; if not, then in accordance with Chapters X and XI of the aforementioned General Corporation Law.

ARTICLE THIRTY-TWO. Mergers, reorganizations and corporate break-ups shall be subject to the provisions of Chapter IX of the General Corporation Law.

ARTICLE THIRTY-THREE. Any matters not expressly contemplated in these Bylaws shall be governed by the provisions of the General Corporation Law.

INCIDENTAL ARTICLES

ONE. The minimum fixed corporate capital established in Article six of these bylaws is hereby fully subscribed and paid in as follows:

SHAREHOLDERS	REGISTERED SHARES	AMOUNT, FACE VALUE
CONSULTORIA DE COMERCIO INTERNACIONAL DE ESPAÑA, SOCIEDAD ANÓNIMA DE CAPITAL VARIABLE	2460 TWO THOUSAND FOUR HUNDRED AND SIXTY	$2,460,000.00 TWO MILLION FOUR HUNDRED AND SIXTY THOUSAND PESOS NATIONAL CURRENCY
SERVICIOS ESPECIALIZADOS EN MONTAJES INDUSTRIALES, SOCIEDAD ANÓNIMA DE CAPITAL VARIABLE	150 ONE HUNDRED AND FIFTY	$150,000.00 ONE HUNDRED AND FIFTY THOUSAND PESOS NATIONAL CURRENCY
AYETH PRICELLA FLORES ROSAS	150 ONE HUNDRED AND FIFTY	$150,000.00 ONE HUNDRED AND FIFTY THOUSAND PESOS NATIONAL CURRENCY
CÉSAR ROMERO RODRÍGUEZ	150 ONE HUNDRED AND FIFTY	$150,000.00 ONE HUNDRED AND FIFTY THOUSAND PESOS NATIONAL CURRENCY
A.A.C.F. MANIOBRAS Y CONSTRUCCIONES ELÉCTRICAS, SOCIEDAD ANÓNIMA DE CAPITAL VARIABLE	45 FORTY-FIVE	$45,000.00 FORTY-FIVE THOUSAND PESOS NATIONAL CURRENCY

LETICIA IVETTE LAZCANO ESQUEDA	45 FORTY-FIVE	$45,000.00 FORTY-FIVE THOUSAND PESOS NATIONAL CURRENCY
TOTAL	**3000 THREE THOUSAND**	**$3,000,000.00 THREE MILLION PESOS NATIONAL CURRENCY**

TWO. The makers of this instrument consider this meeting, in which they render their signatures, to be the first General Shareholders Meeting, and by unanimous vote formulate the following:

RESOLUTIONS

ARTICLE ONE. The parties in this instrument resolve:

I. To entrust the management of the company to a **Board of Directors**. To this effect, they designate the following individuals:

PRESIDENT: C

TREASURER: ALFONSO AVELINO CRUZ SUÁREZ

SECRETARY: AYETH PRICELLA FLORES ROSAS

DIRECTOR: CÉSAR ROMERO RODRÍGUEZ

DIRECTOR: WILBERTH JOSÉ JESÚS CAUICH PENICHE

Messrs. **FONSO AVELINO CRUZ SUÁREZ**, **AYETH PRICELLA FLORES ROS** and **WILBERTH JOSÉ JESÚS CAUICH PENICHE**, in their capacity of President, Treasurer, Secretary, and Directors of the Board of Directors, respectively, shall in the performance of their duties jointly and severally enjoy any and all powers listed in Article **TWENTY-SIX** of these Bylaws which govern this company and are deemed to be reproduced here as if they were inserted verbatim; [such powers] shall be valid as long as they hold their offices, except for the power **TO GRANT, SIGN, GUARANTEE, AND ENDORSE LOAN DOCUMENTS**, which powers shall be exercised jointly or separately solely and exclusively by Messrs. **CÉSAR MARTÍN RODRÍGUEZ** and **ALFONSO AVELINO CRUZ SUÁREZ** in their capacity of President and Treasurer, respectively. The **GENERAL POWER OF ATTORNEY FOR ACTS OF OWNERSHIP** shall be exercised jointly by all members of the Board of Directors.

THREE. In order to acquire shares, partnership or ownership interests, interest portions or obligations of any kind in partnerships or companies, or to participate therein, as may be necessary or desirable to achieving the corporate object, three members of the Board of Directors shall act jointly.

FOUR. The parties in this instrument declare that:

A. The company treasury holds the full amount of the minimum capital not subject to withdrawal.

B. The designated officers have accepted their positions.

FIVE. Mr. **HUMBERTO HOYUELA LÓPEZ** is appointed as the Shareholders' Representative.

SIX. The parties appearing before me authorize the undersigned Notary to handle the administrative paperwork and to have the first certified counterpart of this instrument recorded with the relevant Public Registry of Commerce.

LEGAL STANDINGS

Messrs. [redacted] ALFONSO AVELINO CRUZ SUÁREZ and **WILBERTH JOSÉ JESÚS CAUICH PENICHE** declare that their legal standing has not been revoked or in any way restricted, and prove the lawful existence of their clients by means of the certifications which I add to the appendix of this instrument marked with the letters "**A**", "**B**", and "**C**".

I, the Notary, attest:

I. That the parties appearing before me have legal standing to proceed herein, and I have no knowledge to the contrary. They identified themselves before me with documents, photocopies of which I add to the appendix of this instrument marked with the letter "**D**".

II. That pursuant to Article twenty-seven of the Federal Tax Code, the Federal Taxpayer Registration codes of the shareholders who constitute this company were verified, a photocopy of which I add to the appendix of this instrument marked with the letter "**E**".

III. That I cautioned the parties, pursuant to the provisions of Article one hundred and fifty-two of the Regulation of the General Population Law, that if foreign nationals are officers of the company, the performance of their duties will require the relevant authorization by the Ministry of the Interior.

IV. That I warned the parties that they are to prove to me within the month following the signing of this instrument that they have filed an application to register the company with the Federal Taxpayer Registry and that, should they fail to show me such application, I shall proceed to notify the corresponding tax authorities in accordance with Article twenty-seven of the Federal Tax Code.

V. That the items listed and inserted fully agree with the originals shown to me and to which I have referred.

VI. That based on their **PERSONAL IDENTIFICATION**, they are:

Mr. [redacted] Spaniard by birth, son of Spanish parents, born in Madrid on March thirty-one, nineteen hundred and seventy-six, married, engineer, residing at Hesiodo No. five hundred and forty-four, Apt. five hundred and two, Colonia Polanco, Delegación Miguel Hidalgo in Mexico City, Federal District, temporarily in this Municipality of Naucalpan de Juárez, State of Mexico, in order to sign this instrument. As an immigrant, he proved his legal residence in this country by means of his immigration document issued by the Ministry of the Interior, National Immigration Institute, on November twenty-nine, two thousand and ten, in effect as of November twenty-nine, two thousand eleven, a photocopy of which I add to the appendix of this instrument marked with the letter "**F**".

Mr. **ALFONSO AVELINO CRUZ SUÁREZ**, a Mexican national by birth, son of Mexican parents, born in Mexico City, Federal District on September nineteen, nineteen hundred and seventy-two, married, engineer, residing at Catorce de Julio No. forty-seven A, Colonia Huichapan, Delegación Xochimilco in Mexico City, Federal District, temporarily in this Municipality of Naucalpan de Juárez, State of Mexico in order to sign this instrument, with Federal Taxpayer Number CUSA7209191X7 (CUSA seven two zero nine one nine one X seven), who identified himself with his passport issued by the Ministry of Foreign Affairs on December thirty, two thousand and nine.

Mrs. **AYETH PRICELLA FLORES ROSAS**, a Mexican national by birth, born in Cananea, State of Sonora on April nine, nineteen hundred and sixty-eight, unmarried, entrepreneur, residing at Campos Eliseos No. one hundred and thirty-four, Colonia Polanco Reforma, Delegación Miguel Hidalgo in Mexico City, Federal District, temporarily in this Municipality of Naucalpan de Juárez, State of Mexico in order to sign this instrument, with Federal Taxpayer Number FORA680409TL8 (FORA six eight zero four zero nine TL eight), who identified herself with her passport issued by the Ministry of Foreign Affairs on November seventeen, two thousand and ten.

[REDACTED] a Mexican national by birth, son of Mexican parents, born in Mexico City, Federal District on September twenty-nine, nineteen hundred and sixty-nine, married, engineer, residing at Privada la Cañada No. sixty, Penthouse B, Bosque Real, Huixquilucan, State of Mexico, with Federal Taxpayer Number RORC690929R30 (RORC six nine zero nine two nine R three zero), who identified himself with his passport issued by the Ministry of Foreign Affairs on January twenty-six, two thousand eleven.

Mr. **WILBERTH JOSÉ JESÚS CAUICH PENICHE**, a Mexican national by birth, son of Mexican parents, born in Mérida, State of Yucatán on January nine, nineteen hundred and fifty-nine, married, merchant, residing at Calle Cuarenta No. three hundred and twelve, Colonia Francisco Villa West, Mérida, State of Yucatán, temporarily in this Municipality of Naucalpan de Juárez, State of Mexico in order to sign this instrument, with Federal Taxpayer Number CAPW5901093N5 (CAPW five nine zero one zero nine three N five), who identified himself with his voter's registration card issued by the Federal Electoral Institute.

[*Initials*] CHECKED

Mrs. **LETICIA IVETT LAZCANO ESQUEDA**, a Mexican national by birth, born in Mexico City, Federal District on January twelve, nineteen hundred and seventy, married, B.A. in Communications, residing at Privada la Cañada No. sixty, Penthouse B, Bosque Real, Huixquilucan, State of Mexico, with Federal Taxpayer Number LAEL700112LL2 (LAEL seven zero zero one one two LL two), who identified herself with her voter's registration card issued by the Federal Electoral Institute.

VII. That, having read this instrument to the parties appearing before me, to whom I explained the legal effects and consequences thereof, they indicated their agreement with its terms and signed it for the record on the same date on which I have definitively certified it. I ATTEST HERETO.

I add the supplemental notes to the appendix of this instrument under the corresponding letter. I attest hereto.

Mr. [REDACTED] - Signature.

Mr. Alfonso Avelino Cruz Suárez. - Signature.

Mrs. Ayeth Pricella Flores Rosas. - Signature.

Mr. [REDACTED] - Signature.

Mr. Wilberth José Jesús Cauich Peniche. - Signature.

Mrs. Leticia Ivette Lazcano Esqueda. - Signature.

Witnessed by me: Patricia M. Ruiz de Chávez Rincón Gallardo, Esq. - Signature.

The Notary's Certification Stamp

In compliance with the provisions of Article seven point seven hundred and seventy-one of the Civil Code in effect in the State of Mexico, the wording of which is identical to Article two thousand five hundred and fifty-four of the same legal code in effect in the Federal District in civil matters and in the entire Republic in federal matters, the following is transcribed in its entirety:

ARTICLE 7.771

OF THE CIVIL CODE IN EFFECT IN THE STATE OF MEXICO

"For all powers of attorney for litigation and collections, it shall suffice to say that it is conferred with all general powers and the special powers requiring special clauses in accordance with the law, so as to be understood to be conferred without any restrictions.

For general powers of attorney to manage assets, it shall suffice to say that they are given as such, so that the legal representative has all types of administrative powers.

For general powers of attorney for acts of ownership, it shall suffice that they are given as such, so that the legal representative has all the powers of an owner, both with respect to the assets and taking any and all steps to defend them.

If the powers of a legal representative in the three foregoing cases are to be limited, the restrictions shall be put to paper, otherwise they will be special powers.

All Notaries shall insert this article in legal documents containing the granting of powers of attorney.

THIS IS A CERTIFIED COPY faithfully taken from the original on file in the open document registry in my charge and is issued for the corporation named **CONSORCIO INTEGRADOR SONORA 80M, SOCIEDAD ANÓNIMA DE CAPITAL VARIABLE** on fourteen pages duly sealed and checked.

Naucalpan de Juárez, State of Mexico, on this eighteenth day of July, two thousand eleven. I attest hereto.

[*Signature*]

PERMITTING DEPT. CONSTITUTION
SUBDIRECTORATE FOR CO[illegible]

SRE

PERMIT
FILE
FOLIO

In conformance with the provisions of Article 27, Section I of the Constitution of the United Mexican States, Article 28, Section V of the Charter of the Federal Public Administration, Article 15 of the Foreign Investment Law, and Articles 13, 14, and 18 of the Regulation of the Foreign Investment Law and the National Registry of Foreign Investments, and in response to the application filed by Mr(s). **ALFONSO CRUZ AGUIRRE**, on the basis of the provisions of Article 33, Section IV of the current Internal Regulation of the Ministry of Foreign Affairs and Article SIX, paragraph a), Section VI, and paragraph d), Section I of the DECREE published in the Federal Official Gazette on April 11, 2008, amending Articles six and seven and adding Articles one A and eleven A of the Decree delegating powers to public servants of the Ministry of Foreign Affairs as stated, published on April 28, 2005, we grant a permit to organize an SA DE CV [corporation with variable capital] under the following name:

CONSORCIO INTEGRADOR SONORA 80M

This permit is subject to the condition that the bylaws of the company to be incorporated shall include the Foreigner Exclusion Clause or the agreement contemplated in Section I of Article 27 of the Constitution, in accordance with the provisions of Articles 15 of the Foreign Investment Law and Article 14 of the Regulation of the Foreign Investment Law and of the National Registry of Foreign Investments. We should point out that this permit is granted irrespective of the provisions of Article 91 of the Industrial Property Law.

This permit shall become invalid if the interested parties fail to execute the Incorporation document before a notary public in accordance with the provisions of Article 17 of the Regulation of the Foreign Investment Law and the National Registry of Foreign Investments within ninety business days from the date the permit is granted.

The interested party shall also notify the Ministry of Foreign Affairs of the use of the name being authorized by this permit within six months from its issue in accordance with the provisions of Article 18 of the Regulation of the Foreign Investment Law and the National Registry of Foreign Investments.

[*Initials*]
CHECKED

Mexico City, Fed. District, July 08, 2011

THE DEPUTY DIRECTOR

[*Signature*]

DAVID LOPEZ RODRIGUEZ, Esq.

JUL. 11, 2011
Ministry of
Foreign Affairs
Directorate General of Legal Affairs

THIS PAGE LEFT BLANK

Certification

AT THE REQUEST OF THE INTERESTED PARTY, I hereby certify that I have translated the following document:

Articles of Incorporation of
CONSORCIO INTEGRADOR SONORA 80M, S.A. DE C.V.

from the Spanish into the English language on this 17th day of May 2017, and that the information contained in the translated document is a true, complete and correct reflection of the original text, to the best of my ability as a Professional Translator.

ROSETTA STONE ASSOCIATES IN TRANSLATION

CAROLA P. MYERS
Member, A.C.I.A. - ATA-Certified

LIC. P/ ON GALLARDO
NOTARIO PUBLICO No. 163
ESTADO DE MÉXICO

COPIA CERTIFICADA

ESCRITURA [illegible] CINCO MIL SEISCIENTOS VEINTINUEVE----------

VOLUMEN NÚMERO NOVENTA Y NUEVE----------

FOLIO NÚMERO CIENTO QUINCE ----------

--- En Naucalpan de Juárez, Estado de México, a doce de julio del año dos mil once, Yo, **LICENCIADA PATRICIA M. RUIZ DE CHÁVEZ RINCÓN GALLARDO**, Notario Público Número ciento sesenta y tres, del Estado de México, con residencia en esta Ciudad, actuando en el protocolo ordinario que está a mi cargo, hago constar: ----------

---------- **PROTESTA DE LEY** ----------

--- Para los efectos de los artículos setenta y nueve, fracción ocho romano y ciento sesenta, de la Ley del Notariado del Estado de México, los comparecientes bajo protesta de decir verdad y advertidos de las penas en que incurren quienes declaran con falsedad, manifestaron que las declaraciones que hacen en el presente instrumento son verídicas. ----------

---------- **ANTECEDENTE** ----------

--**ÚNICO**.- PERMISO DE LA SECRETARIA DE RELACIONES EXTERIORES.----------

--- Para el otorgamiento de esta escritura se solicitó y obtuvo de la Secretaría de Relaciones Exteriores el Permiso Número "0925784" (cero nueve dos cinco siete ocho cuatro), Expediente número "20110907925" (dos cero uno uno cero nueve cero siete nueve dos cinco), Folio número "11070809800 1" (uno uno cero siete cero ocho cero nueve ocho cero cero uno) de fecha ocho de julio de dos mil once, otorgada para constituir la sociedad denominada **CONSORCIO INTEGRADOR SONORA 80M, SOCIEDAD ANÓNIMA DE CAPITAL VARIABLE**, documento que agrego al apéndice bajo la letra "**A**".----------

--En virtud de lo anterior, los comparecientes otorgan el presente instrumento al tenor de la siguiente: ----------

---------- **CLAUSULA** ----------

--- **ÚNICA**.- Los comparecientes constituyen una Sociedad Anónima de Capital Variable, de conformidad con las Leyes Vigentes en los Estados Unidos Mexicanos particularmente de acuerdo con los Capítulos Quinto, Octavo y disposiciones conexas de la Ley General de Sociedades Mercantiles, cuyo organización y funcionamiento se regirá por los siguientes----------

---------- **ESTATUTOS SOCIALES** ----------

--- **DENOMINACION, OBJETO, DURACION, DOMICILIO Y NACIONALIDAD** ----------

---**ARTÍCULO PRIMERO**.- La Sociedad se denomina **CONSORCIO INTEGRADOR SONORA 80M**, seguida de las palabras "**SOCIEDAD ANÓNIMA DE CAPITAL VARIABLE**" o de su abreviatura "**S.A. de C.V.**".--

--- **ARTÍCULO SEGUNDO**.- La sociedad tiene por **objeto**: ------------------------------

--- a).- Promoción, comercialización, inversión, realización de ingenierías, adquisición de equipos, construcción, contratación, puesta en marcha y mantenimiento de proyectos de generación de energía y proyectos medioambientales. ------------------------------

--- b).- Adquirir, enajenar, fraccionar y lotificar toda clase de terrenos urbanos y suburbanos, ejecutar toda clase de obras de urbanización y saneamiento, como calles, pavimentos, banquetas, guarniciones, canales, puentes, caminos puentes, redes y líneas eléctricas y subestaciones tanto de distribución como de transmisión, alumbrado, drenaje y demás servicios e instalaciones análogas, contratar y ejecutar con ingenieros y arquitectos, constructores, consultaría y asesoría, toda clase de obras y edificaciones por cuenta propia o ajena, con personas físicas o morales, civiles, comerciales o industriales o con los gobiernos locales y federales de la republica. ------------------------------

--- c).- Celebrar toda clase de contratos de servicios personales con ingenieros, arquitectos, técnicos de obras y constructores; adquirir e instalar para los objetos, implementos de construcción, vehículos, bodegas y oficinas; comprar, vender, importar, exportar y fabricar toda clase de materiales y artículos para la construcción, ya sean de fierro, aluminio, madera, granito, mármol y plásticos o de cualquier otro material; obtener y conceder toda clase de créditos con o sin garantía, reales y personales; y en general ejecutar toda clase de contratos y convenios, y realizar toda clase de operaciones de naturaleza civil o mercantil que se relacione directa o indirectamente con los objetos sociales antes indicados y todo aquello que sirve para su buena marcha y mejor desarrollo. ------------------------------

--- d).- Análisis de suelo , control en construcción, por medio de laboratorio, supervisor, coordinar, revisar técnica y administrativamente, auditar y dictaminar toda clase de obras, construcciones y proyectos, adquirir, enajenar, gravar, arrendar y explotar toda clase de bienes urbanos y sub-urbanos; construir, edificar, ejecutar, instalar, reparar, realizar estudios y proyectos, y adaptar toda clase de obras y de construcciones, como casas, edificios, viviendas populares, condominios, escuelas, comercios, bancos, oficinas y construcciones industriales. ------------------------------

--- e).- Dar o tomar dinero en préstamo con o sin garantía específica y otorgar avales o garantías en operaciones de empresas que estén directamente relacionadas con los objetos o actividades de la sociedad. ------------------------------

--- f).- Comercialización, construcción, fabricación, compra venta, arrendamiento, importación, exportación, maquila, distribución de toda clase de actividades industriales y comerciales, incluyendo la exportación, importación de maquinaria, equipos, herramientas, mercancías y cualquier implemento necesario para el desarrollo de la sociedad.------------------------------

--- g).- El uso, explotación, adquisición, venta y licencia de patentes y marcas nombres comerciales y publicidad. ------------------------------

--- h).- En general emprender cualquier actividad relacionada con los productos, artículos, servicios y derechos descritos en los párrafos anteriores, cualquiera de ellos en la

Republica ... o en países extranjeros, incluyendo aquellas actividades realizadas por agentes, comisionistas, representantes, intermediarios o distribuidores.---

--- i).- La realización de todos los actos legales necesarios que sean civiles, mercantiles, administrativos o de otra naturaleza, relacionados con el propósito de la sociedad. ---

--- j).- Emitir cedulas, obligaciones, toda clase de títulos de crédito, certificados o documentos similares con intervención de las instituciones que señalen las leyes. ---

--- k).- Establecer, operar, negociar en cualquier forma con fabricas, plantas, laboratorios, almacenes, oficinas, tiendas y demás establecimientos convenientes para la realización de los objetos. ---

--- l).- Proporcionar y recibir toda clase de servicios técnicos, administrativos o de supervisión.---

--- m).- Registrar, adquirir, disponer y negociar con marcas industriales, nombres comerciales, patentes, invenciones y procesos. ---

--- n).- La asociación de profesionistas o sociedades de profesionistas de otras especialidades con el fin de prestar servicios profesionales en otras áreas ya sean de la Republica Mexicana o en el extranjero, otorgándoles la representación o corresponsalía de la sociedad o actuando esta como su representante o corresponsal. ---

--- o).- Administrar y explotar toda clase de establecimientos mercantiles de servicios. ---

--- p).- La celebración de contratos de asistencia técnica, adquisición, transferencia y explotación de toda clase de tecnología nacional o extranjera. ---

--- q).-Emitir, girar, endosar, aceptar, avalar, descontar, contratar o suscribir toda clase de títulos y operaciones de crédito, sin que se ubique en los supuestos del artículo cuarto de la ley de mercado de valores. ---

--- Por lo que enunciativa y no limitativamente podrá: ---

--- 1.- Prestar y contratar todo tipo de servicios profesionales o técnicos adicionales, así como dar y contratar asesorías, relacionadas o convenientes para el desarrollo de su objeto social, así como jurídica y contable.---

--- 2.- Adquirir acciones, partes sociales, participaciones, partes de interés u obligaciones de toda clase de asociaciones o sociedades y formar parte en ellas, según sea necesario o conveniente para el desarrollo de su objeto social.---

--- 3.- Aceptar o conferir toda clase de comisiones mercantiles o mandatos, obrando en su propio nombre o en nombre de terceros. ---

--- 4.- Establecer agencias o representaciones y actuar como comisionista, agente, representante, mediador mercantil o distribuidor.---

--- 5.- Participar en todo tipo de licitaciones y/o concursos, públicos o privados, dentro y fuera de la República Mexicana, así como adquirir, obtener, utilizar o disponer por cualquier título patentes, marcas, nombres comerciales, marcas industriales, franquicias, opciones y preferencias, derechos de propiedad literaria, industrial y artística ya sea en México o en el extranjero, así como concesiones, permisos y/o autorizaciones de alguna autoridad, relacionadas directa o indirectamente con los fines de su objeto social. ---

--- 6.- Adquirir o por cualquier otro título poseer, arrendar, administrar, gravar y disponer o enajenar toda clase de bienes muebles, derechos reales, así como inmuebles, por sí o a través de terceros, que sean necesarios o convenientes para su objeto. ---

--- 7.- Contratar al personal necesario para el cumplimiento de los fines sociales y delegar en una o varias personas el cumplimiento de mandatos, comisiones, servicios y actividades propias de su objeto.--

--- 8.- Prestar y recibir todo tipo de créditos o financiamientos, así como constituir todo tipo de garantías reales o personales para garantizar dichos créditos, incluyendo fianzas o avales así como emitir, avalar, otorgar, suscribir y en general negociar con todo tipo de de títulos de crédito en relación con obligaciones de la sociedad o de terceros, según sea necesario o conveniente para la sociedad.--

--- 9.- En general, ejecutar toda clase de actos y celebrar toda clase de contratos y convenios ya sean laborales, civiles, mercantiles, administrativos o de cualquier otra naturaleza, permitidos por la legislación mexicana, tanto con personas físicas y morales de carácter privado o público, relacionadas directa o indirectamente para la realización de su objeto social.--

--- **ARTÍCULO TERCERO.**- La **DURACIÓN** de la Sociedad será **NOVENTA Y NUEVE AÑOS,** contados a partir de la fecha de firma de la presente escritura. ------------------------------

--- **ARTÍCULO CUARTO.**- El **DOMICILIO** de la sociedad es en la Ciudad de **MEXICO, DISTRITO FEDERAL,** sin embargo, podrá establecer agencias y sucursales y fijar domicilios convencionales en cualquier lugar de la República Mexicana o del Extranjero, sin que por ello se entienda cambiado su domicilio social. ------------------------------

--- **ARTÍCULO QUINTO.**- La sociedad es de **NACIONALIDAD MEXICANA.**- Los accionistas extranjeros, actuales o futuros de la Sociedad, se obligan formalmente ante la Secretaría de Relaciones Exteriores a considerarse como nacionales respecto de las acciones de la sociedad que adquieran o que sean titulares, así como de los bienes, derechos, concesiones, participaciones o intereses de que sea titular la propia sociedad, o bien, de los derechos y obligaciones que deriven de los contratos que sea parte la sociedad con autoridades mexicanas y a no invocar la protección de su Gobierno, bajo la pena en caso contrario de perder en beneficio de la Nación Mexicana, las acciones que hubiesen adquirido. --

--- En virtud de lo anterior, se tiene por convenido ante la Secretaría de Relaciones Exteriores, el pacto previsto en la fracción primera del artículo veintisiete de la Constitución Política de los Estados Unidos --

------------------------------ **CAPITAL SOCIAL Y ACCIONES** ------------------------------

--- **ARTÍCULO SEXTO.** El capital social es variable. El capital mínimo fijo es de **TRES MILLONES DE PESOS MONEDA NACIONAL,** dividido en **TRES MIL** acciones nominativas, con valor nominal de **MIL PESOS MONEDA NACIONAL,** cada una de ellas, totalmente suscritas y pagadas.--

--- El capital variable es ilimitado, representado por acciones de la serie que determine la Asamblea que decrete su emisión.--

--- El capital social es susceptible de aumento por aportaciones posteriores de los socios, o por admisión de nuevos socios, y de disminución por retiro total o parcial de las aportaciones, siempre que dicho retiro no implique el mínimo fijado en la Ley General de Sociedades Mercantiles.--

--- **ARTÍCULO SÉPTIMO.** Las acciones de la Sociedad serán de igual valor y conferirán iguales derechos y obligaciones a sus titulares.--

--- **ARTÍCULO OCTAVO**. La Sociedad llevará un Libro de Registro de Acciones, de acuerdo con los artículos ciento veintiocho y ciento veintinueve de la Ley General de Sociedades Mercantiles.---

--- La Sociedad considerará como propietario a quien aparezca inscrito en dicho registro.-

--- **ARTÍCULO NOVENO**. Los aumentos del capital social en su parte mínima fija se efectuaran por resolución de la Asamblea General Extraordinaria de Accionistas, con la consecuente reforma de estos estatutos sociales. Los aumentos del capital social en su parte variable podrán efectuarse por resolución de la Asamblea General Extraordinaria de Accionistas. Al tomarse los acuerdos respectivos, la Asamblea de Accionistas que decrete el aumento, o cualquier asamblea de accionistas posterior, fijara los términos y bases en los que deberá llevarse a cabo dicho aumento y su correspondiente emisión de acciones.---

--- Los accionistas, tendrán derecho preferente en proporción al número de acciones que ya posean, para suscribir las que se emitan, en caso de aumento de capital social, mismo que deberán ejercitar dentro de los quince días siguientes a la publicación en el periódico oficial del domicilio de la sociedad y/o en uno de los periódicos de mayor circulación en dicho domicilio social, del acuerdo de la asamblea sobre el aumento del capital.---

--- En caso de que algún accionista no ejerciere su derecho para suscribir un aumento de capital, los demás accionistas, en proporción en su tenencia accionaría, podrán suscribir las acciones respecto de las cuales no se hubiesen ejercido el derecho de preferencia respectivo.---

---Si después de expirado el plazo a que se hace mención en los párrafos anteriores, aun quedasen sin suscribir algunas acciones, éstas podrán ser ofrecidas para su suscripción y pago, en las condiciones y plazos que determine la propia asamblea que hubiese decretado el aumento del capital, o en los términos en que disponga el Consejo de Administración o el Administrador Único, o de los delegados designados por la asamblea a dicho efecto, en el entendido de que el precio al cual se ofrezcan las acciones a terceros no podrá ser inferior a aquél al cual hubieran sido ofrecidas a los accionistas de la Sociedad para suscripción y pago.---

--- No podrá decretarse un nuevo aumento de capital sin que las acciones que representen el anteriormente acordado estén totalmente suscritas y pagadas, ni podrá acordarse una disminución que tenga como consecuencia la reducción del capital mínimo acordado.---

--- **ARTÍCULO DÉCIMO**. Las disminuciones en el capital mínimo fijo se efectuarán por resolución de la Asamblea Extraordinaria de Accionistas, con la consecuente reforma de estos estatutos sociales, cumpliendo en todo caso, con lo ordenado por el artículo noveno de la Ley General de Sociedades Mercantiles. Las disminuciones en el capital variable, salvo las derivadas del ejercicio del derecho de retiro a que se refiere este artículo, podrán efectuarse por resolución de la asamblea ordinaria de accionistas. ---

--- En el supuesto de que se realicen reducciones del capital social por reembolso a los accionistas, este se hará a prorrata entre todas las acciones representativas del capital social, en el entendido de que el precio de reembolso no podrá ser inferior al valor contable de las acciones de acuerdo al último estado de posición financiera que haya sido aprobado por la Asamblea General Extraordinaria de Accionistas antes de que se resuelva la reducción.--

--- La disminución del capital social como consecuencia del ejercicio del derecho de retiro de algún accionista propietario de acciones representativas de la parte variable del capital social, deberá ceñirse a lo ordenado en los artículos doscientos veinte y doscientos veintiuno de la Ley General de Sociedades Mercantiles. --

--- El pago del reembolso será exigible a la Sociedad a partir del día siguiente a la celebración de la asamblea ordinaria de accionistas que haya aprobado el estado de posición financiera correspondiente al ejercicio social en que el retiro deba surtir sus efectos. --

--- Todo aumento o disminución del capital social deberá de inscribirse en un libro de registro que para tal efecto llevará la Sociedad.--

--- **ARTÍCULO DÉCIMO PRIMERO**. La Asamblea General Extraordinaria de Accionistas podrá resolver la amortización de acciones con utilidades repartibles sin disminuir el capital social, cumpliendo lo previsto por el artículo ciento treinta y seis de la Ley General de Sociedades Mercantiles. La amortización se llevará a cabo en forma proporcional entre todos los accionistas, en forma tal que después de amortización éstos tengan los mismos porcentajes respecto al capital social y participación accionaria que antes tenían.---------

--- Las acciones amortizadas quedarán anuladas y los títulos correspondientes deberán cancelarse.--

--- **ARTÍCULO DÉCIMO SEGUNDO**. Los títulos definitivos o los certificados provisionales que representen a las acciones serán nominativos y podrán amparar una o mas acciones, contendrán las menciones a que se refiere el artículo ciento veinticinco de la Ley General de Sociedades Mercantiles.--

---------- **ASAMBLEAS DE ACCIONISTAS** ----------

--- **ARTÍCULO DÉCIMO TERCERO.** La Asamblea General de Accionistas es el órgano supremo de la Sociedad. Las Asambleas de Accionistas serán ordinarias o extraordinarias. Serán Asambleas Extraordinarias las convocadas para tratar: 1.- Cualquiera de los asuntos indicados en el artículo ciento ochenta y dos de la Ley General de Sociedades Mercantiles; 2.- La amortización de acciones con utilidades repartibles a que se refiere el artículo décimo primero de estos estatutos, y 3.- Cualquier asunto que requiera de la resolución de los accionistas, relacionada con algún procedimiento de quiebra o suspensión de pagos de la Sociedad. Serán Asambleas Ordinarias las convocadas para tratar cualquiera de los asuntos indicados en el artículo ciento ochenta y uno de la Ley General de Sociedades Mercantiles y para tratar cualquier otro asunto no reservado a las Extraordinarias. Las Asambleas de Accionistas se reunirán en el domicilio social y sin este requisito serán nulas, salvo caso fortuito o de fuerza mayor. ------------------------------

--- **ARTÍCULO DÉCIMO CUARTO.** Las convocatorias para Asambleas de Accionistas deberán ser hechas por el Consejo de Administración o Administrador Único o por el o los Comisarios, salvo lo dispuesto por los artículos ciento sesenta y ocho, ciento ochenta y cuatro y ciento ochenta y cinco de la Ley General de Sociedades Mercantiles.-------------

--- Las convocatorias para las Asambleas deberán publicarse en el Diario Oficial (al que los accionistas dan el carácter de periódico oficial del domicilio social) y/o en uno de los diarios de mayor circulación en dicho domicilio social, por lo menos con quince días de anticip[illegible] fijada para la asamblea. Las convocatorias contendrán el orden del día y deberán estar firmados por la persona o personas que las hagan. Las asambleas podrán ser celebradas sin previa convocatoria si el total del capital social estuviese totalmente representado en el momento de la votación.------------------------------

--- Si en una Asamblea estuvieran reunidos todos los accionistas, dicha asamblea podrá resolver sobre asuntos de cualquier naturaleza y aun sobre aquellos no contenidos en el orden del día respectivo. ------------------------------

--- **ARTÍCULO DÉCIMO QUINTO**. Serán admitidos en las Asambleas, los accionistas que aparezcan inscritos como titulares de una o mas acciones en el registro de acciones nominativas que lleve la Sociedad un día antes de la fecha en que se celebre la Asamblea respectiva, o en su defecto, que acrediten su calidad de accionistas por cualquier otro medio legal, pudiendo ser representados por la persona o las personas que para ello designen mediante carta poder firmada ante dos testigos o por mandatarios con poder general o especial suficiente otorgado en los términos de la legislación aplicable. ------------------------------

--- El Consejo de Administración, o el Administrador Único, y el Comisario o los Comisarios de la Sociedad no podrán representar a accionista alguno en las asambleas. ---------------

--- **ARTÍCULO DÉCIMO SEXTO.** Las Asambleas serán presididas por el Presidente del Consejo de Administración o el Administrador Único, y en su ausencia, por la persona que designen los accionistas presentes por mayoría de votos.------------------------------

--- Actuará como Secretario en las Asambleas de Accionistas quien ocupe el cargo de Secretario de la Sociedad y, a falta de éste la persona que al efecto designen los accionistas presentes por mayoría de votos. El Presidente nombrará uno o más escrutadores de entre los accionistas presentes, para hacer el recuento de las acciones representadas y determinar si se constituye quórum, así como para contar los votos emitidos. ------------------------------

--- **ARTÍCULO DÉCIMO SÉPTIMO**. Las Actas de las Asambleas serán elaboradas por el Secretario, asentadas en el libro respectivo y firmadas por el Presidente y el Secretario de la Asamblea, así como por el o los Comisarios que asistieren. A las Actas se agregará la Lista de Asistencia y los documentos que justifiquen que la convocatoria se hizo en los términos que previene la Ley y los presentes Estatutos.------------------------------

--- Cuando por cualquier circunstancia no pudiere asentarse el acta de asamblea en el libro respectivo se protocolizará ante notario.------------------------------

--- Las Actas de las Asambleas Extraordinarias serán protocolizadas ante Notario e inscritas en el Registro Público de Comercio. ------------------------------

--- **ARTÍCULO DÉCIMO OCTAVO**. Las Asambleas Generales Ordinarias de accionistas se celebrarán por lo menos una vez al año, dentro de los cuatro meses siguientes a la clausura de cada ejercicio social y cuando sea convocada para tratar alguno de los asuntos de su competencia.------------------------------

--- Las Asambleas Extraordinarias se reunirán cuando sean convocadas para tratar alguno de los asuntos de su competencia. ------------------------------

--- **ARTÍCULO DÉCIMO NOVENO**. Para que las Asambleas se consideren legalmente reunidas y sus resoluciones sean válidas, se atenderá a lo dispuesto por los artículos ciento ochenta y nuevo, ciento noventa y ciento noventa y uno de la Ley General de Sociedades Mercantiles. ---

--- No obstante lo anterior, podrán adoptarse resoluciones fuera de asamblea por unanimidad de los accionistas que representen la totalidad de las acciones en que se divida el capital social o de la categoría especial de acciones de que se trate, en su caso, y dichas resoluciones tendrán, para todos los efectos legales, la misma validez que si hubieren sido adoptadas reunidos en asamblea general o especial, respectivamente, siempre que se confirmen por escrito. El documento en el que consta la confirmación escrita deberá ser enviado al Secretario de la Sociedad, quien transcribirá las resoluciones respectivas en el libro de actas correspondiente, indicando que dichas resoluciones fueron adoptadas de conformidad con estos estatutos.---------------------------------------

--- **ARTÍCULO VIGÉSIMO.** Las resoluciones legalmente adoptadas por las Asambleas de accionistas son obligatorias aún para los ausentes o disidentes, salvo el derecho de oposición que les confiere la Ley General de Sociedades Mercantiles.---------------------

--------------------**ADMINISTRACIÓN Y VIGILANCIA DE LA SOCIEDAD**--------------------

--- **ARTÍCULO VIGÉSIMO PRIMERO.** La administración, según decisión de la Asamblea, podrá estar a cargo de un Administrador Único o de un Consejo de Administración, formado por el número de consejeros propietarios que acuerde la Asamblea que los elija y podrán elegirse suplentes que actuarán a falta o en ausencia de los respectivos propietarios.-------

---**ARTÍCULO VIGÉSIMO SEGUNDO.** Los miembros del Consejo de Administración o el Administrador Único podrán ser o no accionistas; duraran en su cargo un año, pero continuarán en su desempeño hasta que las personas designadas para substituirlo tomen posesión; podrá ser reelecto y recibirá las remuneraciones que determine la Asamblea Ordinaria de Accionistas. En caso de que la administración de la sociedad sea confiada en un Consejo de Administración, se cuidará el derecho que tienen las minorías para designar a un Consejero, de acuerdo con el artículo ciento cuarenta y cuatro de la Ley General de Sociedades Mercantiles---

--- **ARTÍCULO VIGÉSIMO TERCERO.** El Consejo de Administración celebrará sesiones cuando sea convocado al efecto por su Presidente, por el Secretario, por el o los Comisarios o por cualesquiera de los Consejeros.---

--- La sesiones del Consejo de Administración serán convocadas por medio de un aviso por escrito enviado por correo certificado con acuse de recibo que deberá contener el Orden del Día, el lugar, la fecha y la hora de Sesión ha de celebrarse, misma que deberá ser recibida por todos los miembros del Consejo de Administración con por lo menos quince días de anticipación a la fecha fijada por la sesión.-------------------------------------

--- **ARTÍCULO VIGÉSIMO CUARTO.** Las Sesiones del Consejo de Administración de la Sociedad para las cuales se hayan satisfecho las disposiciones relativas a convocatorias que establece el Artículo Vigésimo Tercero de estos estatutos, se consideraran legalmente instaladas en virtud de primera convocatoria, si se encuentran presentes la mayoría del total de los Consejeros en funciones. En caso de que en primera convocatoria no se alcance el quórum requerido, se podrán emitir segunda o ulterior convocatorias, y se consideraran legalmente instaladas independientemente del número de Consejeros que asistieran, siempre que sean más de dos; en lo entendido, sin embargo, de que cada consejero deberá ser notificado de que dicha segunda o ulterior convocatoria no menos de quince [illegible] de la fecha en que ha de celebrarse la sesión y el Orden del Día deberá ser igual al especificado en la primera convocatoria.------------------------------

--- Salvo que votación mayor sea requerida de conformidad con la Ley General de Sociedades Mercantiles, el Consejo de Administración adoptara sus resoluciones por mayoría de votos de los presentes. En caso de empate, el Presidente del Consejo decidirá con voto de calidad. Adicionalmente, las resoluciones podrán ser tomadas fuera de Sesión de Consejo, por unanimidad de votos, teniendo para todos los efectos legales, la misma validez que si hubieren adoptado en sesión de consejo, siempre y cuando se confirmen por escrito. ------------------------------

--- No obstante lo anterior, las resoluciones que tome el Consejo de Administración, reunido en virtud de primera, segunda o ulteriores convocatorias, para tratar de los siguientes asuntos, deberán de contar con el voto unánime de todos sus miembros. ---------

---1.- Autorización para la venta, gravamen, transferencia, cesión o transmisión por cualquier título legal de las acciones o partes sociales representativas del capital social de aquellas sociedades en las que la Sociedad tenga el carácter de accionista o socio, cualquiera que sea el monto o porcentaje de su participación accionaria. ----------------

---2.- Aprobación de modificaciones o desviaciones al presupuesto anual, por montos que excedan del diez por ciento de lo presupuestado o en el rubro respectivo. ---------------

---3.- Otorgamiento de poderes para realizar actos de dominio a nombre de la Sociedad. --

---4.- Autorización para la venta o gravamen de cualesquiera activos (incluyendo intangibles) de la Sociedad o cualquiera de su subsidiarias, que representan en lo individual o en su conjunto un monto que exceda del cinco por ciento del valor contable de la totalidad de los activos de la Sociedad, a nivel consolidado, según los últimos estados financieros de la Sociedad aprobados por los accionistas. ----------------------

--- **ARTÍCULO VIGÉSIMO QUINTO.** A falta de designación expresa de la Asamblea de Accionistas que acuerde su designación, en la primera sesión del Consejo de Administración que se reúna inmediatamente después de que se celebre la Asamblea en que hubieran sido designados, los Consejeros nombraran de entre ellos al Presidente. Asimismo designarán a un Secretario, quien podrá o no ser Consejero, así como a las demás personas que ocupen cargos que se crearen para el mejor desempeño de sus funciones. Las ausencias temporales o definitivas en el Consejo de Administración, serán cubiertas por los suplentes respectivos. --

--- **ARTÍCULO VIGÉSIMO SEXTO.** El Consejo de Administración o el Administrador Único es el representante Legal de la Sociedad y, por consiguiente, estará investido y tendrá las mas amplias facultades para realizar el objeto social, dirigir y administrar la sociedad, por lo que de manera enunciativa y no limitativa, actuarán con las siguientes facultades: --------

---I.- ***PODER GENERAL PARA PLEITOS Y COBRANZAS*** con todas las facultades generales y aún los especiales que de acuerdo con la Ley requieran cláusula especial, en los términos del párrafo primero del artículo siete punto setecientos setenta y uno y del artículo siete punto ochocientos seis del Código Civil vigente del Estado de México y sus correlativos de las Entidades donde lo ejercite.--

--- De manera enunciativa y no limitativa, se mencionan entre otras facultades, las siguientes:--

--- I.- Para desistirse, de toda clase de procedimientos, inclusive el amparo.----------------

--- II.- Para transigir.---

--- III.- Para comprometer en árbitros.---

--- IV.- Para absolver y articular posiciones.---

--- V. - Para recusar.---

--- VII.- Para recibir pagos.---

--- VIII. - Para los demás actos que expresamente determine la Ley.---

--- Se ejercerá ante particulares y ante toda clase de autoridades administrativas o judiciales, inclusive de carácter Federal o Local y ante las Juntas de Conciliación y arbitraje.---

--- II. **_PODER GENERAL PARA ACTOS DE ADMINISTRACIÓN_** en términos del segundo párrafo del citado artículo siete punto setecientos setenta y uno del Código Civil del Estado de México y su correlativo en las Entidades donde se ejercite.---

--- III. **_PODER GENERAL PARA ACTOS DE DOMINIO_**, de acuerdo con el párrafo tercero del citado artículo siete punto setecientos setenta y uno del Código Civil del Estado de México y su correlativo en las Entidades donde se ejercite.---

--- IV. **_REPRESENTACIÓN EN MATERIA LABORAL_**, con facultades expresas para comparecer ante cualquier autoridad laboral, Juntas Federales y Locales de Conciliación, Juntas Federales y Locales de Conciliación y Arbitraje y en especial audiencias en la etapa conciliatoria en los juicios de orden laboral, facultados para celebrar convenios que de dichas audiencias pudieren resultar, así como en forma especial para absolver y articular posiciones, conciliar, transigir, formular convenios, presentar denuncias y querellas, desistirse de toda clase de juicios y recursos aún el amparo, representar a la sociedad ante toda clase de autoridades, ya sean judiciales, administrativas o cualesquiera otras que se avoquen al conocimiento de conflictos laborales, en términos de los artículos once, ochocientos setenta y ocho, seiscientos noventa y dos fracciones primera, segunda y tercera, setecientos ochenta y seis y ochocientos setenta y seis de la Ley Federal del Trabajo.---

--- V.- **_PODER PARA OTORGAR, SUSCRIBIR, AVALAR Y ENDOSAR TÍTULOS DE CRÉDITO_**, en los términos de la Ley General de Títulos y Operaciones de Crédito así como para verificar toda clase de operaciones bancarias, de comercio y abrir o cerrar cuentas corrientes en bancos y demás instituciones financieras.---

--- VI. Para delegar sus facultades en uno o varios Consejeros para que actúen separadamente o en comité.---

--- VII. Facultad para otorgar poderes generales o especiales y para revocar unos y otros -

--- VIII. Para nombrar y remover libremente Director o Gerente General, Gerentes, Directores y demás funcionarios, asesores técnicos y empleados de la sociedad y para delegar todo o parte de éstas facultades en una o más personas, fijándoles a aquellos sus retribución.---

--- IX.- Facultad para participar en todo tipo de Licitaciones, así como ante la SECRETARIA DE HACIENDA Y CRÉDITO PÚBLICO, INSTITUTO MEXICANO DEL SEGURO SOCIAL (IMSS) e INSTITUTO DEL FONDO NACIONAL DE LA VIVIENDA PARA LOS TRABAJADORES (INFONAVIT)---

--- X. Conforme al artículo número siete punto setecientos sesenta y ocho del Código Civil para el Estado de México, la vigencia de las facultades antes establecidas para el Consejo de Administración o Administrador Único en su caso, será de noventa y nueve años.---

--- Las facultades antes relacionadas, podrán ser restringidas por la Asamblea General de Accionistas, la que se reserva el derecho de delegarlas total o parcialmente en la persona de uno o más miembros del Consejo de Administración de la Sociedad o persona ajena a ésta.---

--- **ARTÍCULO VIGÉSIMO SÉPTIMO.**- La vigilancia de la Sociedad estará a cargo de uno o más Comisarios que designará la Asamblea de Accionistas, los cuales podrán tener sus respectivos suplentes. Los accionistas tenedores de acciones que representen por lo menos el veinticinco por ciento de las acciones representativas del capital social tendrán en todo tiempo el derecho de designar a un Comisario. Los Comisarios y, en su caso, sus suplentes no necesitaran ser accionistas de la Sociedad, serán nombrados anualmente, podrán ser reelectos una o más veces, y continuaran en el desempeño de sus funciones hasta en tanto la asamblea haga nuevos nombramientos y los designados tomen posesión de sus cargos. ---

--- Los Comisarios tendrán las atribuciones y obligaciones que se enumeran en el artículo ciento sesenta y seis de la Ley General de Sociedades Mercantiles, así como todas aquellas que les sean delegadas por la Asamblea de Accionistas y percibirán la remuneración que anualmente ésta les señale.---

---------------------EJERCICIO SOCIAL E INFORMACIÓN FINANCIERA ---------------------

--- **ARTÍCULO VIGÉSIMO OCTAVO.** El ejercicio social coincidirá con el año calendario, con excepción del primero, que comenzará en la fecha de firma de la presente escritura y terminará el treinta y uno de diciembre del mismo año.---

--- **ARTICULO VIGÉSIMO NOVENO.** Dentro de los cuatro meses siguientes a la clausura de cada ejercicio social, el Consejo de Administración o el Administrador Único preparará la siguiente información financiera y cualquier otra que sea necesaria conforme a los artículos ciento setenta y dos de la Ley General de Sociedades Mercantiles. Respecto de dicho informe se procederá a lo ordenado en los artículos, ciento setenta y tres, ciento setenta y seis y ciento setenta y siete de la misma Ley y deberá quedar concluido y ponerse a disposición de los accionistas por lo menos quince días antes de la fecha en que se verifique la Asamblea que haya discutirlo.---

---------------------------------UTILIDADES Y PÉRDIDAS ---------------------------------

---**ARTÍCULO TRIGÉSIMO** Para la distribución de utilidades deberá observarse lo dispuesto en los artículos dieciséis, diecisiete, dieciocho, diecinueve, veinte y veintiuno de la ley General de Sociedades Mercantiles, lo que solo podrá hacerse después de que hayan sido debidamente aprobados por la Asamblea General, los estados financieros que las arrojen.---

--- De las utilidades netas deberá separarse anualmente un cinco por ciento, cuando menos, para constituir, incrementar o en su caso reponer el fondo de reserva legal, hasta que dicho fondo sea igual al veinte por ciento del capital social.---

--- Las utilidades que se obtengan se distribuirán entre todos los accionistas, en proporción al número de sus acciones, o en su caso, al importe exhibido de las mismas.---

--- Las pérdidas, en su caso, serán soportadas en la misma proporción y hasta por el importe de sus acciones.---

--- Los fundadores no se reservan participación especial alguna, aparte de la que corresponda al número de sus acciones.--

--DISOLUCIÓN Y LIQUIDACIÓN --

--- **ARTÍCULO TRIGÉSIMO PRIMERO**. Para la Disolución y Liquidación de la sociedad se observará lo ordenado por la Ley General de Sociedades Mercantiles. Disuelta la Sociedad se pondrá en liquidación. La Asamblea Extraordinaria de Accionistas designará uno o más liquidadores quienes tendrán las facultades que establece la Ley o que determine la Asamblea Extraordinaria de Accionistas que los designe.--

--- El o los liquidadores practicarán la liquidación con arreglo a las bases que, en su caso, determinare dicha Asamblea y, en su defecto, con arreglo los capítulos décimo y décimo primero romanos, de la mencionada Ley General de Sociedades Mercantiles.--

--- **ARTÍCULO TRIGÉSIMO SEGUNDO.** La Fusión, Transformación y Escisión de la Sociedad, se sujetará a lo dispuesto en el capítulo noveno romano de la Ley General de Sociedades Mercantiles.--

--- **ARTÍCULO TRIGÉSIMO TERCERO.** En todo lo no previsto expresamente en estos estatutos, regirán las disposiciones de la Ley General de Sociedades Mercantiles--

--**ARTÍCULOS TRANSITORIOS** --

--- **PRIMERO.** El Capital Social Mínimo Fijo establecido en el artículo sexto de los estatutos en éste acto queda íntegramente suscrito y pagado de la siguiente manera:--

ACCIONISTAS	ACCIONES NOMINATIVAS	IMPORTE, VALOR NOMINAL
CONSULTORIA DE COMERCIO INTERNACIONAL DE ESPAÑA, SOCIEDAD ANÓNIMA DE CAPITAL VARIABLE	2460 DOS MIL CUATROCIENTAS SESENTA	$2'460,000.00 DOS MILLONES CUATROCIENTOS SESENTA MIL PESOS MONEDA NACIONAL
SERVICIOS ESPECIALIZADOS EN MONTAJES INDUSTRIALES, SOCIEDAD ANONIMA DE CAPITAL VARIABLE	150 CIENTO CINCUENTA	$150,000.00 CIENTO CINCUENTA MIL PESOS MONEDA NACIONAL
AYETH PRICELLA FLORES ROSAS	150 CIENTO CINCUENTA	$150,000.00 CIENTO CINCUENTA MIL PESOS MONEDA NACIONAL
CÉSAR ROMERO RODRIGUEZ	150 CIENTO CINCUENTA	$150,000.00 CIENTO CINCUENTA MIL PESOS MONEDA NACIONAL
A.A.C.F. MANIOBRAS Y CONSTRUCCIONES ELECTRICAS, SOCIEDAD ANONIMA DE CAPITAL VARIABLE	45 CUARENTA Y CINCO	$45,000.00 CUARENTA Y CINCO MIL PESOS MONEDA NACIONAL

LETICIA IVETTE LAZCANO ESQUEDA	45 CUARENTA Y CINCO	$45,000.00 CUARENTA Y CINCO MIL PESOS MONEDA NACIONAL
TOTAL	**3000 TRES MIL**	**$ 3'000,000.00 TRES MILLONES DE PESOS MONEDA NACIONAL**

--- **SEGUNDO**.- Los otorgantes de esta escritura, consideran la reunión para su firma como la primera Asamblea General de Accionistas y toman por unanimidad de votos, los siguientes: --

-- **ACUERDOS** --

--- **ARTICULO PRIMERO**.- Los comparecientes de esta escritura acuerdan: --------------------

--- **I.**- Confiar la administración de la sociedad a un **CONSEJO DE ADMINISTRACIÓN**, y para tal efecto designan a las siguientes personas: --

--- Los señores **CÉSAR MARTÍN RODRÍGUEZ, ALFONSO AVELINO CRUZ SUÁREZ, AYETH PRICELLA FLORES ROSAS, CÉSAR ROMERO RODRÍGUEZ** y **WILBERTH JOSE JESUS CAUICH PENICHE**, en su carácter de Presidente, Tesorero, Secretario y Vocales del Consejo de Administración, respectivamente, quienes para el desempeño de sus funciones, gozaran conjunta o separadamente de todas y cada de las facultades que señala el artículo **VIGÉSIMO SÉXTO** de los estatutos que rigen esta sociedad, mismas que se tienen aquí por reproducidas como si a la letra se insertasen, las cuales tendrán una vigencia del tiempo que duren en sus cargos, a excepción de la facultad para **PARA OTORGAR, SUSCRIBIR, AVALAR Y ENDOSAR TÍTULOS DE CRÉDITO**, dichas facultades serán ejercidas conjunta o separadamente única y exclusivamente por los señores y **ALFONSO AVELINO CRUZ SUÁREZ**, en su carácter de Presidente y Tesorero respectivamente, el **PODER GENERAL PARA ACTOS DE DOMINIO** deberá ejercerse de manera conjunta por todos los miembros del Consejo de Administración.--------------------

--- **TERCERO**.- Para efectos de adquirir acciones, partes sociales, participaciones, partes de interés u obligaciones de toda clase de asociaciones o sociedades y formar parte en ellas, según sea necesario o conveniente para el desarrollo de su objeto social, se deberá de actuar de manera conjunta por tres miembros del Consejo de Administración.----------

--- **CUARTO**.- Los comparecientes de esta escritura, manifiestan: --------------------

--- A.- Que obra en las cajas de la sociedad, el importe total del capital mínimo sin derecho a retiro.--

---- B.- Que los funcionarios designados aceptaron sus cargos.--------------------

--- **QUINTO**.- Designan como Comisario al señor **HUMBERTO HOYUELA LÓPEZ**.--------------------

--- **SEXTO**.- Los comparecientes autorizan a la suscrita notario para realizar los trámites administrativos y para llevar a cabo la inscripción del primer testimonio que de esta escritura se expida, en el Registro Público de Comercio correspondiente. ----------

-- **PERSONALIDADES** --

---Yo, la Notario, Doy Fe: ---

--- I.- Que a mi juicio los comparecientes tienen capacidad legal para la celebración de este acto, pues nada me consta en contrario, y que se identificaron ante mí con los documentos que en fotocopia agrego al apéndice de esta escritura con la letra "D". ------

--- II.- Que en términos del artículo veintisiete del Código Fiscal de la Federación, se verificaron las claves del Registro Federal de Contribuyentes de los accionista que constituyen la presente sociedad y que en copia fotostática agrego al apéndice de esta escritura, bajo la letra "E".---

--------- --- III.- Que previne a los comparecientes, en términos de lo dispuesto por el Artículo Ciento Cincuenta y Dos del Reglamento de la Ley General de Población, que en caso de que personas extranjeras sean funcionarios de la Sociedad, el desempeño de sus cargos estará sujeto a la autorización correspondiente que emita la Secretaría de Gobernación.----IV.- Que advertí a los comparecientes que deberán acreditarme dentro del mes siguiente a la fecha de firma de la presente escritura, haber presentado la solicitud de inscripción de la sociedad en el Registro Federal de Contribuyentes y que en caso de no exhibirme dicha solicitud, procederé a dar el aviso a las autoridades fiscales correspondientes, en términos del artículo veintisiete del Código Fiscal de la Federación.---

---V.- Que lo relacionado e inserto concuerda fielmente con los originales que tuve a la vista a los cuales me remití.---

---VI.- Que manifestaron por sus **GENERALES** ser: ---

[redacted] español por nacimiento, hijo de padres españoles, originario de Madrid, España, lugar donde nació el día treinta y uno de marzo de mil novecientos setenta y seis, casado, ingeniero, con domicilio en con domicilio en Hesiodo número quinientos cuarenta y cuatro, interior quinientos dos, colonia Polanco, Delegación Miguel Hidalgo, en México, Distrito Federal y de paso por este Municipio de Naucalpan de Juárez, Estado de México, para la firma del presente instrumento, acreditando su legal estancia en el país como inmigrante con su documento Migratorio, expedido por la Secretaría de Gobernación, Instituto Nacional de Migración, el día veintinueve de noviembre de dos mil diez y vigente al día veintinueve de noviembre de dos mil once, documento que en copia agrego al apéndice de este instrumento con la letra "F".--------

--- **SEÑOR ALFONSO AVELINO CRUZ SUÁREZ**, mexicano por nacimiento, hijo de padres mexicanos, originario de México, Distrito Federal, lugar donde nació el día diecinueve de septiembre de mil novecientos setenta y dos, casado, Ingeniero, con domicilio en Catorce de Julio número cuarenta y siete A, Colonia Huichapan, Delegación Xochimilco, en México, Distrito Federal y de paso por este Municipio de Naucalpan de Juárez, Estado de México, para la firma del presente instrumento, con Registro Federal de Contribuyentes número CUSA7209191X7 (CUSA siete dos cero nueve uno nueve uno X siete), quien se identifica con Pasaporte expedido por la Secretaría de Relaciones Exteriores, el día treinta de diciembre de dos mil nueve.---

--- **SEÑORA [illegible]RICELLA FLORES ROSAS,** mexicana por nacimiento, originaria de Cananea, Estado de Sonora, lugar donde nació el día nueve de abril de mil novecientos sesenta y ocho, soltera, Empresaria, con domicilio en Campos Elíseos número ciento treinta y cuatro, colonia Polanco Reforma, Delegación Miguel Hidalgo, en México, Distrito Federal y de paso por este Municipio de Naucalpan de Juárez, Estado de México, para la firma del presente instrumento, con Registro Federal de Contribuyentes número FORA680409TL8 (FORA seis ocho cero cuatro cero nueve TL ocho), quien se identifica con con Pasaporte expedido por la Secretaría de Relaciones Exteriores, el día diecisiete de noviembre de dos mil diez.---

--- **SEÑOR CÉSAR ROMERO RODRÍGUEZ,** mexicano por nacimiento, hijo de padres mexicanos, originario de México, Distrito Federal, lugar donde nació el día veintinueve de septiembre de mil novecientos sesenta y nueve, casado, Ingeniero, con domicilio en Privada la Cañada número sesenta, Pent House B, Bosque Real, Huixquilucan, Estado de México, con Registro Federal de Contribuyentes número RORC690929R30 (RORC seis nueve cero nueve dos nueve R tres cero), quien se identifica con Pasaporte expedido por la Secretaría de Relaciones Exteriores, el día veintiséis de enero de dos mil once.---

--- **SEÑOR WILBERTH JOSE JESUS CAUICH PENICHE,** mexicano por nacimiento, hijo de padres mexicanos, originario de Mérida, Estado de Yucatán, lugar donde nació el día nueve de enero de mil novecientos cincuenta y nueve, casado, Comerciante, con domicilio en calle Cuarenta número trescientos doce, colonia Francisco Villa Poniente, Mérida, Estado de Yucatán y de paso por este Municipio de Naucalpan de Juárez, Estado de México, para la firma del presente instrumento, con Registro Federal de Contribuyentes número CAPW5901093N5 (CAPW cinco nueve cero uno cero nueve tres N cinco), quien se identifica con Credencial para Votar, expedida por el Instituto Federal Electoral.---

--- **SEÑORA LETICIA IVETT LAZCANO ESQUEDA,** mexicana por nacimiento, originaria de México, Distrito Federal, lugar donde nació el día doce de enero de mil novecientos setenta, casada, Licenciada en Comunicación, con domicilio con domicilio en Privada la Cañada número sesenta, Pent House B, Bosque Real, Huixquilucan, Estado de México, con Registro Federal de Contribuyentes número LAEL700112LL2 (LAEL siete cero cero uno uno dos LL dos), quien se identifica con Credencial para Votar, expedida por el Instituto Federal Electoral.---

--- VII.- De que leído este instrumento a los comparecientes a quienes expliqué el valor y consecuencias legales del mismo, se manifestaron conformes con sus términos y firman, para constancia el mismo día de su fecha en que Autorizo Definitivamente.- DOY FE.---

--- Agrego al apéndice de este instrumento las notas complementarias bajo la letra que les corresponda.- Doy Fe.---

--- Para cumplir con lo dispuesto por el artículo siete punto setecientos setenta y uno del Código Civil vigente en el Estado de México, mismo que tiene idéntica redacción al artículo dos mil quinientos cincuenta y cuatro del mismo ordenamiento legal vigente en el Distrito Federal en materia común y en toda la República en materia Federal, se transcribe íntegramente a continuación: --

--ARTICULO 7.771--

-------------------------DEL CODIGO CIVIL VIGENTE EN EL ESTADO DE MEXICO.-------------------------

--- " En todos los poderes para pleitos y cobranzas, bastará que se diga que se otorga con todas las facultades generales y las especiales que requieran cláusulas especiales conforme a la ley, para que se entiendan conferidos sin limitación alguna.-----------------

--- En los poderes generales para administrar bienes bastará expresar que se dan con ese carácter, para que el apoderado tenga toda clase de facultades administrativas.----------

--- En los poderes generales, para ejercer actos de dominio, bastará que se den con ese carácter para que el apoderado tengo todas las facultades de dueño, tanto en lo relativo a los bienes, como para hacer toda clase de gestiones a fin de defenderlos.---------

--- Cuando se quisieren limitar en los tres casos antes mencionadas las facultades de los apoderados se consignarán las limitaciones o los poderes serán especiales.-----------------

--- Los notarios insertarán este artículo en los testimonios de los poderes que otorguen".-----

--- **ES COPIA CERTIFICADA**, sacada fielmente de su original que obra en el protocolo abierto que está mi cargo, se expide para la sociedad denominada **CONSORCIO INTEGRADOR SONORA 80M, SOCIEDAD ANÓNIMA DE CAPITAL VARIABLE**, va en catorce páginas debidamente selladas y cotejadas.--

--- En Naucalpan de Juárez, Estado de México a los dieciocho días del mes de julio del año dos mil once. Doy Fe.--

LIC. PATRICIA M. RUIZ DE CHAVEZ RINCON GALLARDO NOTARIO PUBLICO No. 103 NAUCALPAN DE JUAREZ ESTADO DE MEXICO

SUBDIRECCIÓN DE SOCIE

PERMISO	0925784
EXPEDIENTE	20110907925
FOLIO	110708098001

De conformidad con lo dispuesto por los artículos 27, fracción [illegible] Constitución Política de los Estados Unidos Mexicanos, 28, fracción V de la Ley Orgánica de la Administración Pública Federal, 15 de la Ley de Inversión Extranjera y 13, 14 y 18 del Reglamento de la Ley de Inversión Extranjera y del Registro Nacional de Inversiones Extranjeras, y en atención a la solicitud presentada por el (la) Sr(a). **ALFONSO CRUZ AGUIRRE**, con fundamento en lo dispuesto por los artículos 33 fracción IV del Reglamento Interior de la Secretaría de Relaciones Exteriores en vigor y [illegible] XIO incisos a) fracción VI y d) fracción I del ACUERDO publicado en el Diario Oficial de la Federación el 11 de abril de 2008, por el que se reforman los artículos sexto y séptimo; y se adicionan los artículos primero bis y décimo primero bis, del Acuerdo por el que se delegan facultades en los servidores públicos de lo Secretaría de Relaciones Exteriores que se indican, publicado el 28 de abril de [illegible], se concede el permiso para constituir una **SA DE CV** bajo la siguiente denominación:

CONSORCIO INTEGRADOR SONORA 80M

Este permiso, quedará condicionado a que en los estatutos de la sociedad que se constituya, se inserte la cláusula de exclusión de extranjeros o el convenio previsto en la fracción I del artículo 27 Constitucional, de conformidad con lo que establecen los artículos 15 de la Ley de Inversión Extranjera y 14 del Reglamento de la Ley de Inversión Extranjera y del Registro Nacional de Inversiones Extranjeras. Cabe señalar que el presente permiso se otorga sin perjuicio de lo dispuesto por el artículo [illegible] de la Ley de la Propiedad Industrial.

COTEJADO

Este permiso quedará sin efectos si dentro de los noventa días hábiles siguientes a la fecha de otorgamiento del mismo, los interesados no acuden a otorgar ante fedatario público el instrumento correspondiente a la Constitución de que se trata, de conformidad con lo establecido por el artículo 17 del Reglamento de la Ley de Inversión Extranjera y del Registro Nacional de Inversiones Extranjeras.

Asimismo, el interesado deberá dar aviso del uso de la denominación que se autoriza mediante el presente permiso a la Secretaría de Relaciones Exteriores dentro de los seis meses siguientes a la expedición del mismo, de conformidad con lo dispuesto por el artículo 18 del Reglamento de la Ley de Inversión Extranjera y del Registro Nacional de Inversiones Extranjeras.

México, DF. a 08 de julio de 2011

EL SUBDIRECTOR

LIC. DAVID LOPEZ RODRIGUEZ

11 JUL. 2011

SRE

SIN TEXTO

Exhibit 4

Translation from Spanish
20 July 2017

Tax Identification Card

SHCP
MINISTRY OF THE TREASURY AND PUBLIC CREDIT

SAT
Tax Administration Service

CIS110712JQ2
Federal Taxpayer Registry

CONSORCIO INTEGRADOR SONORA 80 M SA DE CV

Name, Company or Business Name
idCIF: 150 503 588 46
VALIDATE YOUR TAX INFORMATION

ROSETTA STONE *ASSOCIATES IN TRANSLATION*

7375 N. Calle sin Celo, Tucson, AZ 85718 • (520) 575-9200 • rosettrans@aol.com • www.rosettrans.com
• ATA-Certified •

Certification

AT THE REQUEST OF THE INTERESTED PARTY, I hereby certify that I have translated the following document:

Consorcio Integrador Sonora 80 M S.A. de C.V. Tax Documents ████

from the Spanish into the English language on this 20th day of July 2017, and that the information contained in the translated documents is a true, complete and correct reflection of the original text, to the best of my ability as a Professional Translator.

ROSETTA STONE ASSOCIATES IN TRANSLATION

Carola P. Myers

CAROLA P. MYERS
Member, A.C.I.A. - ATA-Certified

Your Dependable Source of Foreign Language Translation and Interpretation

Cédula de Identificación Fiscal

SHCP

SAT

CIS110712JQ2

Registro Federal de Contribuyentes

CONSORCIO INTEGRADOR SONORA 80M SA DE CV

Nombre, denominación o razón social

idCIF:15050358846

VALIDA TU INFORMACIÓN FISCAL

Exhibit
5

Translation from Spanish
20 July 2017

gob.mx

TAX IDENTIFICATION CARD

SHCP SAT Tax Administration Service

CIS110712JQ2
Federal Taxpayer Registry

CONSORCIO INTEGRADOR SONORA 80M
Name, Business Name

idCIF: 15050358846
VALIDATE YOUR TAX INFORMATION

SHCP SAT Tax Administration Service

CERTIFICATE OF TAX STATUS

Place and Date of Issue
BENITO JUAREZ, MEXICO CITY, JUNE 19, 2017

CIS110712JQ2

Taxpayer Identification Data:	
Federal Taxpayer Registration Number:	CIS110712JQ2
Name/Business Name:	CONSORCIO INTEGRADOR SONORA 80M
Capitalization Type	SOCIEDAD ANÓNIMA DE CAPITAL VARIABLE
Commercial Name:	CONSORCIO INTEGRADOR SONORA 80M
Operational Start-Up Date:	JULY 12, 2011
Registry Status:	ACTIVE
Date of Last Status Change:	SEPTEMBER 13, 2011

Information on Location:	
Zip Code: 03810	**Road Type:** STREET
Road Name: MONTECITO	**Exterior Number:** 38 FLOOR 28
Interior Number: 12 & 13	**Name of Section:** NAPOLES
Place Name:	**Municipality or Territorial Demarcation:** BENITO JUAREZ
Name of State or Federal District: MEXICO CITY	**Street Corner:** AVENIDA INSURGENTES
Street: CALLE DAKOTA	**E-mail:**

Page [1] of [3]

MEXICO
GOVERNMENT OF THE REPUBLIC

Contact
Av. Hidalgo 77, col. Guerrero, 06300, Mexico City
Hotline: 627 22 728 from Mexico City
or 01 (55) 627 22 728 from elsewhere in the country
From U.S. and Canada: 1 877 44 88 728
denuncias@sat.gob.mx

gob.mx

Landline Tel. Area Code: 55	**Number:** 11070436

Business Activities:

Sequence	Business Activities:	Percentage	Start Date	End Date
1	Environmental consulting services		12/07/2011	
2	Management and supervision of building projects for 40 electric power generation and conduction and telecommunications		12/07/2011	

Regimens:

Regimen		Start Date	End Date
General Regimen, Corporate Entities		12/07/2011	
		12/07/2011	

Requirements:

Description of Requirement	Due Date Description	Start Date	End Date
Payment of monthly withholdings of income tax for wages and salaries	Not later than day 17 of the month immediately following the relevant period	12/07/2011	
Informational annual return on customers and suppliers of goods and services. Income tax	Not later than February 15 of the following year	12/07/2011	
Informational annual return on withholdings of income tax for wages and salaries and wage-like earnings	Not later than February 15 of the following year	12/07/2011	
Informational return on Value Added Tax together with annual income tax return.	Together with the annual return for the fiscal year	12/07/2011	
Definitive monthly Value Added Tax payment.	Not later than day 17 of the month immediately following the relevant period	12/07/2011	
Annual income tax return for fiscal year (corporate entities)	Within three months following the close of the business year	12/07/2011	
Suppliers' Value Added Tax return.	Not later than the last day of the month immediately following the relevant period.	12/07/2011	
Informational annual return on employment subsidy	Not later than February 15 of each year	12/07/2011	
Provisional monthly income tax payment (corporate entities filing under general regimen)	Not later than day 17 of the month immediately following the relevant period	01/04/2011	

Your personal information is recorded and protected in the SAT system pursuant to applicable legal provisions for the protection of private information and various tax and legal provisions on confidentiality and data protection, allowing the tax authority to exercise its responsibilities.

If you wish to amend or correct your personal information, you may visit any Tax Service Office and/or go to the administration at http://sat.gob.mx

Original seal chain: ||2017/06/19|CIS110712JQ2|CONSTANCIA DE SITUACIÓN FISCAL|200001000007001121 88||

Digital seal: fxoV9Ajwr5Nke6lyxXspYGS4XRDbCh2Nx7MppfnQ6HlC4bBmWvwmdRJSR22kUFOssFsF8yhtDXq5I/Xb//xCXY
3IQ4KRTnCh6SZzpIMs7EITYE3M2LGiTcBiv7hNDcXODTu9QUM7FiacomVqg7NFHr823NF87+kVqxfzs270jA=

MEXICO
GOVERNMENT OF THE REPUBLIC

COFEMER

Contact
Av. Hidalgo 77, col. Guerrero, 06300, Mexico City
Hotline: 627 22 728 from Mexico City
or 01 (55) 627 22 728 from elsewhere in the country
From U.S. and Canada: 1 877 44 88 728
denuncias@sat.gob.mx

Translation from Spanish
20 July 2017

MEXICO
GOVERNMENT OF THE REPUBLIC

COFEMER

Contact
Av. Hidalgo 77, col. Guerrero, 06300, Mexico City
Hotline: 627 22 728 from Mexico City
or 01 (55) 627 22 728 from elsewhere in the country
From U.S. and Canada: 1 877 44 88 728

ROSETTA STONE *ASSOCIATES IN TRANSLATION*

7375 N. Calle sin Celo, Tucson, AZ 85718 • (520) 575-9200 • rosettrans@aol.com • www.rosettrans.com
• ATA-Certified •

Certification

AT THE REQUEST OF THE INTERESTED PARTY, I hereby certify that I have translated the following document:

Consorcio Integrador Sonora 80 M S.A. de C.V. Tax Documents

from the Spanish into the English language on this 20th day of July 2017, and that the information contained in the translated documents is a true, complete and correct reflection of the original text, to the best of my ability as a Professional Translator.

ROSETTA STONE ASSOCIATES IN TRANSLATION

Carola P. Myers

CAROLA P. MYERS
Member, A.C.I.A. - ATA-Certified

gob.mx

CEDULA DE IDENTIFICACION FISCAL

SHCP

SAT Servicio de Administración Tributaria

CIS110712JQ2
Registro Federal de Contribuyentes

CONSORCIO INTEGRADOR SONORA 80M
Nombre, denominación o razón social

IdCIF: 15050358846
VALIDA TU INFORMACIÓN FISCAL

SHCP

SAT Servicio de Administración Tributaria

CONSTANCIA DE SITUACIÓN FISCAL

Lugar y Fecha de Emisión

CIS110712JQ2

Datos de Identificación del Contribuyente:

RFC:	CIS110712JQ2
Denominación/Razón Social:	CONSORCIO INTEGRADOR SONORA 80M
Régimen Capital:	SOCIEDAD ANONIMA DE CAPITAL VARIABLE
Nombre Comercial:	CONSORCIO INTEGRADOR SONORA 80M
Fecha inicio de operaciones:	12 DE JULIO DE 2011
Estatus en el padrón:	ACTIVO
Fecha de último cambio de estado:	13 DE SEPTIEMBRE DE 2011

Datos de Ubicación:

Código Postal: 03810	Tipo de Vialidad: CALLE
Nombre de Vialidad: MONTECITO	Número Exterior: 38 PISO 28
Número Interior: 12 Y 13	Nombre de la Colonia: NAPOLES
Nombre de la Localidad:	Nombre del Municipio o Demarcación Territorial: BENITO JUAREZ
Nombre de la Entidad Federativa: CIUDAD DE MEXICO	Entre Calle: AVENIDA INSURGENTES
Y Calle: CALLE DAKOTA	Correo Electrónico:

Página [1] de [3]

MÉXICO

COFEMER

Contacto
Av. Hidalgo 77, col. Guerrero, c.p. 06300, Ciudad de México.
Atención telefónica: 627 22 728 desde la Ciudad de México,
o 01 (55) 627 22 728 del resto del país.
Desde Estados Unidos y Canadá 1 877 44 83 728
denuncias@sat.gob.mx

gob.mx

Tel. Fijo Lada: 55	Número: 11070436

Actividades Económicas:

Orden	Actividad Económica	Porcentaje	Fecha Inicio	Fecha Fin
1	Servicios de consultoría en medio ambiente	60	12/07/2011	
2	Administración y supervisión de construcción de obras de generación y conducción de energía eléctrica y telecomunicaciones	40	12/07/2011	

Regímenes:

Régimen	Fecha Inicio	Fecha Fin
Régimen General de Ley Personas Morales	12/07/2011	

Obligaciones:

Descripción de la Obligación	Descripción Vencimiento	Fecha Inicio	Fecha Fin
Entero de retenciones mensuales de ISR por sueldos y salarios	A más tardar el día 17 del mes inmediato posterior al periodo que corresponda.	12/07/2011	
Declaración informativa anual de clientes y proveedores de bienes y servicios. Impuesto sobre la renta.	A más tardar el 15 de febrero del año siguiente	12/07/2011	
declaración informativa anual de retenciones de ISR por sueldos y salarios e ingresos asimilados a salarios	A más tardar el 15 de febrero del año siguiente	12/07/2011	
Declaración informativa de IVA con la anual de ISR	Conjuntamente con la declaración anual del ejercicio.	12/07/2011	
Pago definitivo mensual de IVA.	A más tardar el día 17 del mes inmediato posterior al periodo que corresponda.	12/07/2011	
Declaración anual de ISR del ejercicio Personas morales.	Dentro de los tres meses siguientes al cierre del ejercicio.	12/07/2011	
Declaración de proveedores de IVA	A más tardar el último día del mes inmediato posterior al periodo que corresponda.	12/07/2011	
Informativa anual del subsidio para el empleo	A más tardar el 15 de febrero de cada año	12/07/2011	
Pago provisional mensual de ISR personas morales régimen general	A más tardar el día 17 del mes inmediato posterior al periodo que corresponda.	01/04/2012	

Sus datos personales son incorporados y protegidos en los sistemas del SAT, de conformidad con los Lineamientos de Protección de Datos Personales y con diversas disposiciones fiscales y legales sobre confidencialidad y protección de datos, a fin de ejercer las facultades conferidas a la autoridad fiscal.

Si desea modificar o corregir sus datos personales, puede acudir a cualquier Módulo de Servicios Tributarios y/o a través de la dirección http://sat.gob.mx

Cadena Original Sello: ||2017/06/19|CIS110712JQ2|CONSTANCIA DE SITUACIÓN FISCAL|200001000007000112188||

Sello Digital:
IxoV9Ajwr5Nke6lvxXspYGS4XRDbCh2Nx7MpplnQ6HC4bBmWvymdRJPSR22kUFOssFsF8yhIDXq5I/Xb//xCXY
3tQ4KRTnCh6SZzplMs7EITYE3M2LGITcBiv7hNDcXODTu9QUM7FlaomVqg7NFHr82z3NF87+kVqxfzs270jA=

MÉXICO

COFEMER

Contacto
Av. Hidalgo 77, col. Guerrero, c.p. 06300, Ciudad de México
Atención telefónica: 627 22 728 desde la Ciudad de México
o 01 (55) 627 22 728 del resto del país
Desde Estados Unidos y Canadá 1 877 44 88 728
denuncias@sat.gob.mx

gob.mx

MÉXICO
GOBIERNO DE LA REPÚBLICA

COFEMER Comisión Federal de Mejora Regulatoria

Contacto
Av. Hidalgo 77, col. Guerrero, c.p. 06300, Ciudad de México.
Atención telefónica: 627 22 728 desde la Ciudad de México,
o 01 (55) 627 22 728 del resto del país.
Desde Estados Unidos y Canadá 1 877 44 88 728.
denuncias@sat.gob.mx

Exhibit 6

Translation from Spanish
26 May 2017

TAX ID CERTIFICATE

FEDERAL TAX I.D. CODE

NAME, DESCRIPTION OR NAME OF FIRM

CONSULTORIO DE COMERCIO INTERNACIONAL DE ESPAÑA SA DE CV

FOLIO

THE REVENUE ADMINISTRATION SERVICE HEREBY INFORMS YOU OF YOUR TAXPAYER IDENTIFICATION NUMBER, WHICH WAS ASSIGNED TO YOU BASED ON THE INFORMATION YOU HAVE PROVIDED, AND WHICH HAS BEEN RECORDED AS FOLLOWS:

NAME, DESCRIPTION OR NAME OF FIRM
CONSULTORIO DE COMERCIO INTERNACIONAL DE ESPAÑA SA DE CV

ADDRESS
CALLE MONTECITO 38 PISO 28 13 NAPOLES DISTRITO FEDERAL 03810

TAX I.D. No.

LOCAL TAX COLLECTION OFFICE **ALR CENTER, FEDERAL DISTRICT**

TYPE OF BUSINESS **OTHER SCIENTIFIC AND TECHNICAL CONSULTING SERVICES**

REGISTRATION STATUS
ACTIVE

DATE REGISTERED **12-01-2009** START DATE OF OPERATIONS **11-13-2009**

OBLIGATIONS

DESCRIPTION	START DATE
File annual Income Tax Return (ISR) listing clients and suppliers of goods and services.	11-13-2009
File annual Income Tax Return (ISR) listing payments and withholdings for professional services (legal entities).	11-13-2009
Provide information on Value Added Tax (IVA) requested on Income Tax Returns (ISR).	11-13-2009
Submit quarterly estimated Income Tax return (ISR) and payment for legal entities due to start of second fiscal year.	01-01-2010
Submit monthly estimated Income Tax return (ISR) and payment for legal entities under general regimen.	04-01-2010
File annual Income Tax return (ISR) for legal entities.	11-13-2009
File monthly return listing transactions with third parties for Value Added Tax (IVA) purposes.	11-13-2009
Submit monthly estimated return and payment of Flat-Rate Business Tax (IETU).	11-13-2009
Submit monthly estimated tax return and payment of Income Tax (ISR) on withholdings on professional services.	11-13-2009
Submit annual estimated return and payment of Flat-Rate Business Tax (IETU).	11-13-2009
Submit monthly return and payment of Value Added Tax (IVA) withholdings.	11-13-2009
Submit final monthly return and payment of Value Added Tax (IVA).	11-13-2009

PROCEDURAL STEPS TAKEN	FILING DATE	PROCEDURE PAGE
Fed. Taxpayer Reg. / Update / Change of Address	02-12-2010	RF201020248792
Fed. Taxpayer Reg. / Update / Change of Address	12-15-2009	RF200919317011
Fed. Taxpayer Reg. / Registration / Registration of Legal Entity	12-01-2009	RF200919065848

Date printed: February 12, 2010
CITIZEN HOTLINE
(Complaints and Suggestions) 01-800-463-6728

M3fxAbSGCpqy3BbcrWVZ5JmkQKp1C+DaPvOrR2bSVxDpfSotMVWySdpxKmdie8EIBayjEn/PnrTE8PgnCFU/TE4kowJUfK72nUFtqx6FMCOVp3d+sChdkfW27Wx
jf4hOzt592VIH7Ku5Ebc9210GtU/TN3pVcTlyYjYmZdj7c=

ROSETTA STONE *ASSOCIATES IN TRANSLATION*
7375 N. Calle sin Celo, Tucson, AZ 85718 • (520) 575-9200 • rosettrans@aol.com • www.rosettrans.com
• ATA-Certified •

Certification

AT THE REQUEST OF THE INTERESTED PARTY, I hereby certify that I have translated the following document:

Registration with the Federal Taxpayer Registry by
CONSULTORIA DE COMERCIO INTERNACIONAL DE ESPAÑA, S.A. DE C.V.
on December 1, 2009

from the Spanish into the English language on this 26th day of May 2017, and that the information contained in the translated document is a true, complete and correct reflection of the original text, to the best of my ability as a Professional Translator.

ROSETTA STONE ASSOCIATES IN TRANSLATION

CAROLA P. MYERS
Member, A.C.I.A. - ATA-Certified

Servicio de Administración Tributaria

CÉDULA DE IDENTIFICACIÓN FISCAL

CLAVE DE REG. FED. DE CONTRIBUYENTE

CCI091113FK9

NOMBRE, DENOMINACIÓN O RAZÓN SOCIAL

CONSULTORIA DE COMERCIO INTERNACIONAL DE ESPAÑA SA DE CV

FOLIO

B1279203

OF-12/02/2010-R 1eGgG0+Cso

INSCRIPCIÓN EN EL R.F.C

EL SERVICIO DE ADMINISTRACIÓN TRIBUTARIA, LE DA A CONOCER EL REGISTRO FEDERAL DE CONTRIBUYENTES, QUE LE HA SIDO ASIGNADO CON BASE EN LOS DATOS QUE PROPORCIONÓ, LOS CUALES HAN QUEDADO REGISTRADOS CONFORME A LO SIGUIENTE:

NOMBRE, DENOMINACIÓN O RAZÓN SOCIAL

CONSULTORIA DE COMERCIO INTERNACIONAL DE ESPAÑA SA DE CV

DOMICILIO

CALLE MONTECITO 38 PISO 28 13 NAPOLES DISTRITO FEDERAL 03810

CLAVE DEL R.F.C CCI091113FK9

ADMINISTRACIÓN LOCAL ALR CENTRO DEL D.F.

ACTIVIDAD Otros servicios de consultoría científica y técnica

SITUACIÓN DE REGISTRO

ACTIVO

FECHA DE INSCRIPCIÓN 01-12-2009 FECHA DE INICIO DE OPERACIONES 13-11-2009

OBLIGACIONES

DESCRIPCIÓN	FECHA ALTA
Presentar la declaración anual de Impuesto Sobre la Renta (ISR) donde se informe sobre los clientes y proveedores de bienes y servicios.	13-11-2009
Presentar la declaración anual de Impuesto Sobre la Renta (ISR) donde informen sobre los pagos y retenciones de servicios profesionales. (personas morales).	13-11-2009
Proporcionar la información del Impuesto al Valor Agregado (IVA) que se solicite en las declaraciones del Impuesto Sobre la Renta (ISR)	13-11-2009
Presentar la declaración y pago provisional trimestral de Impuesto Sobre la Renta (ISR) de personas morales por inicio del segundo ejercicio fiscal.	01-01-2010
Presentar la declaración y pago provisional mensual de Impuesto Sobre la Renta (ISR) de personas morales del régimen general.	01-04-2010
Presentar la declaración anual de Impuesto Sobre la Renta (ISR) de personas morales	13-11-2009
Presentar la declaración mensual donde se informe sobre las operaciones con terceros para efectos de Impuesto al Valor Agregado (IVA).	13-11-2009
Presentar la declaración y pago provisional mensual del Impuesto Empresarial a Tasa Única (IETU).	13-11-2009
Presentar la declaración y pago provisional mensual de Impuesto Sobre la Renta (ISR) por las retenciones realizadas por servicios profesionales.	13-11-2009
Presentar la declaración y pago anual del Impuesto Empresarial a Tasa Única (IETU).	13-11-2009
Presentar la declaración y pago mensual de retenciones de Impuesto al Valor Agregado (IVA).	13-11-2009
Presentar la declaración y pago definitivo mensual de Impuesto al Valor Agregado (IVA) .	13-11-2009

TRÁMITES EFECTUADOS	FECHA DE PRESENTACIÓN	FOLIO DEL TRÁMITE
Reg. Federal Contribuyente / Actualización / Cambio de Domicilio	12-02-2010	RF201020248792
Reg. Federal Contribuyente / Actualización / Cambio de Domicilio	15-12-2009	RF200919317011
Reg. Federal Contribuyente / Inscripción / Inscripción de Persona Moral	01-12-2009	RF200919065848

Fecha de Impresión: 12 de Febrero de 2010
TELEFONO DE ATENCION CIUDADANA
(Quejas Y Sugerencias) 01-800-463-6728

M3lxAb5GCpqy3BbcrWVZ5JmkQKp1C+DaPvOrR2bSVxDpfSotMVWySdpxKmdlo8EIBayjEn/PnrTE8PgnCFU/TE4kowJUfK72nUFtqx6FMZCOVp3d+sChdkfW27Wx
jf4hOzI592V1H7Ku5Ebc9210GIU/TN3pVcTlyYjYmZdj7c=

Exhibit 7

Translated from Spanish
20 July 2017

SHCP
MINISTRY OF THE TREASURY AND PUBLIC CREDIT

ANNUAL TAX RETURN
CORPORATE ENTITIES - GENERAL REGIMEN F18

SAT
Tax Administration Service

IDENTIFYING INFORMATION

TAX I.D.	[redacted]
NAME OR CORPORATE NAME	[redacted]

GENERAL INFORMATION

TYPE OF RETURN	Normal	SUPPLEMENT TYPE	
PERIOD	Fiscal Year	FISCAL YEAR	2016
DATE/TIME FILED	06/19/2017 21:02	TRANSACTION NUMBER	[redacted]

INITIAL INFORMATION

STATE IF YOU ELECT TO AUDIT YOUR FINANCIAL STATEMENTS	No	STATE IF YOU ARE EXCLUSIVELY ENGAGED IN RENEWABLE ENERGY PRODUCTION OR EFFICIENT ELECTRICITY CO-GENERATING SYSTEMS	No
STATE IF THIS IS THE FINAL POST-LIQUIDATION RETURN	Unselected	IF A DAUGHTER COMPANY, INDICATE TAX ID NUMBER OF PARENT COMPANY	
		IF AN INTEGRATED COMPANY, STATE TAX ID NUMBER OF INTEGRATOR	

Translated from Spanish
20 July 2017

SHCP

ANNUAL TAX RETURN
CORPORATE ENTITIES - GENERAL REGIMEN F18

SAT
Tax Administration Service

PROFIT AND LOSS STATEMENT

	RELATED PARTIES	UNRELATED PARTIES	TOTAL
DOMESTIC SALES AND/OR SERVICES	0		0
FOREIGN SALES AND/OR SERVICES			
REFUNDS, DISCOUNTS AND BONUSES ON DOMESTIC SALES			
REFUNDS, DISCOUNTS AND BONUSES ON FOREIGN SALES			
NET EARNINGS	0		0
INITIAL INVENTORY			
DOMESTIC NET PURCHASES			
IMPORTED NET PURCHASES			
FINAL INVENTORY			
COST OF GOODS			
LABOR			
MAQUILAS (ASSEMBLY)			
INDIRECT MANUFACTURING COSTS			
COST OF SALES AND/OR SERVICES			
GROSS PROFIT			0
GROSS LOSS			
OVERHEAD	12,514,525		12,514,525
OPERATING PROFIT			
OPERATING LOSS			12,514,525
DOMESTIC ACCRUED INTEREST RECEIVABLE			
FOREIGN ACCRUED INTEREST RECEIVABLE			
DOMESTIC LATE FEES RECEIVABLE			
FOREIGN ENTITY'S LATE FEES RECEIVABLE			
EXCHANGE RATE EARNINGS			
DOMESTIC ACCRUED INTEREST PAYABLE			

Translated from Spanish
20 July 2017

SHCP
MINISTRY OF THE TREASURY AND PUBLIC CREDIT

ANNUAL TAX RETURN
CORPORATE ENTITIES - GENERAL REGIMEN F18

SAT
Tax Administration Service

PROFIT AND LOSS STATEMENT

	RELATED PARTIES	UNRELATED PARTIES	TOTAL
DOMESTIC LATE FEES PAYABLE			
FOREIGN LATE FEES PAYABLE			
EXCHANGE RATE LOSS			
GAIN DUE TO MONETARY POSITION			
LOSS DUE TO MONETARY POSITION			
OTHER DOMESTIC FINANCIAL TRANSACTIONS			
OTHER FOREIGN FINANCIAL TRANSACTIONS			
OTHER FINANCIAL TRANSACTIONS			
OVERALL FINANCING GAIN OR LOSS			
OTHER DOMESTIC COSTS			
OTHER FOREIGN COSTS			
OTHER COSTS			
OTHER DOMESTIC PROCEEDS			
OTHER FOREIGN PROCEEDS			
OTHER PROCEEDS			
EARNINGS FROM DISCONTINUED AND EXTRAORDINARY ITEMS			
COSTS FROM DISCONTINUED AND EXTRAORDINARY ITEMS			
PROFIT BEFORE TAX			12,514,525
LOSS BEFORE TAX			
INCOME TAX (ISR)			
BUSINESS FLAT TAX (IETU)			
ASSET TAX (IMPAC)			
EMPLOYEE PROFIT SHARING PLAN (PTU) EARNINGS			
FROM SHARE IN SUBSIDIARY			
LOSS FROM SHARE IN SUBSIDIARY			
FAVORABLE RESTATEMENT EFFECTS NOT INCLUDING RESULTS FROM MONETARY POSITION			

Translated from
Spanish 20 July 2017

SHCP
MINISTRY OF THE TREASURY AND PUBLIC CREDIT

ANNUAL TAX RETURN
CORPORATE ENTITIES - GENERAL REGIMEN F18

SAT
Tax Administration Service

PROFIT AND LOSS STATEMENT

	RELATED PARTIES	UNRELATED PARTIES	TOTAL
UNFAVORABLE RESTATEMENT EFFECTS NOT INCLUDING RESULTS FROM MONETARY POSITION			
NET EARNINGS			
NET LOSS			12,514,525

Translated from Spanish
20 July 2017

SHCP

ANNUAL TAX RETURN
CORPORATE ENTITIES - GENERAL REGIMEN F18

SAT
Tax Administration Service

STATEMENT OF FINANCIAL POSITION (BALANCE SHEET)

ASSETS	
CASH ON HAND AND DEPOSITS IN DOMESTIC CREDIT INSTITUTIONS	50,000
CASH ON HAND AND DEPOSITS IN FOREIGN CREDIT INSTITUTIONS	
INVESTMENTS IN SECURITIES AT DOMESTIC INSTITUTIONS (EXCLUDING SHARES)	
INVESTMENTS IN SECURITIES AT FOREIGN INSTITUTIONS (EXCLUDING SHARES)	
DOMESTIC ACCOUNTS AND NOTES RECEIVABLE (RELATED PARTIES)	22,941,021
DOMESTIC ACCOUNTS AND NOTES RECEIVABLE (UNRELATED PARTIES)	
DOMESTIC ACCOUNTS AND NOTES RECEIVABLE (TOTAL)	22,941,021
FOREIGN ACCOUNTS AND NOTES RECEIVABLE (RELATED PARTIES)	
FOREIGN ACCOUNTS AND NOTES RECEIVABLE (UNRELATED PARTIES)	
FOREIGN ACCOUNTS AND NOTES RECEIVABLE (TOTAL)	
TAXES RECEIVABLE	
INVENTORIES	
OTHER CURRENT ASSETS	
INVESTMENTS IN DOMESTIC SHARES	
INVESTMENTS IN FOREIGN SHARES	
INVESTMENTS IN SHARES (TOTAL)	
LAND	
BUILDINGS	
CONSTRUCTIONS UNDERWAY	
MACHINERY AND EQUIPMENT	
FURNISHINGS AND OFFICE EQUIPMENT	
COMPUTER EQUIPMENT	
TRANSPORTATION EQUIPMENT	803,445
OTHER FIXED ASSETS	
ACCRUED DEPRECIATION	-110,165
DEFERRED CHARGES AND	

LIABILITIES	
DOMESTIC ACCOUNTS AND NOTES PAYABLE (RELATED PARTIES)	39,482,549
DOMESTIC ACCOUNTS AND NOTES PAYABLE (UNRELATED PARTIES)	
DOMESTIC ACCOUNTS AND NOTES PAYABLE (TOTAL)	39,482,549
FOREIGN ACCOUNTS AND NOTES PAYABLE (RELATED PARTIES)	
FOREIGN ACCOUNTS AND NOTES PAYABLE (UNRELATED PARTIES)	
FOREIGN ACCOUNTS AND NOTES PAYABLE (TOTAL)	
TAXES PAYABLE	0
ADVANCES FROM CUSTOMERS (RELATED PARTIES)	
ADVANCES FROM CUSTOMERS (UNRELATED PARTIES)	
ADVANCES FROM CUSTOMERS (TOTAL)	
CONTRIBUTIONS TOWARD FUTURE CAPITAL INCREASES	
OTHER LIABILITIES	
TOTAL LIABILITIES	39,482,549

EQUITY CAPITAL	
CORPORATE CAPITAL FROM CAPITAL CONTRIBUTIONS	3,000,000
CORPORATE CAPITAL FROM CAPITALIZATION	
RESERVES	
OTHER CAPITAL ACCOUNTS	
CONTRIBUTIONS TOWARD FUTURE CAPITAL INCREASES	
ACCRUED PROFIT	
PROFIT FOR YEAR	
ACCRUED LOSS	-6,283,723
LOSS FOR FISCAL YEAR	-12,514,525
EXCESS IN CAPITAL RESTATEMENT	

Translated from Spanish
20 July 2017

SHCP
MINISTRY OF THE TREASURY AND PUBLIC CREDIT

ANNUAL TAX RETURN
CORPORATE ENTITIES - GENERAL REGIMEN F18

SAT
Tax Administration Service

STATEMENT OF FINANCIAL POSITION (BALANCE SHEET)

ASSETS		EQUITY CAPITAL	
ACCRUED AMORTIZATION	-	EQUITY CAPITAL RESTATEMENT	
TOTAL ASSETS	23,684,301	TOTAL EQUITY CAPITAL	-15,798,248
		TOTAL LIABILITIES PLUS EQUITY CAPITAL	23,684,301

Translated from Spanish
20 July 2017

SHCP
MINISTRY OF THE TREASURY AND PUBLIC CREDIT

ANNUAL TAX RETURN
CORPORATE ENTITIES - GENERAL REGIMEN F18

SAT
Tax Administration Service

RECONCILIATION BETWEEN ACCOUNTING INCOME AND TAXABLE INCOME

NET PROFIT OR LOSS	-12,514,525	DEDUCTIBLE ANNUAL ADJUSTMENT FOR INFLATION	
RESTATEMENT EFFECTS		COST OF GOODS SOLD FOR TAX PURPOSES	
PROFIT OR LOSS DUE TO MONETARY POSITION		DEDUCTION OF INVESTMENTS	
HISTORICAL NET PROFIT OR LOSS	-12,514,525	FISCAL STIMULUS BY IMMEDIATE DEDUCTION OF INVESTMENTS	
NON-ACCOUNTING REVENUE		FISCAL STIMULUS OF THE DISABLED OR THE ELDERLY	
ANNUAL ACCUMULATED INFLATION ADJUSTMENT		TAX LOSS ON SALE OF SHARES	
ADVANCES FROM CUSTOMERS		TAX LOSS ON SALE OF LAND AND FIXED ASSETS	
LATE CHARGES ALREADY COLLECTED		LATE FEES ACTUALLY PAID	
GAINS FROM SALE OF LAND AND FIXED ASSETS		OTHER NON-ACCOUNTING TAX DEDUCTIONS	
INVENTORY INCREASE FOR BUSINESS YEAR		NON-FISCAL BOOK INCOME	
OTHER NON-ACCOUNTING INCOME		ACCRUED LATE FEES RECEIVABLE, WHETHER OR NOT COLLECTED	
NON-ALLOWABLE DEDUCTIONS		ADVANCES FROM CUSTOMERS FROM PREVIOUS BUSINESS YEARS	
NON-ACCOUNTING TAX DEDUCTIONS		TAX BALANCES RECEIVABLE AND THEIR RESTATEMENT	
BOOK COST OF SALES		BOOK PROFIT ON SALE OF FIXED ASSETS	
BOOK DEPRECIATION AND AMORTIZATION		BOOK PROFIT ON SALE OF SHARES	
EXPENSES NOT SUBJECT TO TAX REQUIREMENTS		PROFIT FROM SHARE IN SUBSIDIARY	
INCOME, BUSINESS, AND ASSET TAX AND EMPLOYEE PROFIT SHARING PLAN		OTHER NON-TAXABLE BOOK INCOME	
BOOK LOSS ON SALE OF SHARES		FISCAL PROFIT OR LOSS BEFORE EMPLOYEE PROFIT SHARING PLAN	-12,514,525
BOOK LOSS ON SALE OF FIXED ASSETS			
LOSS FROM SHARE IN SUBSIDIARY			
INTEREST EARNED THAT EXCEED MARKET VALUE AND LATE FEES, WHETHER PAID OR NOT			
OTHER NON-ALLOWABLE DEDUCTIONS			
NON-ACCOUNTING DEDUCTIONS			

Translated from Spanish
20 July 2017

SHCP
MINISTRY OF THE TREASURY AND PUBLIC CREDIT

ANNUAL TAX RETURN
CORPORATE ENTITIES - GENERAL REGIMEN F18

SAT
Tax Administration Service

STATE HOW YOU DETERMINED THE BASIC INVENTORY

BASIC INVENTORY INFORMATION

STATE HOW YOU DETERMINED THE BASIC INVENTORY	Initial inventory

INFORMATIONAL DATA

INITIAL INVENTORY AMOUNT		AMOUNT OF DEDUCTIBLE RAW MATERIAL CONSUMED, LABOR, AND OVERHEAD	

ACCRUED INVENTORY OPTION

STATE VALUATION METHOD FOR BASIC INVENTORY	Unselected	COMPARATIVE DIFFERENCE OF IMPORTED INVENTORIES		REDUCED INVENTORY	
BASIC INVENTORY AS OF DECEMBER 31, 2004		AMOUNT OF ACCRUED INVENTORY FOR YEAR OF RETURN	0	ACCRUED INVENTORY FOR BUSINESS YEAR	
UNDEDUCTED BALANCE AS OF JANUARY 1, 2005		PERCENTAGE OF ACCRUAL		COST OF SALES OF GOODS SOLD ON INSTALLMENTS, NOT YET DEDUCTED	
TAX LOSSES NOT YET DECREASED AS OF DECEMBER 31, 2004		ACCRUED INVENTORY			

VALUATION OF SYSTEMS AND BASES

STATE YOUR CHOICE FOR DETERMINING COST OF SALES	Unselected	STATE COST BASIS USED	Unselected

VALUATION METHODS

STATE VALUATION METHOD USED	Unselected

COST EXCEEDING MARKET OR REPLACEMENT PRICE

COST EXCEEDING MARKET OR REPLACEMENT PRICE		PRICING TYPE CONSIDERED	Unselected

AUTHORIZED DEDUCTIONS

WAGES AND SALARIES		PRE-TAX WAGE CREDIT	
PROFESSIONAL FEES PAID TO INDIVIDUALS	360,538	SAR, INFONAVIT AND OLD-AGE PENSION CONTRIBUTIONS	
ROYALTIES AND TECHNICAL SUPPORT		CONTRIBUTIONS TO PENSION AND RETIREMENT FUNDS	
DONATIONS		IMSS CONTRIBUTIONS	
TEMPORARY USE OR ENJOYMENT OF GOODS PAID TO INDIVIDUALS		RESTAURANT MEALS	19,899
FREIGHT AND HAULING CHARGES PAID TO INDIVIDUALS		LOSS FROM DERIVATIVE FINANCIAL TRANSACTIONS	
CONTRIBUTIONS PAID OTHER THAN ISR, IETU, IMPAC, IVA AND IEPS (SPECIAL TAX ON PRODUCTION AND SERVICES)		DEDUCTION FOR NUTRITIONAL ASSISTANCE TO WORKERS	
		TOTAL AMOUNT OF PAYMENTS THAT ARE EXEMPT INCOME FOR WORKERS	
INSURANCE AND FINANCING			
LOSS FROM UNRECOVERABLE LOANS		DEDUCTIBLE AMOUNT AT 47% (PAYMENTS THAT ARE EXEMPT INCOME FOR WORKERS)	

Translated from Spanish
20 July 2017

SHCP
MINISTRY OF THE TREASURY AND PUBLIC CREDIT

ANNUAL TAX RETURN
CORPORATE ENTITIES - GENERAL REGIMEN F18

SAT
Tax Administration Service

AUTHORIZED DEDUCTIONS

FUEL AND LUBRICANTS		DEDUCTIBLE AMOUNT AT 53% (PAYMENTS THAT ARE EXEMPT INCOME FOR WORKERS)	
		OTHER AUTHORIZED DEDUCTIONS	12,018,088
		TOTAL AUTHORIZED DEDUCTIONS	12,514,525

Translated from Spanish
20 July 2017

SHCP
MINISTRY OF THE TREASURY AND PUBLIC CREDIT

ANNUAL TAX RETURN
CORPORATE ENTITIES - GENERAL REGIMEN F18

SAT
Tax Administration Service

END-OF-BUSINESS YEAR FIGURES

TAX LOSSES FROM PREVIOUS BUSINESS YEARS YET TO BE AMORTIZED AND UPDATED	6,417,617	UPDATED BALANCE OF CAPITAL CONTRIBUTION ACCOUNT	3,656,400
PRIOR YEAR TAX LOSSES PENDING UPDATED AMORTIZATION (DEEP WATERS)		AMOUNT OF NET TAX PROFIT FROM INTEGRABLE PARTICIPATION	
AVERAGE ANNUAL LOAN BALANCE		AMOUNT OF NET TAX PROFIT FROM INTEGRABLE PARTICIPATION FOR WHICH THE FISCAL YEAR TAX HAS BEEN PAID	
AVERAGE ANNUAL DEBT BALANCE		AMOUNT OF NET TAX PROFIT FROM INTEGRABLE PARTICIPATION FOR WHICH PAYMENT OF FISCAL YEAR TAX HAS BEEN DEFERRED	
PROFIT COEFFICIENT TO BE APPLIED IN COMING BUSINESS YEAR	0.0000	AMOUNT OF NET TAX PROFIT FROM NON-INTEGRABLE PARTICIPATION	
PERCENTAGE OF FUNDABLE PARTICIPATION			
INCOME TAX INCURRED OVER AND ABOVE IMPAC IN THE 3 PRIOR BUSINESS YEARS, NOT YET APPLIED			
UPDATED BALANCE OF NET TAX PROFIT ACCOUNT			
UPDATED BALANCE OF NET TAX PROFIT ACCOUNT (GENERATED SINCE 2014 BUSINESS YEAR)			
UPDATED BALANCE OF REINVESTED TAX PROFIT ACCOUNT			

Translated from Spanish
20 July 2017

SHCP
MINISTRY OF THE TREASURY AND PUBLIC CREDIT

ANNUAL TAX RETURN
CORPORATE ENTITIES - GENERAL REGIMEN F18

SAT
Tax Administration Service

END-OF-BUSINESS YEAR FIGURES

INFORMATION ON PRODUCTION COOPERATIVE ELECTING TO DEFER PAYMENT OF INCOME TAX

TAXABLE PROFITS NOT DISTRIBUTED IN PREVIOUS BUSINESS YEAR		TAXABLE PROFIT DISTRIBUTED IN BUSINESS YEAR	
AMOUNT OF INCOME TAX TO BE DEFERRED IN PREVIOUS BUSINESS YEAR		AMOUNT OF TAXABLE PROFIT TRANSFERRED DUE TO MERGER OR EXCISSION	
TAXABLE PROFIT NOT DISTRIBUTED IN BUSINESS YEAR		AMOUNT IN PRODUCTIVE INVESTMENTS EQUAL TO DEFERRED INCOME TAX	
UPDATED BALANCE OF TAXABLE PROFIT ACCOUNT			

SHCP

ANNUAL TAX RETURN
CORPORATE ENTITIES - GENERAL REGIMEN F18

SAT
Tax Administration Service

DETERMINATION OF INCOME TAX

TOTAL ACCRUABLE INCOME	0
TOTAL AUTHORIZED DEDUCTIONS AND IMMEDIATE INVESTMENT DEDUCTION	
ADDITIONAL DEDUCTION DUE TO PAYMENT OF PERSONAL SERVICES IN MAQUILA OPERATION	
TAX PROFIT OR LOSS BEFORE PTU	0
PTU PAID FOR BUSINESS YEAR	
TAX PROFIT FOR BUSINESS YEAR	0
TAX LOSS FOR BUSINESS YEAR	
TAX LOSSES IN PRIOR FISCAL YEARS BEING APPLIED THIS BUSINESS YEAR	
ADDITIONAL DEDUCTION FOR FIRST EMPLOYMENT INCENTIVE	
TAX PROFIT/LOSS	0
INCOME TAX FOR BUSINESS YEAR	0
TAX INCURRED IN BUSINESS YEAR	0
PERCENTAGE OF INTEGRABLE PARTICIPATION	
INTEGRABLE PARTICIPATION TAX	
INTEGRATED TAX PROFIT/LOSS FACTOR	
AMOUNT OF TAX ON INTEGRABLE PARTICIPATION	
PERCENTAGE OF NON-INTEGRABLE PARTICIPATION	
AMOUNT OF TAX ON NON-INTEGRABLE PARTICIPATION	
REPORTABLE TAX FOR FISCAL YEAR	
INCENTIVE FOR TECHNOLOGICAL RESEARCH AND DEVELOPMENT	
INCENTIVE FOR NATIONAL FILM PRODUCTION AND DISTRIBUTION	
INCENTIVE FOR INVESTMENT PROJECTS IN NATIONAL THEATER PRODUCTION	
OTHER INCENTIVES	
TOTAL INCENTIVES	
ESTIMATED TAX PAYMENTS TURNED OVER TO PARENT COMPANY	
ESTIMATED TAX PAYMENTS PAID TO GOVERNMENT	
OTHER AMOUNTS DUE	
OTHER AMOUNTS IN FAVOR	
DIFFERENCE DUE	0
DIFFERENCE IN FAVOR	0
DEFERRED INCOME TAX DUE PAID DURING THE BUSINESS YEAR (INTEGRATED)	
REPORTABLE DEFERRED INCOME TAX DUE TO DIVESTITURE	
DEFERRABLE INCOME TAX AMOUNT FOR YEAR (PRODUCTION CO-OP)	
DEFERRED INCOME TAX AMOUNT FROM PRIOR YEARS PAID THIS BUSINESS YEAR (PRODUCTION CO-OP)	
INCOME TAX DUE FOR FISCAL YEAR	0
INCOME TAX IN FAVOR FOR FISCAL YEAR	

TAX ON EARNINGS SUBJECT TO PREFERENTIAL TAX REGIMENS

TAX ON EARNINGS SUBJECT TO PREFERENTIAL TAX REGIMENS	

Translated from Spanish
20 July 2017

SHCP
MINISTRY OF THE TREASURY AND PUBLIC CREDIT

ANNUAL TAX RETURN
CORPORATE ENTITIES - GENERAL REGIMEN F18

SAT
Tax Administration Service

DETERMINATION OF INCOME TAX

TAX PAID ABROAD, TO BE CREDITED	
TAX TO BE CREDITED ON DIVIDENDS OR PROFIT DISTRIBUTIONS	
TAX ON FISCAL CONSOLIDATION DUE	
TAX ON FISCAL CONSOLIDATION PAID (OVERPAID)	

INFORMATIONAL DATA ON INCOME TAX

TOTAL INCENTIVE FOR TECHNOLOGICAL RESEARCH AND DEVELOPMENT IN PRIOR YEARS APPLIED IN BUSINESS YEAR	
TOTAL INCENTIVE FOR NATIONAL FILM PRODUCTION AND DISTRIBUTION IN PREVIOUS YEARS APPLIED IN BUSINESS YEAR	
TOTAL INCENTIVE FOR INVESTMENT PROJECTS IN NATIONAL THEATER PRODUCTION IN PREVIOUS YEARS APPLIED IN BUSINESS YEAR	
ADDITIONAL DEDUCTION FOR UNAPPLIED FIRST EMPLOYMENT INCENTIVE	
AMOUNT APPLIED FOR SCRAP PROGRAM INCENTIVE	
AMOUNT DEDUCTIBLE FROM PAYMENTS MADE FOR TEMPORARY USE OR ENJOYMENT OF AUTOMOBILES	
IMPAC RECOVERED DURING FISCAL YEAR DERIVING FROM DECONSOLIDATION	
AMOUNT OF DEFERRABLE INCOME TAX FOR BUSINESS YEAR (INTEGRATED)	
STATE FISCAL YEAR THAT CORRESPONDS TO THE DEFERRED INCOME TAX YOU ARE PAYING (INTEGRATED)	
YEAR OF DEFERRED INCOME TAX BEING PAID DUE TO DIVESTITURE (DEL)	
DEFERRED INCOME TAX YEAR PAID DUE TO DIVESTITURE (AL)	
WAGES, SALARIES AND BENEFITS FOR DISABLED WORKERS AND/OR THE ELDERLYISCAPACIDAD Y/O ADULTOS MAYORES	Unselected
APPLIED DEDUCTION PERCENTAGE FOR INVESTMENT IN RENEWABLE ENERGY SOURCES	
INITIAL BALANCE FOR FISCAL YEAR (NET TAXABLE PROFIT ACCOUNT FOR INVESTMENTS IN RENEWABLE ENERGY SOURCES)	
WITHDRAWALS IN FISCAL YEAR (NET TAXABLE PROFIT ACCOUNT FOR INVESTMENTS IN RENEWABLE ENERGY SOURCES)	
WITHDRAWALS IN PRIOR FISCAL YEARS (NET TAXABLE PROFIT ACCOUNT FOR INVESTMENTS IN RENEWABLE ENERGY SOURCES)	
TOTAL AMOUNT OF WITHDRAWALS DURING FISCAL YEAR IN QUESTION (NET TAXABLE PROFIT ACCOUNT FOR INVESTMENTS IN RENEWABLE ENERGY SOURCES)	
AMOUNT OF EARNINGS FROM RENEWABLE ENERGY PRODUCTION OR EFFICIENT ELECTRICITY CO-GENERATING SYSTEMS	

INFORMATIONAL DATA ON TAX INCENTIVE RELATED TO TAX ON VEHICLE USE OR OWNERSHIP

NUMBER OF NEW VEHICLES SOLD TO INDIVIDUALS FOR WHICH IT WAS DECIDED TO PAY VEHICLE USE AND OWNERSHIP TAX (ISTUV)	
TOTAL ISTUV PAID FOR VEHICLES SOLD TO INDIVIDUALS	
TOTAL ISTUV TAX INCENTIVE APPLICABLE TO NEW VEHICLES SOLD TO INDIVIDUALS FROM PREVIOUS YEARS, APPLIED THIS FISCAL YEAR	
AMOUNT OF ISTUV TAX INCENTIVE CREDITED AGAINST INCOME TAX IN ESTIMATED PAYMENTS	
REMAINING ISTUV TAX INCENTIVE NOT YET CREDITED	
TOTAL ISTUV TAX INCENTIVE APPLICABLE TO NEW VEHICLES ACQUIRED BY CORPORATE ENTITIES FROM PRIOR BUSINESS YEARS, AND APPLIED IN THIS FISCAL YEAR	

Translated from Spanish
20 July 2017

SHCP
MINISTRY OF THE TREASURY AND PUBLIC CREDIT

ANNUAL TAX RETURN
CORPORATE ENTITIES - GENERAL REGIMEN F18

SAT
Tax Administration Service

DETERMINATION OF PAYMENT
INCOME TAX R1 - CORPORATE ENTITIES

DUE	0	SWEEPSTAKE CREDIT	
IN FAVOR		MARITIME FUEL	
UPDATED PORTION		TOTAL APPLICATIONS	0
SURCHARGES		DATE OF PRIOR PAYMENT	
CORRECTION FINE		AMOUNT OF PRIOR PAYMENT	
TOTAL CONTRIBUTIONS	0	AMOUNT DUE	0
SALARY CREDIT		DO YOU WISH TO PAY IN INSTALLMENTS?	Unselected
EMPLOYMENT SUBSIDY		AMOUNT OF FIRST INSTALLMENT	
OFFSETS		AMOUNT EXCLUDING FIRST INSTALLMENT	
CREDIT IEPS, DIESEL, PRIMARY SECTOR AND MINING INDUSTRY		AMOUNT IN FAVOR	
AUTOMOTIVE DIESEL FOR TRANSPORTATION		AMOUNT DUE	0
USE OF INFRASTRUCTURE, TOLL ROADS			
OTHER INCENTIVES			

Translated from Spanish
12 July 2017

SHCP
MINISTRY OF THE TREASURY AND PUBLIC CREDIT

RECEIPT
FISCAL YEAR RETURN FOR FEDERAL TAX

SAT
Tax Administration Service

Taxpayer Reg. Number:	CIS110712JQ2		
Name/Business Name:	CONSORCIO INTEGRADOR SONORA BOM SA DE CV		

Type of Return:	Normal		
Period Covered by Return:	Fiscal Year	**Fiscal Year:**	2016
Date and Time filed:	06-19-2017 21:02	**How filed:**	Internet
Transaction Number:	170000358778		

Tax declared:

Reason for Payment 1:	INCOME TAX, LEGAL ENTITIES
Due:	0
Amount due:	0
Amount payable:	0

We recommend you verify that the amount calculated of the updated portion is correct, inasmuch as the domestic consumer price index may have changed, and the amount must be based on the most recently published index.

Personal information is recorded and protected in the SAT system pursuant to applicable legal provisions.

To amend or correct personal information, please visit sat.gob.mx.

This receipt is being issued without prejudging the veracity of the information it contains or whether it meets the established deadlines, and the tax authority is free to audit it.

Digital seal: EEODBPOzXlzrjqlRqmOX5253HrKvsopqPu37GMkqjq5JOop2Hu1Y1WOsJSpnn!JowsjqQfbTPdyKBalrXkWIUcenOpFK9vdLCKBg
vze94uUCkVLAe0+6B1x58XQNM3QTg3woSzkauEyh4sjQVluv6kKUm2pYQKUQ4C7hXcQWqvA=

ROSETTA STONE *ASSOCIATES IN TRANSLATION*

7375 N. Calle sin Celo, Tucson, AZ 85718 • (520) 575-9200 • rosettrans@aol.com • www.rosettrans.com
• ATA-Certified •

Certification

AT THE REQUEST OF THE INTERESTED PARTY, I hereby certify that I have translated the following document:

Consorcio Integrador Sonora 80 M S.A. de C.V. Tax Documents (Martín)

from the Spanish into the English language on this 20th day of July 2017, and that the information contained in the translated documents is a true, complete and correct reflection of the original text, to the best of my ability as a Professional Translator.

ROSETTA STONE ASSOCIATES IN TRANSLATION

Carola P. Myers

CAROLA P. MYERS
Member, A.C.I.A. - ATA-Certified

SHCP

DECLARACIÓN DEL EJERCICIO
PERSONAS MORALES DEL RÉGIMEN GENERAL F18

SAT
Servicio de Administración Tributaria

DATOS DE IDENTIFICACIÓN

RFC	CIS110712JQ2
DENOMINACIÓN O RAZÓN SOCIAL	CONSORCIO INTEGRADOR SONORA BBM SA DE CV

DATOS GENERALES

TIPO DE DECLARACIÓN	Normal	TIPO DE COMPLEMENTARIA	
PERIODO	Del Ejercicio	EJERCICIO	2016
FECHA Y HORA DE PRESENTACIÓN	19/06/2017 21:02	NÚMERO DE OPERACIÓN	170000358778

DATOS INICIALES

INDIQUE SI OPTA POR DICTAMINAR SUS ESTADOS FINANCIEROS	No	INDIQUE SI SE DEDICA EXCLUSIVAMENTE A LA GENERACIÓN DE ENERGÍA PROVENIENTE DE FUENTES RENOVABLES O DE SISTEMAS DE COGENERACIÓN DE ELECTRICIDAD EFICIENTE	No
INDIQUE SI SE TRATA DE LA ÚLTIMA DECLARACIÓN DEL EJERCICIO DE LIQUIDACIÓN	Sin selección	EN CASO DE SER CONTROLADA INDIQUE EL RFC DE LA CONTROLADORA	
		EN CASO DE SER INTEGRADA INDIQUE EL RFC DE LA INTEGRADORA	

SHCP

DECLARACIÓN DEL EJERCICIO
PERSONAS MORALES DEL RÉGIMEN GENERAL F18

SAT

ESTADO DE RESULTADOS

	PARTES RELACIONADAS	PARTES NO RELACIONADAS	TOTAL
VENTAS Y/O SERVICIOS NACIONALES	0		0
VENTAS Y/O SERVICIOS EXTRANJEROS			
DEVOLUCIONES, DESCUENTOS Y BONIFICACIONES SOBRE VENTAS NACIONALES			
DEVOLUCIONES, DESCUENTOS Y BONIFICACIONES SOBRE VENTAS AL EXTRANJERO			
INGRESOS NETOS	0		0
INVENTARIO INICIAL			
COMPRAS NETAS NACIONALES			
COMPRAS NETAS DE IMPORTACIÓN			
INVENTARIO FINAL			
COSTO DE LAS MERCANCÍAS			
MANO DE OBRA			
MAQUILAS			
GASTOS INDIRECTOS DE FABRICACIÓN			
COSTO DE VENTAS Y/O SERVICIOS			
UTILIDAD BRUTA			0
PÉRDIDA BRUTA			
GASTOS DE OPERACIÓN	12,514,525		12,514,525
UTILIDAD DE OPERACIÓN			
PÉRDIDA DE OPERACIÓN			12,514,525
INTERESES DEVENGADOS A FAVOR NACIONALES			
INTERESES DEVENGADOS A FAVOR DEL EXTRANJERO			
INTERESES MORATORIOS A FAVOR NACIONALES			
INTERESES MORATORIOS A FAVOR DEL EXTRANJERO			
GANANCIA CAMBIARIA			
INTERESES DEVENGADOS A CARGO NACIONALES			
INTERESES DEVENGADOS A CARGO DEL EXTRANJERO			

ESTADO DE RESULTADOS

	PARTES RELACIONADAS	PARTES NO RELACIONADAS	TOTAL
INTERESES MORATORIOS A CARGO NACIONALES			
INTERESES MORATORIOS A CARGO DEL EXTRANJERO			
PÉRDIDA CAMBIARIA			
RESULTADO POR POSICIÓN MONETARIA FAVORABLE			
RESULTADO POR POSICIÓN MONETARIA DESFAVORABLE			
OTRAS OPERACIONES FINANCIERAS NACIONALES			
OTRAS OPERACIONES FINANCIERAS EXTRANJERAS			
OTRAS OPERACIONES FINANCIERAS			
RESULTADO INTEGRAL DE FINANCIAMIENTO			
OTROS GASTOS NACIONALES			
OTROS GASTOS EXTRANJEROS			
OTROS GASTOS			
OTROS PRODUCTOS NACIONALES			
OTROS PRODUCTOS EXTRANJEROS			
OTROS PRODUCTOS			
INGRESOS POR PARTIDAS DISCONTINUAS Y EXTRAORDINARIAS			
GASTOS POR PARTIDAS DISCONTINUAS Y EXTRAORDINARIAS			
UTILIDAD ANTES DE IMPUESTOS			
PÉRDIDA ANTES DE IMPUESTOS			12,514,525
ISR			
IETU			
IMPAC			
PTU			
UTILIDAD EN PARTICIPACIÓN SUBSIDIARIA			
PÉRDIDA EN PARTICIPACIÓN SUBSIDIARIA			
EFECTOS DE REEXPRESIÓN FAVORABLES EXCEPTO RESULTADO POR POSICIÓN MONETARIA			

SHCP

DECLARACIÓN DEL EJERCICIO
PERSONAS MORALES DEL RÉGIMEN GENERAL F18

SAT

ESTADO DE RESULTADOS

	PARTES RELACIONADAS	PARTES NO RELACIONADAS	TOTAL
EFECTOS DE REEXPRESIÓN DESFAVORABLES EXCEPTO RESULTADO POR POSICIÓN MONETARIA			
UTILIDAD NETA			
PÉRDIDA NETA			12,514,525

SHCP

DECLARACIÓN DEL EJERCICIO
PERSONAS MORALES DEL RÉGIMEN GENERAL F18

SAT

ESTADO DE POSICIÓN FINANCIERA (BALANCE)

ACTIVO

EFECTIVO EN CAJA Y DEPÓSITOS EN INSTITUCIONES DE CRÉDITO NACIONALES	50,000
EFECTIVO EN CAJA Y DEPÓSITOS EN INSTITUCIONES DE CRÉDITO DEL EXTRANJERO	
INVERSIONES EN VALORES CON INSTITUCIONES NACIONALES (EXCEPTO ACCIONES)	
INVERSIONES EN VALORES CON INSTITUCIONES EXTRANJERAS (EXCEPTO ACCIONES)	
CUENTAS Y DOCUMENTOS POR COBRAR NACIONALES (PARTES RELACIONADAS)	22,941,021
CUENTAS Y DOCUMENTOS POR COBRAR NACIONALES (PARTES NO RELACIONADAS)	
CUENTAS Y DOCUMENTOS POR COBRAR NACIONALES (TOTAL)	22,941,021
CUENTAS Y DOCUMENTOS POR COBRAR DEL EXTRANJERO (PARTES RELACIONADAS)	
CUENTAS Y DOCUMENTOS POR COBRAR DEL EXTRANJERO (PARTES NO RELACIONADAS)	
CUENTAS Y DOCUMENTOS POR COBRAR DEL EXTRANJERO (TOTAL)	
CONTRIBUCIONES A FAVOR	
INVENTARIOS	
OTROS ACTIVOS CIRCULANTES	
INVERSIONES EN ACCIONES NACIONALES	
INVERSIONES EN ACCIONES DEL EXTRANJERO	
INVERSIONES EN ACCIONES (TOTAL)	
TERRENOS	
CONSTRUCCIONES	
CONSTRUCCIONES EN PROCESO	
MAQUINARIA Y EQUIPO	
MOBILIARIO Y EQUIPO DE OFICINA	
EQUIPO DE CÓMPUTO	
EQUIPO DE TRANSPORTE	803,445
OTROS ACTIVOS FIJOS	
DEPRECIACIÓN ACUMULADA	-110,165
CARGOS Y GASTOS DIFERIDOS	

PASIVO

CUENTAS Y DOCUMENTOS POR PAGAR NACIONALES (PARTES RELACIONADAS)	39,482,549
CUENTAS Y DOCUMENTOS POR PAGAR NACIONALES (PARTES NO RELACIONADAS)	
CUENTAS Y DOCUMENTOS POR PAGAR NACIONALES (TOTAL)	39,482,549
CUENTAS Y DOCUMENTOS POR PAGAR DEL EXTRANJERO (PARTES RELACIONADAS)	
CUENTAS Y DOCUMENTOS POR PAGAR DEL EXTRANJERO (PARTES NO RELACIONADAS)	
CUENTAS Y DOCUMENTOS POR PAGAR DEL EXTRANJERO (TOTAL)	
CONTRIBUCIONES POR PAGAR	0
ANTICIPOS DE CLIENTES PARTES RELACIONADAS	
ANTICIPOS DE CLIENTES PARTES NO RELACIONADAS	
ANTICIPOS DE CLIENTES (TOTAL)	
APORTACIONES PARA FUTUROS AUMENTOS DE CAPITAL	
OTROS PASIVOS	
SUMA PASIVO	39,482,549

CAPITAL CONTABLE

CAPITAL SOCIAL PROVENIENTE DE APORTACIONES	3,000,000
CAPITAL SOCIAL PROVENIENTE DE CAPITALIZACIÓN	
RESERVAS	
OTRAS CUENTAS DE CAPITAL	
APORTACIONES PARA FUTUROS AUMENTOS DE CAPITAL	
UTILIDADES ACUMULADAS	
UTILIDAD DEL EJERCICIO	
PÉRDIDAS ACUMULADAS	-6,283,723
PÉRDIDA DEL EJERCICIO	-12,514,525
EXCESO EN LA ACTUALIZACIÓN DEL CAPITAL	
INSUFICIENCIA EN LA ACTUALIZACIÓN DEL CAPITAL	

SHCP

DECLARACIÓN DEL EJERCICIO
PERSONAS MORALES DEL RÉGIMEN GENERAL F18

SAT
Servicio de Administración Tributaria

ESTADO DE POSICIÓN FINANCIERA (BALANCE)

ACTIVO		CAPITAL CONTABLE	
AMORTIZACIÓN ACUMULADA		ACTUALIZACIÓN DEL CAPITAL CONTABLE	
SUMA ACTIVO	23,684,301	SUMA CAPITAL CONTABLE	-15,798,248
		SUMA PASIVO MÁS CAPITAL CONTABLE	23,684,301

SHCP

DECLARACIÓN DEL EJERCICIO
PERSONAS MORALES DEL RÉGIMEN GENERAL F18

SAT

CONCILIACIÓN ENTRE EL RESULTADO CONTABLE Y EL FISCAL

UTILIDAD O PÉRDIDA NETA	-12,514,525	AJUSTE ANUAL POR INFLACIÓN DEDUCIBLE	
EFECTOS DE REEXPRESIÓN		COSTO DE LO VENDIDO FISCAL	
RESULTADO POR POSICIÓN MONETARIA		DEDUCCIÓN DE INVERSIONES	
UTILIDAD O PÉRDIDA NETA HISTÓRICA	-12,514,525	ESTÍMULO FISCAL POR DEDUCCIÓN INMEDIATA DE INVERSIONES	
INGRESOS FISCALES NO CONTABLES		ESTÍMULO FISCAL DE LAS PERSONAS CON DISCAPACIDAD Y/O ADULTOS MAYORES	
AJUSTE ANUAL POR INFLACIÓN ACUMULABLE		PÉRDIDA FISCAL EN ENAJENACIÓN DE ACCIONES	
ANTICIPOS DE CLIENTES		PÉRDIDA FISCAL EN ENAJENACIÓN DE TERRENOS Y ACTIVO FIJO	
INTERESES MORATORIOS EFECTIVAMENTE COBRADOS		INTERESES MORATORIOS EFECTIVAMENTE PAGADOS	
GANANCIA EN LA ENAJENACIÓN DE ACCIONES O POR REEMBOLSO DE CAPITAL		OTRAS DEDUCCIONES FISCALES NO CONTABLES	
GANANCIA EN LA ENAJENACIÓN DE TERRENOS Y ACTIVO FIJO		INGRESOS CONTABLES NO FISCALES	
INVENTARIO ACUMULABLE DEL EJERCICIO		INTERESES MORATORIOS DEVENGADOS A FAVOR COBRADOS O NO	
OTROS INGRESOS FISCALES NO CONTABLES		ANTICIPOS DE CLIENTES DE EJERCICIOS ANTERIORES	
DEDUCCIONES CONTABLES NO FISCALES		SALDOS A FAVOR DE IMPUESTOS Y SU ACTUALIZACIÓN	
COSTO DE VENTAS CONTABLE		UTILIDAD CONTABLE EN ENAJENACIÓN DE ACTIVO FIJO	
DEPRECIACIÓN Y AMORTIZACIÓN CONTABLE		UTILIDAD CONTABLE EN ENAJENACIÓN DE ACCIONES	
GASTOS QUE NO REÚNEN REQUISITOS FISCALES		UTILIDAD EN PARTICIPACIÓN SUBSIDIARIA	
ISR, IETU, IMPAC Y PTU		OTROS INGRESOS CONTABLES NO FISCALES	
PÉRDIDA CONTABLE EN ENAJENACIÓN DE ACCIONES		UTILIDAD O PÉRDIDA FISCAL ANTES DE PTU	-12,514,525
PÉRDIDA CONTABLE EN ENAJENACIÓN DE ACTIVO FIJO			
PÉRDIDA EN PARTICIPACIÓN SUBSIDIARIA			
INTERESES DEVENGADOS QUE EXCEDEN DEL VALOR DE MERCADO Y MORATORIOS PAGADOS O NO			
OTRAS DEDUCCIONES CONTABLES NO FISCALES			
DEDUCCIONES FISCALES NO CONTABLES			

SHCP

DECLARACIÓN DEL EJERCICIO
PERSONAS MORALES DEL RÉGIMEN GENERAL F18

SAT
Servicio de Administración Tributaria

DATOS INFORMATIVOS DEL COSTO DE VENTA FISCAL

DATOS DEL INVENTARIO BASE

INDIQUE EL MÉTODO PARA DETERMINAR EL VALOR DEL INVENTARIO BASE	Inventario Inicial

DATOS INFORMATIVOS

MONTO DEL INVENTARIO INICIAL		MONTO DE LA MATERIA PRIMA CONSUMIDA, MANO DE OBRA Y LOS GASTOS INDIRECTOS DEDUCIBLES	

OPCIÓN DE ACUMULACIÓN DE INVENTARIOS

INDIQUE EL MÉTODO DE VALUACIÓN DEL INVENTARIO BASE	Sin selección	DIFERENCIA DE LA COMPARACIÓN DE INVENTARIOS DE IMPORTACIÓN		INVENTARIO REDUCIDO	
INVENTARIO BASE AL 31 DE DICIEMBRE DE 2004		VALOR DEL INVENTARIO ACUMULABLE DEL EJERCICIO QUE DECLARA	0	INVENTARIO ACUMULABLE DEL EJERCICIO	
SALDO PENDIENTE POR DEDUCIR AL 1° DE ENERO DE 2005		PORCENTAJE DE ACUMULACIÓN		COSTO DE LO VENDIDO PENDIENTE DE DEDUCIR DE MERCANCÍAS ENAJENADAS A PLAZO	
PÉRDIDAS FISCALES PENDIENTES DE DISMINUIR AL 31 DE DICIEMBRE DE 2004		INVENTARIO ACUMULABLE			

SISTEMAS Y BASES DE VALUACIÓN

INDIQUE LA OPCIÓN PARA DETERMINAR EL COSTO DE LO VENDIDO	Sin selección	INDIQUE LA BASE DE COSTOS UTILIZADA	Sin selección

MÉTODOS DE VALUACIÓN

INDIQUE EL MÉTODO DE VALUACIÓN UTILIZADO	Sin selección

COSTO SUPERIOR AL PRECIO DE MERCADO O AL DE REPOSICIÓN

COSTO SUPERIOR AL PRECIO DE MERCADO O DE REPOSICIÓN		TIPO DE PRECIO CONSIDERADO	Sin selección

DEDUCCIONES AUTORIZADAS

SUELDOS Y SALARIOS		CRÉDITO AL SALARIO NO DISMINUIDO DE CONTRIBUCIONES	
HONORARIOS PAGADOS A PERSONAS FÍSICAS	360,536	APORTACIONES SAR, INFONAVIT Y JUBILACIONES POR VEJEZ	
REGALÍAS Y ASISTENCIA TÉCNICA		APORTACIONES PARA FONDOS DE PENSIONES Y JUBILACIONES	
DONATIVOS OTORGADOS		CUOTAS AL IMSS	
USO O GOCE TEMPORAL DE BIENES PAGADOS A PERSONAS FÍSICAS		CONSUMOS EN RESTAURANTES	19,899
FLETES Y ACARREOS PAGADOS A PERSONAS FÍSICAS		PÉRDIDA POR OPERACIONES FINANCIERAS DERIVADAS	
CONTRIBUCIONES PAGADAS, EXCEPTO ISR, IETU, IMPAC, IVA Y IEPS		DEDUCCIÓN POR CONCEPTO DE AYUDA ALIMENTARIA PARA LOS TRABAJADORES	
SEGUROS Y FIANZAS		MONTO TOTAL DE LOS PAGOS QUE SEAN INGRESOS EXENTOS PARA EL TRABAJADOR	
PÉRDIDA POR CRÉDITOS INCOBRABLES		MONTO DEDUCIBLE AL 47% (PAGOS QUE SON INGRESOS EXENTOS PARA EL TRABAJADOR)	
VIÁTICOS Y GASTOS DE VIAJE	116,000		

SHCP

DECLARACIÓN DEL EJERCICIO
PERSONAS MORALES DEL RÉGIMEN GENERAL F18

SAT
Servicio de Administración Tributaria

DEDUCCIONES AUTORIZADAS

COMBUSTIBLE Y LUBRICANTES		MONTO DEDUCIBLE AL 53% (PAGOS QUE SON INGRESOS EXENTOS PARA EL TRABAJADOR)	
		OTRAS DEDUCCIONES AUTORIZADAS	12,018,098
		TOTAL DE DEDUCCIONES AUTORIZADAS	12,514,525

SHCP

DECLARACIÓN DEL EJERCICIO
PERSONAS MORALES DEL RÉGIMEN GENERAL F18

SAT

CIFRAS AL CIERRE DEL EJERCICIO

PÉRDIDAS FISCALES DE EJERCICIOS ANTERIORES PENDIENTES DE AMORTIZAR ACTUALIZADAS	6,417,617
PÉRDIDAS FISCALES DE EJERCICIOS ANTERIORES PENDIENTES DE AMORTIZAR ACTUALIZADAS (AGUAS PROFUNDAS)	
SALDO PROMEDIO ANUAL DE LOS CRÉDITOS	
SALDO PROMEDIO ANUAL DE LAS DEUDAS	
COEFICIENTE DE UTILIDAD POR APLICAR EN EL EJERCICIO SIGUIENTE	0.0000
PORCENTAJE DE PARTICIPACIÓN CONSOLIDABLE	
ISR CAUSADO EN EXCESO DEL IMPAC EN LOS 3 EJERCICIOS ANTERIORES, PENDIENTES DE APLICAR	
SALDO ACTUALIZADO DE LA CUENTA DE UTILIDAD FISCAL NETA	
SALDO ACTUALIZADO DE LA CUENTA DE UTILIDAD FISCAL NETA (GENERADA A PARTIR DEL EJERCICIO 2014)	
SALDO ACTUALIZADO DE LA CUENTA DE UTILIDAD FISCAL REINVERTIDA	

SALDO ACTUALIZADO DE LA CUENTA DE CAPITAL DE APORTACIÓN	3,656,400
MONTO DE LA UTILIDAD FISCAL NETA DE LA PARTICIPACIÓN INTEGRABLE	
MONTO DE LA UTILIDAD FISCAL NETA DE LA PARTICIPACIÓN INTEGRABLE POR LA QUE SE PAGÓ EL IMPUESTO DEL EJERCICIO	
MONTO DE LA UTILIDAD FISCAL NETA DE LA PARTICIPACIÓN INTEGRABLE POR LA QUE SE DIFIRIÓ EL IMPUESTO DEL EJERCICIO	
MONTO DE LA UTILIDAD FISCAL NETA DE LA PARTICIPACIÓN NO INTEGRABLE	

SHCP

DECLARACIÓN DEL EJERCICIO
PERSONAS MORALES DEL RÉGIMEN GENERAL F18

SAT

CIFRAS AL CIERRE DEL EJERCICIO

INFORMACIÓN DE LA SOCIEDAD COOPERATIVA DE PRODUCCIÓN QUE OPTA POR DIFERIR EL ISR

UTILIDAD GRAVABLE NO DISTRIBUIDA EN EL EJERCICIO ANTERIOR		UTILIDAD GRAVABLE DISTRIBUIDA EN EL EJERCICIO	
MONTO DEL ISR A DIFERIR EN EL EJERCICIO ANTERIOR		MONTO DE LA UTILIDAD GRAVABLE TRANSMITIDO POR FUSIÓN O ESCISIÓN	
UTILIDAD GRAVABLE NO DISTRIBUIDA EN EL EJERCICIO		MONTO EN INVERSIONES PRODUCTIVAS EQUIVALENTE AL ISR DIFERIDO	
SALDO ACTUALIZADO DE LA CUENTA DE UTILIDAD GRAVABLE			

DECLARACIÓN DEL EJERCICIO
PERSONAS MORALES DEL RÉGIMEN GENERAL F18

DETERMINACIÓN DEL IMPUESTO SOBRE LA RENTA

TOTAL DE INGRESOS ACUMULABLES	0
TOTAL DE DEDUCCIONES AUTORIZADAS Y DEDUCCIÓN INMEDIATA DE INVERSIONES	
DEDUCCIÓN ADICIONAL POR PAGO DE SERVICIOS PERSONALES EN LA OPERACIÓN DE MAQUILA	
UTILIDAD O PÉRDIDA FISCAL ANTES DE PTU	0
PTU PAGADA EN EL EJERCICIO	
UTILIDAD FISCAL DEL EJERCICIO	0
PÉRDIDA FISCAL DEL EJERCICIO	
PÉRDIDAS FISCALES DE EJERCICIOS ANTERIORES QUE SE APLICAN EN EL EJERCICIO	
DEDUCCIÓN ADICIONAL DEL FOMENTO AL PRIMER EMPLEO	
RESULTADO FISCAL	0
IMPUESTO SOBRE LA RENTA DEL EJERCICIO	0
IMPUESTO CAUSADO EN EL EJERCICIO	0
PORCENTAJE DE PARTICIPACIÓN INTEGRABLE	
IMPUESTO DE LA PARTICIPACIÓN INTEGRABLE	
FACTOR DE RESULTADO FISCAL INTEGRADO	
MONTO DEL IMPUESTO CORRESPONDIENTE A LA PARTICIPACIÓN INTEGRABLE	
PORCENTAJE DE PARTICIPACIÓN NO INTEGRABLE	
MONTO DEL IMPUESTO CORRESPONDIENTE DE LA PARTICIPACIÓN NO INTEGRABLE	
IMPUESTO DEL EJERCICIO A ENTERAR	
ESTÍMULO POR PROYECTOS EN INVESTIGACIÓN Y DESARROLLO TECNOLÓGICO	
ESTÍMULO A LA PRODUCCIÓN Y DISTRIBUCIÓN CINEMATOGRÁFICA NACIONAL	
ESTÍMULO A PROYECTOS DE INVERSIÓN EN LA PRODUCCIÓN TEATRAL NACIONAL	
OTROS ESTÍMULOS	
TOTAL DE ESTÍMULOS	
PAGOS PROVISIONALES EFECTUADOS ENTREGADOS A LA CONTROLADORA	
PAGOS PROVISIONALES EFECTUADOS ENTERADOS A LA FEDERACIÓN	
IMPUESTO RETENIDO AL CONTRIBUYENTE	
OTRAS CANTIDADES A CARGO	
OTRAS CANTIDADES A FAVOR	
DIFERENCIA A CARGO	0
DIFERENCIA A FAVOR	0
ISR DIFERIDO A CARGO QUE PAGA EN EL EJERCICIO (INTEGRADA)	
ISR DIFERIDO A ENTERAR POR DESINCORPORACIÓN	
MONTO DEL ISR DEL EJERCICIO QUE PODRÁ DIFERIRSE (SOCIEDAD COOPERATIVA DE PRODUCCIÓN)	
MONTO DEL ISR DIFERIDO DE EJERCICIOS ANTERIORES PAGADO EN EL EJERCICIO (SOCIEDAD COOPERATIVA DE PRODUCCIÓN)	
ISR A CARGO DEL EJERCICIO	0
ISR A FAVOR DEL EJERCICIO	

IMPUESTO SOBRE INGRESOS SUJETOS A REGÍMENES FISCALES PREFERENTES

IMPUESTO SOBRE INGRESOS SUJETOS A REGÍMENES FISCALES PREFERENTES	

SHCP

SECRETARÍA DE HACIENDA Y CRÉDITO PÚBLICO

DECLARACIÓN DEL EJERCICIO PERSONAS MORALES DEL RÉGIMEN GENERAL F18

SAT

Servicio de Administración Tributaria

DETERMINACIÓN DEL IMPUESTO SOBRE LA RENTA

IMPUESTO ACREDITABLE PAGADO EN EL EXTRANJERO

IMPUESTO ACREDITABLE POR DIVIDENDOS O UTILIDADES DISTRIBUIDOS

IMPUESTO CORRESPONDIENTE A LA CONSOLIDACIÓN FISCAL A CARGO

IMPUESTO CORRESPONDIENTE A LA CONSOLIDACIÓN FISCAL ENTREGADO (EN EXCESO)

DATOS INFORMATIVOS DEL IMPUESTO SOBRE LA RENTA

TOTAL DEL ESTÍMULO POR PROYECTOS EN INVESTIGACIÓN Y DESARROLLO TECNOLÓGICO DE EJERCICIOS ANTERIORES APLICADO EN EL EJERCICIO

TOTAL DEL ESTÍMULO A LA PRODUCCIÓN Y DISTRIBUCIÓN CINEMATOGRÁFICA NACIONAL DE EJERCICIOS ANTERIORES APLICADO EN EL EJERCICIO

TOTAL DEL ESTÍMULO A PROYECTOS DE INVERSIÓN EN LA PRODUCCIÓN TEATRAL NACIONAL DE EJERCICIOS ANTERIORES APLICADO EN EL EJERCICIO

DEDUCCIÓN ADICIONAL DEL FOMENTO AL PRIMER EMPLEO NO APLICADA

MONTO APLICADO DEL ESTÍMULO FISCAL DE CHATARRIZACIÓN

MONTO DEDUCIBLE DE LOS PAGOS EFECTUADOS POR EL USO O GOCE TEMPORAL DE AUTOMÓVILES

IMPAC RECUPERADO EN EL EJERCICIO DERIVADO DE LA DESCONSOLIDACIÓN

MONTO DEL ISR DEL EJERCICIO QUE PODRÁ DIFERIRSE (INTEGRADA)

INDIQUE EL EJERCICIO QUE CORRESPONDE AL ISR DIFERIDO QUE PAGA (INTEGRADA)

EJERCICIO DEL ISR DIFERIDO QUE SE PAGA POR DESINCORPORACIÓN (DEL)

EJERCICIO DEL ISR DIFERIDO QUE SE PAGA POR DESINCORPORACIÓN (AL)

SUELDOS, SALARIOS Y PRESTACIONES A TRABAJADORES CON DISCAPACIDAD Y/O ADULTOS MAYORES

PORCENTAJE DE DEDUCCIÓN APLICADO TRATÁNDOSE DE INVERSIÓN EN ENERGÍAS RENOVABLES — Sin selección

SALDO INICIAL EN EL EJERCICIO (CUENTA DE UTILIDAD FISCAL NETA POR INVERSIONES EN ENERGÍAS RENOVABLES)

RETIROS EN EL EJERCICIO (CUENTA DE UTILIDAD FISCAL NETA POR INVERSIONES EN ENERGÍAS RENOVABLES)

RETIROS REALIZADOS EN EJERCICIOS ANTERIORES (CUENTA DE UTILIDAD FISCAL NETA POR INVERSIONES EN ENERGÍAS RENOVABLES)

MONTO TOTAL DE RETIROS REALIZADOS AL EJERCICIO DE QUE SE TRATE (CUENTA DE UTILIDAD FISCAL NETA POR INVERSIONES EN ENERGÍAS RENOVABLES)

MONTO DE LOS INGRESOS QUE CORRESPONDEN A LA GENERACIÓN DE ENERGÍA PROVENIENTE DE FUENTES RENOVABLES O DE SISTEMAS DE COGENERACIÓN DE ELECTRICIDAD EFICIENTE

DATOS INFORMATIVOS DEL ESTÍMULO FISCAL RELACIONADOS CON EL IMPUESTO SOBRE TENENCIA O USO DE VEHÍCULOS

NÚMERO DE VEHÍCULOS NUEVOS ENAJENADOS A PERSONAS FÍSICAS POR LAS QUE SE OPTÓ POR PAGAR EL ISTUV

MONTO TOTAL DEL ISTUV PAGADO POR VEHÍCULOS ENAJENADOS A PERSONAS FÍSICAS

TOTAL DEL ESTÍMULO FISCAL ISTUV APLICABLE A VEHÍCULOS NUEVOS ENAJENADOS A PERSONAS FÍSICAS, DE EJERCICIOS ANTERIORES APLICADO EN EL EJERCICIO

MONTO DEL ESTÍMULO FISCAL ISTUV ACREDITADO CONTRA EL ISR EN PAGOS PROVISIONALES

REMANENTE DEL ESTÍMULO FISCAL ISTUV PENDIENTE DE ACREDITAR

TOTAL DEL ESTÍMULO FISCAL ISTUV APLICABLE A VEHÍCULOS NUEVOS ADQUIRIDOS POR PERSONAS MORALES, DE EJERCICIOS ANTERIORES APLICADO EN EL EJERCICIO

SHCP

DECLARACIÓN DEL EJERCICIO
PERSONAS MORALES DEL RÉGIMEN GENERAL F18

SAT

Servicio de Administración Tributaria

DETERMINACIÓN DEL PAGO
R1 ISR PERSONAS MORALES

A CARGO	0	ACREDITAMIENTO SORTEOS	
A FAVOR		DIÉSEL MARINO	
PARTE ACTUALIZADA		TOTAL DE APLICACIONES	0
RECARGOS		FECHA DEL PAGO REALIZADO CON ANTERIORIDAD	
MULTA POR CORRECCIÓN		MONTO PAGADO CON ANTERIORIDAD	
TOTAL DE CONTRIBUCIONES	0	CANTIDAD A CARGO	0
CRÉDITO AL SALARIO		¿OPTA POR PAGAR EN PARCIALIDADES?	Sin selección
SUBSIDIO PARA EL EMPLEO		IMPORTE DE LA PRIMERA PARCIALIDAD	
COMPENSACIONES		IMPORTE SIN LA PRIMERA PARCIALIDAD	
CRÉDITO IEPS DIÉSEL, SECTOR PRIMARIO Y MINERO		CANTIDAD A FAVOR	
DIÉSEL AUTOMOTRIZ PARA TRANSPORTE		CANTIDAD A PAGAR	0
USO DE INFRAESTRUCTURA, CARRETERA DE CUOTA			
OTROS ESTÍMULOS			

SHCP

SECRETARÍA DE HACIENDA Y CRÉDITO PÚBLICO

ACUSE DE RECIBO
DECLARACIÓN DEL EJERCICIO DE IMPUESTOS FEDERALES

SAT
Servicio de Administración Tributaria

RFC: CIS110712JQ2

Denominación o razón social: CONSORCIO INTEGRADOR SONORA 80M SA DE CV

Tipo de declaración:	Normal		
Período de la declaración:	Del Ejercicio	**Ejercicio:**	2016
Fecha y hora de presentación:	19/06/2017 21:02	**Medio de presentación:**	Internet
Número de operación:	170000358778		

Impuestos que declara:

Concepto de pago 1:	ISR PERSONAS MORALES
A cargo:	0
Cantidad a cargo:	0
Cantidad a pagar:	0

Es recomendable verificar que el importe calculado de la parte actualizada esté correcto, en virtud de que puede haber cambiado el índice nacional de precios al consumidor y el cálculo debe estar basado en el último publicado.

Los datos personales son incorporados y protegidos en los sistemas del SAT, de conformidad con las disposiciones legales en la materia.

Para modificar o corregir datos personales visita sat.gob.mx.

Este acuse es emitido sin prejuzgar la veracidad de los datos asentados ni el cumplimiento dentro de los plazos establecidos. Quedan a salvo las facultades de revisión de la autoridad fiscal.

Sello digital :
EEODBPOzX1zrjq1RqmOX52S3HrKvsopqPu37GMkQjq5J0op2Hu1Y1W0sJ5pnn1JowsjqQfb1PdyK8a1rXkW1UcenOpFK9vdLCK8g
vze94uUCkVLAeO+6B1x58XQNM3QTg3woSzkauEyh4sjQV1uv6kKUm2pYQKUQ4C7hXcQWqvA=

Exhibit 8

AMENDED AND RESTATED SHARES PURCHASE AGREEMENT

THIS AMENDED AND RESTATED SHARES PURCHASE AGREEMENT (this "**Agreement**") is entered into as of February 2, 2016 (the "**Effective Date**"), by and between Consorcio Integrador Sonora 80M S.A. de C.V., a Mexican variable capital corporation ("Seller"), and **General Energy Solutions USA, Inc.**, a corporation incorporated under the laws of the state of Nevada, U.S.A. ("**Buyer**"). Seller and Buyer are sometimes referred to herein each as a "**Party**" and collectively, as the "**Parties.**"

Recitals

A. Munisol S.A.P.I. de C.V. is developing a solar power generating project totaling approximately 21.56 MW DC to be located in or near Hermosillo, Sonora (the "**Project**").

B. Seller owns twenty-nine thousand seven hundred (29,700) of the Series A shares of the Project Company, an individual named Alfonso Avelino Cruz Sanchez owns three hundred (300) Series A Shares of the Project Company, and an individual named Jose Hugo Barceló Durazo owns twenty-one (21) Series B shares of the Project Company (the combined thirty thousand (30,000) Series A Shares and twenty-one (21) Series B shares are collectively referred to as the "**Equity Interests**").

C. Munisol S.A.P.I. de C.V. is party to that certain Letter of Intent dated October 16, 2015 ("**Letter of Intent**") with US Topco Energy, Inc. ("**US Topco**") whereby Munisol S.A.P.I. de C.V. and US Topco agreed to negotiate on an exclusive basis for a period of time for the purchase of 100% of the ownership interests in Munisol S.A.P.I. de C.V. and all rights to the Project;

D. US Topco and Buyer have entered that certain Engagement Letter dated December 7, 2015, by which US Topco relinquished to Buyer all rights granted by the Letter of Intent and granted Buyer the right to execute this Agreement with Seller;

E. The Parties entered into that certain Shares Purchase Agreement effective January 8, 2016, under which Buyer and Seller agreed to the terms of the Shares Purchase Agreement and agreed that the Shares Purchase Agreement would expire on the earlier of January 22, 2016 or the execution of an amended and restated Shares Purchase Agreement;

F. The Parties desire to amend and restate in its entirety the Shares Purchase Agreement entered on January 8, 2016; and

G. Buyer wishes to purchase, acquire and accept from Seller, and Seller wishes to sell and assign to Buyer, the Equity Interests in accordance with the terms and conditions hereof.

Agreement

In consideration of the foregoing, the mutual promises contained herein and other good and valuable consideration, the receipt and sufficiency of which are hereby acknowledged, the Parties hereby agree to amend and restate in its entirety the January 8, 2016 Shares Purchase Agreement as follows:

81081928.2 0046936-00031

ARTICLE 1
DEFINITIONS

1.1 **Definitions.** As used in this Agreement, the following terms have the following meanings:

"**Acquisition**" has the meaning given to such term in ARTICLE 2 of this Agreement.

"**Action**" means any litigation, cause of action, arbitration, audit, hearing, claim, suit, demand, charge, complaint, dispute, grievance, investigation or proceeding (whether civil, criminal, administrative, investigative, or informal) commenced, brought, conducted, or heard by or before, or otherwise involving, any Governmental Authority, arbitrator or any other Person.

"**Actual Constructed Capacity**" means the total nameplate generating capacity of the Project for any phases of the Project reaching a Commercial Operation Date at any time from the Effective Date until three (3) years thereafter.

"**Affiliate**" means any Person that directly or indirectly through one of more intermediaries, controls or is controlled by or is under common control with the Person specified. For purposes of this definition, control of a Person means the power, direct or indirect, to direct or cause the direction of the management and policies of such Person, whether through the ownership of voting securities, by contract or otherwise. For the avoidance of doubt, the Project Company shall be deemed to be an Affiliate of Seller prior to the Closing and an Affiliate of Buyer after the Closing.

"**Agreement**" has the meaning given to such term in the introduction to this Agreement.

"**Ancillary Documents**" means the Assignment and Conveyance and all other agreements, documents, certificates or other instruments to be executed and delivered in connection with the transactions contemplated hereby.

"**Apportioned Obligations**" has the meaning given to such term in Section 7.1.

"**Assignment and Conveyance**" means that certain Assignment and Conveyance, substantially in the form attached hereto as EXHIBIT A, to be entered into by Buyer and Seller.

"**Books and Records**" means all files, documents, instruments, papers, books and records related to the ownership, business or condition of the Project Company or the Project, including, where applicable, financial statements, Tax Returns and related work papers and letters from accountants, budgets, ledgers, journals, minute books, membership interest certificates and books, membership interest transfer ledgers, Contracts, Permits, Orders, governmental authorizations, computer files and programs, retrieval programs, operating data and plans and environmental studies and plans, if any.

"**Business Day**" means a day other than Saturday, Sunday or any day on which banks located in Los Angeles, California or Hermosillo, Sonora, Mexico are authorized or obligated to close.

"**Buyer**" has the meaning given to such term in the introduction to this Agreement.

"**Buyer Indemnified Persons**" means Buyer and its Affiliates and its and their respective directors, officers, employees and agents, and after the Closing shall include the Project Company.

"**CFE**" has the meaning given to such term in Section 3.7(a) of this Agreement.

"**Clarification Letter Threshold**" means Seller obtains PPA Clarification Letters from Non-Hermosillo Municipal Offtakers representing at least 2.653MW DC of total generating capacity, as shown by the offtake amounts established in the PPA with such Non-Hermosillo Municipal Offtakers.

"**Closing**" means the consummation of the transactions contemplated by this Agreement.

"**Closing Date**" means the date on which the Closing occurs.

"**Commercial Operation Date**" means that for a given unit of electricity produced by the Project, the Project Company has satisfied the following conditions: (a) the completion, testing and successful operation of the transmission upgrades necessary to interconnect the Project to the national electrical system of Mexico; (b) all authorizations, approvals or permits from all applicable Government Authorities necessary to build and operate the Project have been obtained and are in effect; (c) the interconnection agreement with the applicable Government Authority has been executed and is in effect; (d) the construction works and the tests of the Project allowing the normal generation of power have been satisfactorily concluded; (e) the interconnection works and equipment have been tested and completed; and (f) the synchronization tests for the interconnection have been satisfactorily completed.

"**Confidential Information**" has the meaning given to such term in Section 10.11 of this Agreement.

"**Contract**" means any agreement, instrument, lease, license, permit, evidence of indebtedness, guaranty, mortgage, indenture, security agreement or other contract, arrangement, or commitment, whether written or oral.

"**Damages**" means any damages, losses, costs, expenses, expenditures, claims or liabilities (including reasonable counsel fees and reasonable expenses of investigation, defense and prosecution of Actions), whether or not involving a claim by a third party.

"**Disclosing Party**" has the meaning given to such term in Section 10.11 of this Agreement.

"**Disclosure Schedule**" means the disclosure schedules attached hereto.

"**Effective Date**" has the meaning set forth in the preamble.

"**Environmental Attributes**" means all present or future rights, interests, benefits or characteristics attributable to the Project (and all Renewable Energy Credits and Clean Energy

Certificates (*Certificados de Energias Limpias*) associated with such attributes) that are recognized, created, generated or otherwise exist or arise from the Project (whether before, on or after the Closing). Forms of Environmental Attributes include any and all environmental air quality credits, waste management credits, water quality credits, renewable energy credits, carbon credits, emissions reduction credits, certificates, tags, offsets, allowances, or similar products or rights, howsoever entitled.

"**Environmental Laws**" means all Laws (including rules, regulations, codes, plans, injunctions, judgments, orders, ordinances, decrees, rulings and charges thereunder) of Governmental Authorities concerning pollution or protection of health, natural resources, or the environment, including Laws relating to emissions, discharges, releases, or threatened releases of hazardous materials into the air, surface water, ground water, lands or subsurface, or otherwise relating to the manufacture, processing, distribution, use, treatment, storage, disposal, transport or handling of hazardous materials.

"**Equitable Qualifications**" means applicable bankruptcy, insolvency, reorganization, arrangement, moratorium or other similar Laws relating to or affecting the rights of creditors generally and general equitable principles.

"**Equity Interests**" has the meaning given to such term in the recitals to this Agreement.

"**Fee Simple**" means an interest in real property that allows its holder and his, her or its heirs and assigns to own and possess the property in perpetuity.

"**Final Payment**" means the completion of the last payment required by this Agreement.

"**Financing Parties**" means the Person(s), if any, from time to time issuing or providing any construction, term financing, working capital financing, credit support, credit enhancements, interest rate hedging or other permanent debt, lease financing or tax equity funding for the Project, including any applicable trustee, collateral agent or similar Person.

"**GAAP**" means generally accepted accounting principles, consistently applied.

"**Governmental Authority**" means any domestic or foreign governmental or regulatory authority, agency, court, commission, arbitration tribunal or other governmental or regulatory entity (including any self-regulatory organization or independent system operator or regional transmission operator).

"**Hermosillo**" means the city of Hermosillo, Sonora, Mexico.

"**Hermosillo Capacity**" means an amount of nameplate generating capacity equal to 12.96MW DC.

"**Hermosillo PPA**" means that certain Power Supply Agreement entered into on August 14, 2012 by and between the Seller and Hermosillo, as amended by the November 12, 2014 modification.

"**Hermosillo PPA Deadlines**" means all deadlines applicable to the Seller, or the Project Company as delegatee of Seller, contained in the Hermosillo PPA, including, but not limited to, the following deadlines: (1) Clause 1, Definitions and Interpretations, providing that the Effective Date (*Fecha de Inicio de Vigencia*) of the Hermosillo PPA occurs when the Seller has obtained all permits and authorizations needed to operate the Project and has begun producing at least fifty percent (50%) of the total deliveries required by the Hermosillo PPA, which must occur by June 30, 2016; and (2) Clause 3, Obligations of Sonora 80M, providing that the Hermosillo PPA will be automatically rescinded if Seller: (a) fails to initiate operations in 2016 for reasons imputable solely to Seller; (b) fails to obtain all permits necessary to build and operate the Project in 2015; (c) fails to provide the City of Hermosillo with evidence that the Seller owns the land required to build and operate the Project in accordance with the terms of the Hermosillo PPA within 90 days of having signed the November 12, 2014 modification, the trust agreement, and the power of attorney; or (d) fails to deliver the total amount of energy under the Hermosillo PPA by August 31, 2016.

"**Indebtedness**" means (i) all obligations for borrowed money, (ii) all obligations evidenced by bonds, debentures, notes or other similar instruments, (iii) all capital lease obligations, (iv) all obligations for the reimbursement of any obligor on any letter of credit, banker's acceptance or similar credit transaction, (v) all guarantees of Indebtedness, (vi) all obligations under interest rate agreements or hedging agreements, and (vii) the deferred purchase price of assets or services which in accordance with GAAP would be shown on the liability side of a balance sheet.

"**Indemnified Person**" has the meaning given to such term in Section 8.5(a) of this Agreement.

"**Indemnifying Party**" has the meaning given to such term in Section 8.5(a) of this Agreement.

"**Knowledge**" means the information actually known by the respective officers and directors of a Party only, or such information of which any such person has received written notice, but does not include knowledge or awareness of any other person, or constructive or imputed knowledge.

"**Law**" means any applicable law, international treaty, statute, rule, regulation, ordinance or other pronouncement having the effect of law of the United States, Mexico, any foreign country or any domestic or foreign state, county, city, territory or other political subdivision of any Governmental Authority.

"**Lien**" means any lien, security interest, charge, right of first refusal, option, mortgage, pledge, assessment, transfer for the purpose of subjection to the payment of any indebtedness, or restriction on the creation of any of the foregoing, whether relating to any property or right or the income or profits therefrom, or other encumbrance, but does not include any Permitted Lien.

"**Material Contract**" has the meaning set forth in Section 3.10(a) of this Agreement.

"**Municipal Offtakers**" means the cities of Hermosillo, Empalme, Etchojoa, Alamos, and Caborca.

"**Non-Hermosillo Municipal Offtakers**" means the cities of Empalme, Etchojoa, Alamos, and Caborca.

"**Non-Hermosillo Clarification Letter Capacity**" means the total combined generating capacity of the Project represented by the PPAs with all Non-Hermosillo Municipal Offtakers for which Seller obtains PPA Clarification Letters.

"**Non-Hermosillo *Ramo 28* Guaranty Registrations**" means that by no later than March 31, 2016, Seller has certified in writing to Buyer that the registration of the *Ramo 28* Guaranty in the *Registro de Obligaciones y Empréstitos de Entidades y Municipios, Registro Estatal de Deuda Pública del Estado de Sonora*, and the corresponding *Registro de Deuda Pública Municipal* has occurred for all Non-Hermosillo Municipal Offtakers with a *Ramo 28* Guaranty.

"**Order**" means any order, judgment, decree or ruling of a Governmental Authority (excluding, for the avoidance of doubt, any Permit).

"**Ownership Interest**" means, with respect to any Person, any share, capital stock, partnership, membership or similar interest or other indicia of equity ownership (including, any option, warrant, profits interests or similar right or right or security convertible, exchangeable or exercisable therefor or other instrument or right the value of which is based on any of the foregoing) in such Person.

"**Party**" and "**Parties**" have the meaning given to such terms in the introduction to this Agreement.

"**Permit**" means any authorization, license, permit, certificate of authority, approval, registration, franchise, clearance or similar consent granted or issued by any Governmental Authority relating to the Project.

"**Permitted Liens**" means: (a) Liens for Taxes not yet due and payable or for Taxes being contested in good faith through appropriate proceedings; (b) any Lien arising in the ordinary course of business by operation of Law with respect to a liability that is not yet due or delinquent or which is being contested in good faith by Seller or the Project Company; (c) immaterial imperfections or irregularities of title; (d) Liens created by or through Buyer or any Affiliate of Buyer; and (e) obligations under this Agreement, the Material Contracts and any Permit.

"**Person**" means any natural person, corporation, company, partnership (general or limited), limited liability company, cooperative, trust, estate, joint venture, Governmental Authority or other entity or association.

"**Post-Closing Covenants**" has the meaning given to such term in Section2.3(a).

"**Post-Closing Payment**" has the meaning given to such term in Section 2.3(a).

"**PPA**" means each of the power purchase agreements listed on Schedule 2.

"**PPA Clarification Letter**" means a binding written agreement in the form attached hereto as EXHIBIT B between the Project Company and a Municipal Offtaker that is: (a) approved and authorized by the municipal city council (*Cabildo*) of the applicable Municipal Offtaker prior to the Municipal Offtaker executing the PPA Clarification Letter; and (b) if applicable, registered with all applicable registries of public indebtedness at the municipal, state, and federal level of Mexico applicable to the PPA Clarification Letter.

"**Project**" has the meaning given to such term in the recitals to this Agreement.

"**Project Assets**" means those assets described as such on Schedule 1.

"**Project Company**" means Munisol S.A.P.I. de C.V., a Mexican corporation.

"**Purchase Price**" means the aggregate amounts required to be paid under ARTICLE 2 of this Agreement.

"***Ramo 28*** **Guaranty**" means a guaranty under which tax revenues allocated to a Municipal Offtaker from federal taxes of the federal government of the United Mexican States are used as a guaranty of such Municipal Offtaker's obligations under the PPA applicable to such Municipal Offtaker.

"**Receiving Party**" has the meaning given to such term in Section 10.11 of this Agreement.

"**Renewable Energy Credit**" means any credit, certificate, renewable energy certificate, allowance or similar intangible asset or derivative, whether arising pursuant to Law, regulation, certification, markets, trading, offset, private transaction, renewable portfolio standards, renewable fuel standard(s), voluntary programs or otherwise, that is generated and attributable to the production of any amount of electricity or fuel by the Project.

"**Seller**" has the meaning given to such term in the introduction to this Agreement.

"**Seller Indemnified Persons**" means Seller and its Affiliates and its and their respective directors, officers, employees and agents when entitled to indemnification under ARTICLE 8. For avoidance of doubt the Project Company is not a Seller Indemnified Person.

"**Series B Shareholders**" means all holders of record of Series B shares of the Project Company existing as of the Closing Date.

"**Site**" means the site(s) on which the Project Company shall design, construct, test and operate the Project, including (1) the 100 Hectare parcel, and (2) the 1.83 Hectare parcel.

"**Straddle Period**" means any taxable year or period beginning on or before and ending after the Closing Date.

"**Survival Period**" means a period of time commencing on the Closing Date and terminating three (3) years from the Closing Date.

"**Tax**" or "**Taxes**" means all net income, gross income, gross receipts, excise, real estate excise, stamp, real or personal property, ad valorem, withholding, social security, unemployment, use, license, occupation, business and occupation, net worth, payroll, franchise, severance, transfer, recording, employment, premium, windfall profits, environmental, customs duties, capital stock, transfer, profits, sales, uses, registration, value added, alternative or add-on minimum, estimated or other taxes, assessments, special assessments, levies or charges imposed by any Governmental Authority and any interest, surcharges, penalties, or additions to tax attributable thereto.

"**Tax Advisor**" means a certified accountant or tax attorney.

"**Tax Return**" means any returns, declarations, reports, claims for refund, information returns (including where permitted or required, any consolidated, combined or unitary returns) or other documents (including any related or supporting schedules, statements or information and any amendments thereof) filed or required to be filed in connection with the determination, assessment or collection of any Taxes or in connection with the administration of any Laws relating to any Taxes.

"**Transfer Taxes**" means any sales, use, stamp, documentary, filing, business and occupation, recording, transfer, conveyance, real estate transfer, stock transfer, excise, real estate excise, registration, duty, securities transactions or similar transfer Taxes (together with any interest, penalties or additions to Tax attributable thereto) as levied by any Governmental Authority in connection with the sale of the Equity Interests as contemplated by this Agreement.

1.2 <u>**Other References**</u>. As used in this Agreement, unless otherwise specified or where the context otherwise requires: (a) all references to "**Articles**" and "**Sections**" are to Articles and Sections of this Agreement; (b) all references to "**Exhibits**" are to Exhibits attached to this Agreement, each of which is an integral part of this Agreement and, by this reference, made a part of this Agreement in its entirety for all purposes; (c) terms defined in the singular shall have the corresponding meaning when used in the plural and vice versa; (d) all uses of "include" or "including" mean "including, without limitation;" (e) references to a law, rule, regulation, Contract, agreement, or other document mean that law, rule, regulation, Contract, agreement, or document as amended, modified, or supplemented, if applicable, from time to time and includes (in the case of agreements or documents) references to all attachments thereto and instruments incorporated therein; (f) the word "or" has the inclusive meaning represented by the phrase "and/or;" (g) the words "this Agreement," "hereof," "hereunder," "herein," "hereby" or words of similar import refer to this Agreement as a whole and not to a particular Article, Section, subsection, clause, or other subdivision of this Agreement; (h) any reference to a Person includes such Person's successors and permitted assigns and any reference to a Governmental Authority includes any successor thereto; (i) any definition in one part of speech of a word, such as definition of the noun form of that word, shall have a comparable meaning when used in a different part of speech, such as the verb form of that word; (j) the headings of particular provisions of this Agreement are inserted for convenience only and shall not be construed as a part of this Agreement or serve as a limitation or expansion on the scope of any term or provision of this Agreement; and (k) any provisions hereof including the words "written" or "in writing" means hand-written, type-written, printed or electronically made and resulting in a permanent record.

ARTICLE 2
SALE OF EQUITY INTERESTS

2.1 <u>**Sale of Equity Interests.**</u> On the terms and subject to the conditions of this Agreement, at the Closing, Seller shall sell, assign, transfer, convey and deliver to Buyer, and Buyer shall purchase, acquire and receive from Seller, the Equity Interests, free and clear of any Liens.

2.2 <u>**Closing Payment.**</u> If the Closing occurs, then on the Closing Date, Buyer shall pay to Seller, in immediately available funds by wire transfer, an amount equal to Four Hundred Thirty Thousand Dollars (US $430,000.00).

2.3 <u>**Post-Closing Payment.**</u>

(a) If the Closing occurs, and if Seller complies fully with all covenants in ARTICLE 5 of this Agreement (the "**Post-Closing Covenants**"), then Company shall pay to Seller, in immediately available funds by wire transfer, an amount equal Three Million Seventy-Three Thousand Five Hundred Dollars (US $3,073,500.00) ("**Post-Closing Payment**").

(b) If the Post-Closing Payment is due under Section 2.3(a), then Seller shall provide notice to Buyer that the Post-Closing Payment is due. Within ten (10) Business Days of receiving the notice, Buyer shall pay the Post-Closing Payment to Seller.

2.4 <u>**COD Payment.**</u>

(a) If (i) the Closing occurs, (ii) Seller complies fully with the Post-Closing Covenants, (iii) Seller obtains the Non-Hermosillo Ramo 28 Guaranty Registrations, and (iv) the Project reaches the Commercial Operation Date, then within ten (10) Business Days following the Commercial Operation Date, Buyer shall pay to Seller one of the following values (but no more than one):

(i) If the Actual Constructed Capacity is less than or equal to the Hermosillo Capacity as a result of any factor outside of Buyer's reasonable control, then an amount equal to the result of the following equation:

[Actual Constructed Capacity x US $0.325 per Watt] - US $3,503,500.00;

or

(ii) If (A) Seller meets the Clarification Letter Threshold, and (B) the Actual Constructed Capacity is greater than the Hermosillo Capacity, then an amount equal to the result of the following equation:

[Actual Constructed Capacity x US $0.325 per Watt] - US $3,503,500.00 - [({Actual Constructed Capacity - Hermosillo Capacity} x US $0.1625 per Watt) x ({3.79MW DC - Non-Hermosillo Clarification Letter Capacity}/3.79MW DC)];

or

(iii) If (A) Seller does not meet the Clarification Letter Threshold, and (B) the Actual Constructed Capacity is greater than the Hermosillo Capacity, then an amount equal to the result of the following equation:

> [Actual Constructed Capacity x US $0.325 per Watt] - US $3,503,500.00 - [(Actual Constructed Capacity - Hermosillo Capacity) x US $0.1625 per Watt].

(b) Notwithstanding anything to the contrary in this Agreement, if the result of any equation in Section 2.4(a) is below Zero Dollars (US $0.00), then Seller shall pay to Buyer an amount equal to the amount by which such resulting figure is below Zero Dollars (US $0.00).

(c) Notwithstanding anything to the contrary in this Agreement, in no event will any payment be due to Seller under Section 2.4(a) if Seller has not complied fully with all Post-Closing Covenants.

ARTICLE 3
REPRESENTATIONS AND WARRANTIES OF SELLER

Seller represents and warrants to Buyer that, as of the Effective Date and as of the Closing Date:

3.1 Organization.

(a) Seller is a corporation duly organized and validly existing under the Laws of the Country of Mexico and has all requisite corporate power and authority to conduct its business as it is now conducted and to own its properties and assets.

(b) The Project Company is a corporation duly organized and validly existing under the Laws of the Country of Mexico, and has all requisite corporate power and authority to conduct its business as it is now conducted and to own its properties and assets.

(c) The Project Company and Seller are each duly qualified or licensed to do business and in good standing in all jurisdictions in which the character of the properties owned or held under lease or license by the Project Company, or the nature of the business transacted by it, makes such qualification necessary.

(d) The Project Company has not conducted any business or acquired any property or asset, except in each case in connection with the development of the Project. The Project Company does not own any interest in any Person. The Project Company has good title to the Project Assets, free and clear of any and all Liens except Permitted Liens and Liens related to the Project that will be released upon receipt by Seller of the Final Payment.

3.2 Authority. (a) Seller has all requisite corporate power and authority to execute and deliver this Agreement and each Ancillary Document to which it is a party, to perform its obligations hereunder and thereunder and to consummate the transactions contemplated hereby and thereby. The execution and delivery by Seller of this Agreement and each Ancillary Document to which Seller is a party and the performance of its obligations hereunder and thereunder have been duly and validly authorized by all necessary corporate action on the part of Seller.

(b) The Project Company has all requisite corporate power and authority to execute and deliver each Agreement and each Ancillary Document to which it is a party, to perform its obligations hereunder and thereunder and to consummate the transactions contemplated hereby and thereby. The execution and delivery by the Project Company of each Ancillary Document to which it is a party, and the performance by the Project Company of its obligations thereunder have been duly and validly authorized by all necessary corporate action on the part of the Project Company.

3.3 **Enforceability.** Seller has duly and validly executed and delivered this Agreement, and this Agreement constitutes Seller's legal, valid and binding obligation, enforceable against it in accordance with its terms, and each of Seller and the Project Company has duly and validly executed and delivered each of the Ancillary Documents to which it is a party and such Ancillary Documents constitute the legal, valid and binding obligation of each of Seller and the Project Company, enforceable against it in accordance with their respective terms, except as may be limited by the Equitable Qualifications.

3.4 **No Violation.**

(a) The execution and delivery by Seller of this Agreement and of each Ancillary Document to which it is a party do not, and the performance by Seller hereunder and thereunder, as applicable, and the consummation of the transactions contemplated hereby and thereby will not: (i) conflict with or result in a violation or breach of any of the terms, conditions or provisions of the organizational documents of Seller; (ii) result in a breach of, or (with or without notice or the lapse of time) default under, or give rise to any right of termination, cancellation or acceleration under, or to a loss of material benefits under, any of the terms, conditions or provisions of any Contract to which Seller is a party or by which Seller is bound or an intended third-party beneficiary, except for such breaches or defaults (or rights of termination, cancellation or acceleration or loss of material benefits) as to which requisite waivers or consents have been obtained and are in full force and effect; or (iii) conflict with or result in a violation or breach in any material respect of any term or provision of any Law or Order applicable to Seller or any of its assets and properties or create any Lien upon any Project Asset; provided that, for the representations set forth in the foregoing clause (i), Seller shall not be in breach unless such violations, breaches or conflicts reasonably could be expected to impair the ability or obligation of Seller to perform fully on a timely basis its obligations under this Agreement or any of the Ancillary Documents to which it is a party.

(b) The execution and delivery by the Project Company of each Ancillary Document to which it is a party do not, and the performance by the Project Company thereunder and the consummation of the transactions contemplated thereby will not: (i) conflict with or result in a violation or breach of any of the terms, conditions or provisions of the organizational documents of the Project Company; (ii) result in a breach of, or (with or without notice or the lapse of time) default under, or give rise to any right of termination, cancellation or acceleration under, or to a loss of material benefits under, any of the terms, conditions or provisions of any Contract to which the Project Company is a party or by which the Project Company is bound or an intended third-party beneficiary, except for such breaches or defaults (or rights of termination, cancellation or acceleration or loss of material benefits) as to which requisite waivers or consents have been obtained and are in full force and effect; or (iii) conflict with or result in a violation or breach in any material respect of any term or provision of any Law or Order applicable to the Project Company or any of its assets and properties (including any applicable Permit held by the Project Company), or create any Lien upon any Project Asset; provided that, for the representations set forth in the foregoing clause (i), Seller shall not be in breach unless such violations, breaches or conflicts reasonably could be expected to impair the ability or obligation of Seller or the Project Company to perform fully on a timely basis its obligations under this Agreement or any of the Ancillary Documents to which it is a party.

3.5 **Litigation; Proceedings.** There is no Action pending or, to Seller's Knowledge, contemplated or threatened against or affecting Seller or the Project Company or their respective properties or assets, which relates to or challenges the legality, validity or enforceability of this Agreement or which (individually or in the aggregate) reasonably could be expected to impair the ability or obligation of Seller or the Project Company to perform fully on a timely basis its obligations under this Agreement or any of the Ancillary Documents to which it is a party.

3.6 **Consents and Waivers.** No authorization, consent, approval, waiver, license, qualification or written exemption of or from, nor any notice, filing, declaration, qualification or registration to or with any Governmental Authority or any other Person is required to be obtained by Seller or the Project Company in connection with the execution and delivery of this Agreement or any Ancillary Document to which it is a party and the consummation of the transactions contemplated hereunder and thereunder.

3.7 **Real Estate.**

(a) The real property interests in the Site are sufficient to allow the Project Company to develop, install, construct, operate, maintain, and remove the Project, including the construction of a new substation and interconnection line to interconnect the Project to the Federal Electricity Commission (*Comisión Federal de Electricidad*) ("**CFE**")-controlled national electrical system, in accordance with the terms of the PPA and all Ancillary Documents.

(b) There are no real property interests relating to the Site, including but not limited to any licenses, rights-of-way or easements, except as set forth on Schedule 3.7(b) of the Disclosure Schedules.

(c) Seller has made available to Buyer complete and correct copies of all title insurance policies, title commitments, title opinions, surveys and reports of any engineers, environmental consultants or other consultants or any third parties, including any environmental investigations, structural reports, engineering studies, permits, interconnection documentation, audits or assessments, in each case in the possession of, or accessible to, Seller or any of its affiliates (including the Project Company) related to the Site.

3.8 **Capitalization; Title to Equity Interests.**

(a) Seller together with the individuals specified in Recital B are the record and beneficial owners of the Equity Interests, free and clear of all Liens. The Equity Interests have been duly authorized and validly issued, were not issued in violation of any Person's preemptive rights, and are fully paid and non-assessable. The Equity Interests constitute one hundred percent (100%) of the Series A shares in the Project Company plus twenty-one (21) Series B shares in the Project Company. The capitalization table attached hereto as Schedule 3.8 is a complete and accurate representation of all Ownership Interests in the Project Company and the holders thereof upon completion of the conditions precedent to Buyer's obligations set forth in Section 6.2(e).

(b) Except for this Agreement, there are no (i) outstanding subscriptions, warrants, options, purchase rights, calls or commitments of any character relating to or entitling any Person to purchase or otherwise acquire the Equity Interests or other Ownership Interests in the Project Company, (ii) outstanding securities, instruments or obligations that are or may be convertible into or exercisable or exchangeable for any Ownership Interests in the Project Company or (iii) Contracts under which the Project Company may become obligated to sell or otherwise issue any Ownership Interests in the Project Company.

(c) Upon execution of this Agreement and the Assignment and Conveyance, Buyer will immediately acquire good and valid title to the Equity Interests, free and clear of any Liens.

(d) The Project Company does not own, of record or beneficially, or control, directly or indirectly, any Ownership Interests in any Person (or any option, warrant, security or other right convertible, exchangeable or exercisable therefore) and is not, directly or indirectly, a participant in any joint venture, partnership, trust, association or other limited liability entity.

3.9 Brokers. Seller has not engaged any broker, finder or agent in connection with the Acquisition so as to give rise to any claim against Buyer, the Project Company or any of Buyer's Affiliates for any brokerage or finder's commission, fee or similar compensation.

3.10 Contracts; Project Assets; Permits.

(a) Schedule 3.10(a) contains a true, complete and correct list of all Contracts to which the Project Company is a party or that relate to, are associated with or concern the Project or the Project Assets (each, a "**Material Contract**").

(b) Each Material Contract is in full force and effect, and constitutes a legal, valid, binding and enforceable Contract as to the Project Company, and to Seller's Knowledge, the respective counterparties thereto, and will not be rendered invalid or unenforceable as a result of the Acquisition, except, in each case, as such enforceability may be limited by the Equitable Qualifications.

(c) Neither the Project Company, nor to Seller's Knowledge, any other respective counterparties thereto, is in material breach of or in material default under any Material Contract, and to Seller's Knowledge no event has occurred which with the passage of time or giving of notice or both would constitute such a default, result in a loss of rights or permit termination, modification or acceleration under, or result in the creation of any Lien under any Material Contract.

(d) True, correct and complete copies of all Material Contracts and any amendments thereto have been delivered to Buyer prior to the Closing.

(e) Except for the PPAs, the Project Company has not sold or transferred, agreed, or committed to sell or transfer, or granted any options or rights to purchase electric power, net metering credits, Environmental Attributes or Renewable Energy Credits in connection with or related to the Project.

(f) Other than in connection with the development of the Project, the Project Company has not conducted any business or acquired any property or asset. The Project Company has good title to all Project Assets, free and clear of all Liens.

3.11 **Environmental Laws.** The Project Company has complied and is in compliance with all Environmental Laws affecting it or the Project Assets in all material respects. No Action has been filed or commenced or, to Seller's Knowledge threatened against, the Project Company alleging any failure of the Project Company to comply with any applicable Environmental Law. To Seller's Knowledge, there are no conditions, facts or circumstances that could result in the imposition of liabilities against the Project Company under, or noncompliance by the Project Company with, any Environmental Law.

3.12 **Insurance.** The Project Company does not hold any policies of insurance.

3.13 **Intellectual Property.** The Project Company does not own, use or license any patents, trademarks, copyrights or other intellectual property rights. The Project Company has not infringed, or received any notice that the Project Company has infringed, in either case, upon the patent, trademark, copyright or other intellectual property rights of any Person.

3.14 **Employee Matters.** None of Seller, the Project Company or any of their respective Affiliates has made any commitments or representations to any Person regarding (i) potential employment by Buyer or the Project Company or any other Affiliate of Buyer at the Project after the Effective Date, or (ii) any terms and conditions of such potential employment by Buyer or any Affiliate thereof following the Effective Date. Subject to the foregoing, the Project Company does not employ and has never employed any employees and has no liabilities with respect to any employees of Seller or any Affiliates of Seller or any other individuals (including independent contractors, contract workers, leased employees or temporary employees) that have performed work at or in connection with the Project or in connection with the business of the Project Company.

3.15 **Bank Accounts, Powers of Attorney.** Other than the bank accounts listed in Schedule 3.15, there are no bank accounts, safe deposit boxes, or related powers of attorney for the Project Company. Seller has no outstanding powers of attorney for banking or other purposes related to the Project or the Project Company.

3.16 **Taxes.** Seller has caused to be timely filed all required Tax Returns relating to the Project Company that were due on or before the Closing Date, and Seller has paid or will pay all Taxes shown due on such Tax Returns as and when due.

3.17 Disclosure. No representation or warranty by Seller contained in this Agreement or any statement or certificate furnished or to be furnished by or on behalf of Seller to Buyer or its representatives in connection herewith or pursuant hereto contains any untrue statement of a material fact, or omits to state any material fact required to make the statements contained herein or therein not misleading; *provided, however*, that this representation excludes the effect of any industry or economic conditions or matters that are general in nature. Except for any such events or circumstances that have been disclosed in this Agreement (including the Disclosure Schedule) other than matters of a general economic or political nature which do not affect the business of the Project Company uniquely, there are no facts or other circumstances that would, individually or in the aggregate, be considered material by a reasonable investor in making an investment decision regarding the Project Company.

3.18 Disclaimer. EXCEPT AS EXPRESSLY PROVIDED IN THIS ARTICLE 3, SELLER MAKES NO REPRESENTATIONS OR WARRANTIES TO BUYER, EXPRESS, IMPLIED, STATUTORY, COMMON LAW OR OTHERWISE, AND ASSUMES NO OTHER LIABILITIES, WHETHER IN CONTRACT OR IN TORT, WITH RESPECT TO THE SUBJECT MATTER OF THIS AGREEMENT, AND BOTH PARTIES DISCLAIM, WAIVE AND RELEASE ANY IMPLIED WARRANTIES AND WARRANTIES IMPOSED BY LAW INCLUDING ANY WARRANTY OF MERCHANTABILITY AND ANY WARRANTY OF FITNESS FOR A PARTICULAR PURPOSE. THE PARTIES HEREBY ACKNOWLEDGE AND AGREE THAT, TO THE EXTENT REQUIRED BY APPLICABLE LAW, THE DISCLAIMERS CONTAINED IN THIS AGREEMENT ARE "**CONSPICUOUS**" FOR THE PURPOSES OF SUCH APPLICABLE LAW.

ARTICLE 4
REPRESENTATIONS AND WARRANTIES OF BUYER

Buyer represents and warrants to Seller that, as of the Effective Date and as of the Closing Date:

4.1 Organization. Buyer is a corporation duly formed, validly existing and in good standing under the laws of the state of Nevada, U.S.A. and has all requisite corporate power and authority to conduct its business as it is now being conducted.

4.2 Authority. Buyer has all requisite corporate power and authority to execute and deliver this Agreement and each Ancillary Document to which it is a party, to perform its obligations hereunder and thereunder and to consummate the transactions contemplated hereby and thereby. The execution and delivery by Buyer of this Agreement and each Ancillary Document to which it is a party, and the performance by Buyer of its obligations hereunder and thereunder, have been duly and validly authorized by all necessary action on the part of Buyer.

4.3 Enforceability. Buyer has duly and validly executed and delivered this Agreement, and this Agreement constitutes Buyer's legal, valid and binding obligation, enforceable against it in accordance with its terms, and duly and validly executed and delivered each of the Ancillary Documents to which it is a party and such Ancillary Documents constitute Buyer's legal, valid and binding obligations, enforceable against it in accordance with their respective terms, and in the case of each of the foregoing, except as may be limited by the Equitable Qualifications.

4.4 **No Violation.** The execution and delivery by Buyer of this Agreement and each Ancillary Document to which it is or will be a party do not, and the performance by Buyer of its obligations hereunder and thereunder and the consummation of the transactions contemplated hereby and thereby will not:

(a) conflict with or result in a violation or breach of any of the terms, conditions or provisions of the organizational documents of Buyer;

(b) result in a material breach of, or (with or without notice or the lapse of time) default under, or give rise to any right of termination, cancellation or acceleration under, or to a loss of material benefits under, any of the terms, conditions or provisions of any Contract to which Buyer is a party or by which Buyer is bound or an intended third-party beneficiary, in each case which reasonably could be expected to materially impair the ability or obligation of Buyer to perform fully on a timely basis its obligations under this Agreement or any of the Ancillary Documents to which it is a party; or

(c) to Buyer's Knowledge, conflict with or result in a violation or breach in any material respect of any term or provision of any Law or Order applicable to Buyer or any of its assets and properties, or create any lien or encumbrance upon any assets of Buyer, in each case which reasonably could be expected to impair the ability or obligation of Buyer to perform fully on a timely basis its obligations under this Agreement or any of the Ancillary Documents to which it is a party.

4.5 **Litigation; Proceedings.** There is no Action pending or, to Buyer's Knowledge, contemplated or threatened against or affecting Buyer or its properties or assets, which relates to or challenges the legality, validity or enforceability of this Agreement or which (individually or in the aggregate) reasonably could be expected to materially impair the ability or obligation of Buyer to perform fully on a timely basis its obligations under this Agreement or any of the Ancillary Documents to which it is a party.

4.6 **Consents and Waivers.** No authorization, consent, approval, waiver, license, qualification or written exemption from, nor any filing, declaration, qualification or registration with, any Governmental Authority or any other Person is required to be obtained by Buyer in connection with the execution and delivery of this Agreement or any of the Ancillary Documents to which Buyer is a party and the consummation of the transactions contemplated hereunder and thereunder.

4.7 **Brokers.** With the exception of US Topco Energy, Inc., Buyer has not engaged any broker, finder or agent in connection with the Acquisition. Buyer's engagement with US Topco Energy shall not as to give rise to any claim against Seller or any of its Affiliates for any brokerage or finder's commission, fee or similar compensation.

ARTICLE 5
POST-CLOSING COVENANTS

5.1 **PPA Clarification Letter with Hermosillo.** By no later than June 15, 2016, Seller shall obtain a PPA Clarification Letter with Hermosillo.

5.2 Extension of Hermosillo PPA Deadlines. By no later than June 15, 2016, Seller shall obtain a binding modification of the Hermosillo PPA, duly approved and authorized by the municipal city council (*Cabildo*) of Hermosillo, to extend all Hermosillo PPA Deadlines until the later of December 31, 2016 or nine (9) months from the effective date of the extension of the Hermosillo PPA Deadlines.

5.3 Binding Promissory Purchase Agreements.

(a) By no later than January 30, 2016, Seller shall arrange for the Project Company to enter a binding promissory purchase agreement regarding the Site to acquire ownership of: (i) the 100 Hectare parcel in Fee Simple with a permitted period of payment of not less than six (6) months from the effective date of the promissory purchase agreement; and (ii) the 1.83 Hectare parcel in Fee Simple with a permitted period of payment of not less than six (6) months from the effective date of the promissory purchase agreement.

(b) Buyer shall pay no commission or broker fee to any seller or counterparty to any of the agreements executed pursuant to this Section 5.3. Seller shall be in breach of this Section 5.3 if any person or entity other than the owner of the 100 Hectare parcel, including but not limited to, any broker, consultant, or service provider of any kind, receives any portion of the payment made by Buyer to the owner of the 100 Hectare parcel under any agreement entered pursuant to this Section 5.3.

5.4 Acquisition of Real Estate. By no later than February 2, 2016, Seller shall arrange for the Project Company to obtain a notarized deed (*Escritura*) or deeds duly recorded with the Public Registry of Property of Hermosillo Sonora, transferring all right, title, and interest in Fee Simple to the Site. Seller shall ensure that the parties to the notarized deed or deeds agree to certain terms and conditions as follows:

(a) For the 100 Hectare parcel, the parties shall agree that the period to make payment under the previous deed (notarized on January 9, 2015) has expired and the deed has reverted back to the seller.

(b) For the 100 Hectare parcel, the parties shall agree that the previous promissory purchase agreement (dated December 27, 2012) for the 100 Hectare parcel has terminated.

(c) For the 100 Hectare parcel, the parties shall agree that the December 2, 2015 letter from the representative of the seller of the 100 Hectare parcel is not a legally binding agreement and has no force and effect.

(d) The parties shall satisfy Buyer, in its sole discretion, that title to the 100 Hectare parcel is free, clean of any lien, and marketable despite the issue at the Cadastral Registry of the Municipality of Hermosillo regarding the apparent identification of different parcels in the sale location as the 100 Hectare parcel.

(e) For the 1.83 Hectare parcel, the parties shall satisfy Buyer, in its sole discretion, that Mr. Manuel del Grande Leyva has been recognized in a formal judicial act of the courts of Sonora as being the legal executor of the estate of Josefina Leyva Grande with full legal authority to act on behalf of the estate of Josefina Leyva Grande.

(f) That the Site is up to date on the payment of all applicable taxes, including but not limited to, property taxes.

5.5 Amendment to CFE Agreement. By no later than March 31, 2016, Seller shall obtain an amendment to the Facilities and Assignment Agreement (*Convenio de Instalaciones y Cesión*) entered between the Project Company and CFE on December 7, 2015, Convenio No. NOE-HER-002/2015, to extend all deadlines in the Facilities and Assignment Agreement, including but not limited to, the deadlines in the schedule for payment (*Calendario de pagos*) and the deadlines in any Annex to the Facilities and Assignment Agreement, for the maximum period of time permitted by Law.

5.6 Transfer of Environmental Impact Authorization. By no later than the date Buyer receives notice pursuant to Section 2.3(b), Seller shall transfer to the Project Company the environmental impact authorization issued on March 14, 2013 by the Secretary of Environment and Natural Resources (SEMERNAT), Official No. DS-SG-UGA-IA-0244-13.

5.7 Transfer of Aerial Crossing Permit. By no later than the date Buyer receives notice pursuant to Section 2.3(b), Seller shall transfer to the Project Company the permit for an aerial crossing over the Hermosillo-Bahia Kino highway for interconnecting the Project to the national electrical system, issued on March 7, 2013 by the Junta de Caminos del Estado de Sonora, Official No. JCES-11-01-0173-2013.

5.8 Transfer of Construction Permit. By no later than the date Buyer receives notice pursuant to Section 2.3(b), Seller shall obtain for the Project Company an extension of the permit for construction of the Project, License No. DGDU/CU/EBR/4857/2014, issued by the General Coordination of Infrastructure, Urban Development and Ecology (CIDUE) of the municipality of Hermosillo on October 1, 2014, such extension to ensure the construction permit will continue in effect for as long a time period as permitted under applicable Laws.

5.9 Modification of Energy Permit. By no later than the date Buyer receives notice pursuant to Section 2.3(b), Seller shall obtain for the Project Company a modification of the permit of self-supply of electrical energy, No. E/1017/AUT/2013, Resolution No. RES/325/2013, issued by the Energy Regulatory Commission (CRE) to the Project Company on August 29, 2013, as modified on March 5, 2015 by RES/126/2015, such modification to provide an extension of the time period for achieving operational commencement for as long a time period as permitted under applicable Laws.

5.10 Purchase of Series B Shares. At the request of Buyer, Seller shall effectuate or cause Buyer to effectuate the purchase of one (1) Series B share from each of the City of Guaymas and the City of Santa Ana in favor of Buyer. This shall include: (a) obtaining shareholder approval of such purchase and obtaining an endorsement by the City of Guaymas and City of Santa Ana of the share certificate in favor of Buyer; (b) making an entry into the corporate shareholder registry book to reflect the purchases; and (c) providing documentation to Buyer demonstrating compliance with any tax withholding obligations with respect to such transfer of shares or demonstrating that such transaction was made at nominal value of the shares.

5.11 Call for Series B Shareholders for a General Ordinary and Extraordinary Meeting of the Project Company. Seller shall provide assistance to Buyer to effectuate, by no later than February 15, 2016, the corporate calls to the Series B Shareholders of the Project Company regarding a General Ordinary and Extraordinary Shareholders Meeting of the Project Company in which Buyer will approve, among other matters: (1) the financial statements of the Company for fiscal years ended on 2013 and 2014; (2) the ratification and confirmation of the transfer of one (1) Series B share from Jose Hugo Barcelo Durazo to each of the Series B Share Purchasers (as such terms is defined below); (3) the amendment to the articles of incorporation of the Project Company; (4) the resignation of the statutory auditor of the Project Company; and (5) the appointment of a new statutory auditor of the Project Company. Seller shall, upon Buyer's request, assist with any information and documentation that Buyer may need in order to held the General Ordinary and Extraordinary Shareholders Meeting of the Project Company.

ARTICLE 6
CLOSING

6.1 Closing. The Closing shall take place at such place and time and in such manner as the Parties may agree in writing, which may be by electronic delivery of the applicable documents followed by mailing of originals as necessary.

6.2 Conditions Precedent to Buyer's Obligations. The obligation of Buyer to consummate the transactions under this Agreement is subject to the satisfaction or waiver of the following conditions prior to or concurrently with the Closing:

(a) Each of the representations and warranties made by Seller with respect to this Agreement that were or are qualified as to materiality shall be true and correct, and those not so qualified shall be true and correct in all material respects, as of the date hereof and as of the Closing as if made on and as of the Closing, except, in each case, to the extent that such representations and warranties refer specifically to an earlier date, in which case such representations and warranties shall have been true and correct as of such earlier date.

(b) Seller has performed and complied in all material respects with the agreements, covenants and obligations required by this Agreement to be so performed or complied with by Seller at or before Closing.

(c) All authorizations, approvals or permits, if any, of any governmental authority or regulatory body of the United States, Mexico, or of any state that are required in connection with the lawful issuance and sale of the Equity Interests shall have been obtained and be in full force and effect as of the Closing Date.

(d) Since the Effective Date, no event or condition shall have occurred and be continuing that has had or will have a Material Adverse Effect, and no material portion of the Project Assets shall have been destroyed or damaged by casualty.

(e) The Project Company shall have completed the following actions:

(i) Made the corresponding entry into the corporate shareholder registry book of the Project Company reflecting the purchase of 1,140

Series A shares from Ignacio Ongay Narvaez in favor of Seller. The Project Company shall have provided to Buyer documentation demonstrating compliance with any tax withholding obligations with respect to such transfer of shares or provided documentation demonstrating that such transaction was made at nominal value of the shares.

(ii) Made the corresponding entry into the corporate shareholder registry book of the Project Company reflecting the purchase of 300 Series A shares from Ignacio Ongay Narvaez in favor of Alfonso Avelino Cruz Suarez. The Project Company shall have provided to Buyer documentation demonstrating compliance with any tax withholding obligations with respect to such transfer of shares or provided documentation demonstrating that such transaction was made at nominal value of the shares.

(iii) Made the corresponding entry into the corporate shareholder registry book of the Project Company reflecting the purchase of 180 Series A shares from Francisco Aaron Celaya Bracamontes in favor of Seller. The Project Company shall have provided documentation to Buyer demonstrating compliance with any tax withholding obligations with respect to such transfer of shares or provided documentation demonstrating that such transaction was made at nominal value of the shares.

(iv) Made the corresponding entry into the corporate shareholder registry book of the Project Company reflecting the transfer of one (1) Series B share by Jose Hugo Barcelo Durazo in favor of the each of the following: (i) the Ayuntamiento de Etchojoa; (ii) the Ayuntamiento de Caborca; (iii) the Ayuntamiento de Hermosillo; (iv) the Ayuntamiento de Guaymas; (v) the Ayuntamiento de Empalme; and (vi) Ford Motor Company, S.A. de C.V. (collectively, the "**Series B Share Purchasers**"). The Project Company shall have provided documentation to Buyer demonstrating compliance with any tax withholding obligations with respect to such transfer of shares or provided documentation demonstrating that such transaction was made at nominal value of the shares.

(v) Caused Alfonso Avelino Cruz Sanchez and Jose Hugo Barcelo Durazo to transfer, assign, and convey to Seller: (a) three hundred (300) Series A Shares owned by Alfonso Avelino Cruz Sanchez; and (b) twenty-one (21) Series B Shares owned by Jose Hugo Barcelo Durazo.

(vi) Caused the Series A Shareholders of the Project Company to unanimously adopt the following resolutions without holding a shareholders meeting:

1) The transfer of twenty-one (21) Series B shares from Jose Hugo Barcelo Durazo in favor of Seller;

2) The transfer of three hundred (300) Series A shares from Alfonso Avelino Cruz Suarez in favor of Seller;

3) The transfer of thirty thousand (30,000) Series A shares from Seller in favor of Buyer;

4) The transfer of twenty-one (21) Series B shares from Seller in favor of Buyer;

5) The revocation of all powers of attorney of the Project Company that had been in effect as of the date on which the shareholders adopt the resolutions in this Section 6.2(e)(vi);

6) The resignation of the members of the board of directors and appointment of new board members of the Project Company; and

7) The granting of powers of attorney of the Project Company to the individuals designated by Buyer;

(vii) Endorsed thirty thousand (30,000) Series A Shares from Seller in favor of Buyer;

(viii) Endorsed twenty-one (21) Series B Shares from Seller in favor of Buyer; and

(ix) Made all entries corresponding to all actions required herein on the following corporate books of the Project Company: (A) shareholder registry book; (B) shareholders meeting minute book; (C) board of directors meeting minute book; and (D) capital variations book.

(f) The Seller shall have held a General Shareholders Meeting of Seller in which the shareholders entitled to vote on such actions duly approved:

(i) The individuals named in this Agreement to act on behalf of the Seller with full authority to execute this Agreement and the Ancillary Documents; and

(ii) The sale of thirty thousand (30,000) Series A Shares of the Project Company from Seller in favor of Buyer, evidencing such transfer by the proper endorsement of the relevant shares and the withholding of any applicable taxes thereon. This shall include authorization to endorse the share certificates in favor of Buyer.

(g) Seller shall have made all deliveries required of them under Section 6.5.

(h) Seller shall have made available to Buyer a complete and correct copy of a title report for the Site.

6.3 Conditions Subsequent to Buyer's Obligations.

(a) By February 28, 2016, Buyer shall have completed a General Ordinary and Extraordinary Shareholders Meeting of the Project Company, duly noticed in compliance with the Project Company's articles of incorporation, bylaws, and all applicable Laws, at which the shareholders entitled to vote on such actions duly approve:

(i) The ratification and confirmation of all unanimous written resolutions of the Series A Shareholders undertaken pursuant to Section 6.2(c)(vi);

(ii) The ratification and confirmation of the transfer of one (1) Series B share from Jose Hugo Barcelo Durazo to each of the Series B Share Purchasers; and

(iii) Amending the Articles of Incorporation to allow Series B shareholders to transfer Series B shares to third parties with prior written approval obtained at a General Shareholders Meeting or by action by the Board of Directors of the Project Company and to allow that only holders of Series A shares attend the General Shareholders Meetings of the Project Company.

(b) If Buyer, acting in good faith, is unable to complete the actions in Section 6.3(a) of this Agreement by February 28, 2016, then Seller shall refund to Buyer, in immediately available funds by wire transfer, an amount equal to the all payments made by Buyer to Seller under ARTICLE 2 as of such date.

6.4 Conditions Precedent to Seller's Obligations. The obligation of Seller to consummate the transactions under this Agreement is subject to the satisfaction or waiver of the following conditions prior to or concurrently with the Closing:

(a) Each of the representations and warranties made by Buyer with respect to this Agreement that were or are qualified as to materiality shall be true and correct, and those not so qualified shall be true and correct in all material respects, as of the date hereof and as of the Closing as if made on and as of the Closing, except, in each case, (i) to the extent that such representations and warranties refer specifically to an earlier date, in which case such representations and warranties shall have been true and correct as of such earlier date, and (ii) as would not reasonably be expected to materially impair or delay the ability of Buyer to perform its obligations under this Agreement and consummate the Closing.

(b) Buyer has performed and complied in all material respects with the agreements, covenants and obligations required by this Agreement to be so performed or complied with by Buyer at or before Closing.

(c) The Buyer has made all deliveries required of it under Section 6.6.

6.5 Seller's Closing Deliverables.

Prior to Closing, Seller shall deliver or cause to be delivered to Buyer the following:

(a) a duly executed counterpart of this Agreement, the Assignment and Conveyance, and each other Ancillary Document, if any.

(b) all Books and Records of the Project Company to the extent held by Seller, including but not limited to, the shareholder registry book, shareholders meeting minute book, board of directors meeting minute book, and capital variations book, each updated to reflect all actions undertaken pursuant to Section 6.2(e).

(c) copies of the Material Contracts and all consents and approvals required to be obtained, made or delivered by Seller or the Project Company in connection with the Acquisition.

(d) a certificate of an authorized officer of Seller, dated as of the Closing Date, setting forth and attesting to the matters set forth in Section 6.2.

(e) powers of attorney executed by the Project Company demonstrating the representatives of the Project Company who have executed Contracts or obtained permits on behalf of the Project Company have had all necessary authorization to execute such Contracts or obtain such permits on behalf of the Project Company.

(f) copies of the duly executed and notarized meeting minutes of the General Shareholders Meeting of Seller held pursuant to Section 6.2(f).

6.6 <u>Buyer's Closing Deliverables</u>. At the Closing, Buyer shall deliver or cause to be delivered to Seller the following:

(a) payment of the Closing Payment, in immediately available funds, according to Seller's wire instructions.

(b) a duly executed counterpart of this Agreement, the Assignment and Conveyance, and each other Ancillary Document to which Buyer is a party.

(c) a certificate of an authorized officer of Buyer, dated as of the Closing Date, setting forth and attesting to the matters set forth in Section 6.4.

ARTICLE 7
TAX MATTERS

7.1 <u>Certain Taxes</u>.

(a) Notwithstanding any provision of this ARTICLE 7 or elsewhere to this Agreement to the contrary, all Transfer Taxes (and costs incurred in connection with the filing of the appropriate Tax Returns in respect of such Transfer Taxes) shall be borne by Buyer, and Seller shall file all necessary Tax Returns and other documentation with respect to all Transfer Taxes and, if required by applicable Law, Buyer shall join in the execution of any such Tax Returns or other documentation and shall cooperate with Seller to minimize any Transfer Taxes.

(b) All real property Taxes that are due or become due with respect to the assets and properties of the Project Company for Tax periods within which the Closing Date occurs (collectively, the "**Apportioned Obligations**") shall be apportioned between Seller and Buyer as of the Closing Date based on the ratio of the number of days in the current property Tax year elapsed through the Closing Date to 365 days. Seller shall be responsible for the portion of such Apportioned Obligations attributable to the period or portion of the period ending on or before the Closing Date. Buyer shall be responsible for the portion of such Apportioned Obligations attributable to the period or portion of the period after the Closing Date. Each Party shall cooperate in assuring that Apportioned Obligations that are the responsibility of Seller pursuant to this Section 7.1(b) are paid by Seller, and that Apportioned Obligations that are the responsibility of Buyer pursuant to this Section 7.1(b) are paid by Buyer.

7.2 Tax Indemnity.

(a) From and after the Closing, Seller shall defend, indemnify and hold harmless each Buyer Indemnified Person from and against, and will pay to Buyer on behalf of any such Buyer Indemnified Person the amount of, any Damages incurred by any Buyer Indemnified Person arising from: (i) any Taxes imposed on the Project Company or the Project, or for which the Project Company may otherwise be liable, for any taxable year or period that ends on or before the Closing Date and, with respect to any Straddle Period, the portion of such Straddle Period ending on and including the Closing Date; (ii) any Transfer Taxes owing from Seller pursuant to this Agreement; and (iii) any Taxes imposed on any Buyer Indemnified Person resulting from a breach by Seller of any of its covenants relating to Tax matters provided in this Agreement or of any representation or warranty in Section 3.16.

(b) From and after the Closing, Buyer shall defend, indemnify and hold harmless each Seller Indemnified Person from and against, and will pay to Seller on behalf of any such Seller Indemnified Person the amount of, any Damages incurred by any Seller Indemnified Person arising from: (i) any Taxes imposed on the Project Company or the Project for any taxable year or period that begins after the Closing Date and, with respect to any Straddle Period, the portion of such Straddle Period beginning after the Closing Date; (ii) any Transfer Taxes owing from Buyer pursuant to this Agreement; and (iii) any Taxes imposed on any Seller Indemnified Person resulting from a breach by Buyer of any of its covenants relating to Tax matters provided herein.

(c) Subject to Section 7.1(b), with respect to any Straddle Period, the amount of Taxes allocable to the portions thereof ending on the Closing Date and beginning on the day after the Closing Date shall be determined using a closing of the books method as of the close of business on the Closing Date.

(d) Each Party agrees to pay to the other Party any refund or rebate received (whether by payment, credit, offset or otherwise) by it or any of its Affiliates in respect of any Taxes for which the other Party is liable under this ARTICLE 7 within thirty (30) days after such refund or rebate is received. The Parties shall cooperate in order to take any necessary steps to claim any such refund or rebate, *provided* that the out-of-pocket costs of obtaining such a refund or rebate shall be borne by the Party entitled to such refund or rebate.

7.3 Tax Returns.

(a) Seller shall prepare and file all Tax Returns required to be filed by the Project Company for any taxable period ending on or before the Closing Date. Buyer and the Project Company shall provide Seller with such information and cooperation as Seller shall reasonably request in order to prepare and file any such Tax Returns. No such Tax Returns shall be amended without the prior written consent of Seller.

(b) Buyer shall prepare and file all Tax Returns required to be filed by the Project Company for any taxable period ending after the Closing Date. Any such Tax Return for a Straddle Period shall be prepared on a basis consistent with past practices unless otherwise required by applicable Law. Not later than sixty (60) days prior to the filing of a Tax Return of the Project Company for a Straddle Period, Buyer shall deliver a copy of such Tax Return to Seller for Seller's review and comment. Seller shall provide to Buyer any comments Seller may have with respect to any such Tax Return within twenty (20) days of receiving such Tax Return. Seller and Buyer shall attempt to mutually resolve any disputes regarding any such Tax Returns within five (5) days of Buyer receiving Seller's comments, *provided* that if any such dispute cannot be resolved within such time period, the dispute shall be settled in the manner provided in Section 7.5(c) and the determination rendered by a national accounting firm mutually agreed to Buyer and Seller shall be final and binding on the Parties for all purposes and such Tax Return shall be filed in a manner that is consistent with such determination. Not later than thirty (30) days after filing any Tax Return of the Project Company for a Straddle Period, Buyer shall deliver a copy of such Tax Return as filed to Seller.

7.4 Tax Cooperation. Seller and Buyer shall reasonably cooperate, and shall cause their respective Affiliates, directors, officers, employees and representatives reasonably to cooperate, in preparing and filing all Tax Returns, including maintaining and making available to each other all records that are necessary for the preparation of any Tax Returns that the other is required to file under this ARTICLE 7 and in resolving any disputes between the Parties with respect to such Tax Returns.

7.5 Tax Contests.

(a) Buyer shall notify Seller in writing upon receipt by Buyer, the Project Company, or any of Buyer's other Affiliates of a notice of any pending or threatened federal, state or local Tax audits or assessments which may materially affect the Tax liabilities of the Project Company for which Seller is liable pursuant to Section 7.2(a), *provided* that failure to comply with this provision shall not affect Buyer's right to indemnification hereunder except to the extent such failure materially impairs Seller's ability to contest any such Tax liabilities.

(b) Subject to Section 7.5(c), Seller shall have the sole right to represent the Project Company's interests in any Tax audit or administrative or court proceeding relating solely to Tax liabilities for which Seller is liable pursuant to Section 7.2(a) and which relate to taxable periods ending on or before the Closing Date, and to employ counsel of Seller's choice at Seller's expense; *provided, however*, that Seller shall have no right to represent the Project Company's interests in any Tax audit or administrative or court proceeding unless Seller shall have first notified Buyer in writing (i) of Seller's intention to do so, and (ii) that Seller agrees with Buyer that, as between Buyer and Seller, Seller shall be liable for any Taxes and Damages relating to Taxes that result from such audit or proceeding; *provided, further*, that Buyer and its representatives shall be permitted, at Buyer's expense, to be present at, and participate in, any such audit or proceeding. Notwithstanding the foregoing, without the prior written consent of Buyer, which consent may not be unreasonably withheld, delayed or conditioned, neither Seller nor any Affiliate of Seller shall be entitled to settle, either administratively or after the commencement of litigation, any claim for Taxes which could materially adversely affect the liability for Taxes of Buyer, the Project Company or any other Affiliate thereof for any period after the Closing.

(c) Seller and Buyer shall jointly control any Tax audit or administrative or court proceeding relating to Tax liabilities for a Straddle Period, with any disputes as to the conduct of such audit or administrative or court proceeding being resolved in the manner set forth as follows. The objecting Party shall notify the other Party in writing of the area or areas of disagreement. If the Parties are unable to resolve their dispute within twenty (20) days, the matter shall be referred to a Tax Advisor agreed to by both Parties. The decision of the Tax Advisor shall be binding on all Parties. The Tax Advisor's fees shall be shared equally between Seller and Buyer. No Party or its Affiliates shall take a position on any Tax Return, or in any Tax audit or administrative or court, that is in any manner inconsistent with such determination, without the prior written consent of the other Party. Buyer shall have the sole right to represent the Project Company's interests in any Tax audit or administrative or court proceeding relating to Tax liabilities other than any proceeding for a Straddle Period and any proceeding in respect of which Seller has the representation right pursuant to Section 7.5(b) and to employ counsel of Buyer's choice at Buyer's expense. In addition, notwithstanding anything to the contrary in Section 7.5(b) or this Section 7.5(c), Buyer shall have the sole right to defend the Project Company with respect to any issue arising in connection with any Tax audit or administrative or court proceeding to the extent Seller shall have agreed in writing to forego any indemnification under this Agreement with respect to such issue.

(d) Nothing herein shall be construed to impose on Buyer any obligation to defend the Project Company in any Tax audit or administrative or court proceeding.

(e) Seller and Buyer shall reasonably cooperate, and shall cause their respective Affiliates, directors, officers, employees and representatives reasonably to cooperate, in connection with any audit, litigation or other proceeding with respect to Taxes. Such cooperation shall include the retention and (upon the other Party's request) the provision of records and information that is reasonably relevant to any such Tax audit, or administrative or court proceeding and making employees available on a mutually convenient basis to provide additional information and explanation of any material provided hereunder. Each of Seller and Buyer agrees to retain all books and records with respect to Tax matters pertinent to the Project Company relating to any taxable period beginning before the Closing Date until the expiration of the applicable statute of limitations (and, to the extent notified by a Party, any extensions thereof).

7.6 Miscellaneous Tax Covenants.

(a) Seller and Buyer agree to treat all payments under this ARTICLE 7 or ARTICLE 8, to the extent the amount of the Purchase Price, as adjustments to the Purchase Price, for Tax purposes and that such treatment shall govern for all purposes hereof.

(b) Notwithstanding any provision in this Agreement to the contrary, the obligations of either Party to defend, indemnify and hold harmless the other Party pursuant to this ARTICLE 7 shall terminate on the later of (i) the expiration of the applicable statute of limitations with respect to the Tax liabilities in question, taking into account any waiver or extension of such applicable statute of limitations, and (ii) sixty (60) days after the final, non-appealable administrative or judicial determination of such Tax liabilities.

(c) Notwithstanding any other provision of this Agreement, claims for indemnification with respect to Taxes and the procedures with respect thereto shall be governed exclusively by this ARTICLE 7, *provided* that to the extent that the provisions of this ARTICLE 7 are not inconsistent with and do not conflict with ARTICLE 8, the provisions of ARTICLE 8 shall apply. For example, ARTICLE 8 procedures shall apply in connection with Damages relating to Taxes arising from inaccuracies of representations or warranties for which a procedure is not provided in this ARTICLE 7 and for breaches or defaults of covenants or agreements relating to Taxes for which a procedure is not otherwise provided in this ARTICLE 7.

ARTICLE 8
INDEMNIFICATION AND LIABILITY

8.1 **Time Limits.** All claims for indemnification pursuant to this ARTICLE 8 resulting from breaches of representations or warranties in ARTICLE 3 or ARTICLE 4 shall be forever barred unless the Party seeking indemnification notifies the other Party of the indemnification claim within the Survival Period. Any representation, warranty, covenant or agreement as to which an indemnification claim shall have been asserted during the Survival Period shall continue in effect with respect to such claim until such claim shall have been finally resolved or settled. All representations and warranties, covenants, agreements and obligations in this Agreement or any Ancillary Document shall survive the Closing until the expiration of the Survival Period.

8.2 **Indemnification by Seller.** From and after the Closing, subject to the other provisions of this ARTICLE 8, Seller shall defend, indemnify and hold harmless each Buyer Indemnified Person from and against, and will pay to Buyer on behalf of any such Buyer Indemnified Person the amount of, any Damages incurred by any Buyer Indemnified Person as a result of, caused by, arising out of, or in any way relating to: (a) any breach of any representation or warranty as set forth in ARTICLE 3; (b) any breach by Seller of any agreement or covenant of Seller under this Agreement; or (c) any claims against any Buyer Indemnified Party related to the Project Company arising prior to the Closing Date.

8.3 **Indemnification by Buyer.** From and after the Closing, subject to the other provisions of this ARTICLE 8, Buyer shall defend, indemnify and hold harmless each Seller Indemnified Person from and against, and will pay to Seller on behalf of any such Seller Indemnified Person the amount of, any Damages incurred by any Seller Indemnified Person as a result of, caused by, arising out of, or in any way relating to: (a) any breach of any representation or warranty contained in ARTICLE 4; (b) any breach by Buyer of any agreement or covenant of Buyer under this Agreement; or (c) any claims against any Seller Indemnified Party related to the Project Company arising on or after the Closing Date.

8.4 **Liability Limitation.** Except for claims based on such Party's fraud, intentional misrepresentation or willful misconduct and indemnification of third party claims hereunder, the aggregate Damages of either Party to the other under or arising out of or in connection with this Agreement (whether based on negligence, breach of contract or otherwise) shall in no case exceed the Purchase Price to the extent actually paid by Buyer to Seller pursuant to this

Agreement. EACH PARTY'S LIABILITY IS LIMITED TO DIRECT ACTUAL DAMAGES ONLY, SUCH DIRECT ACTUAL DAMAGES WILL BE THE SOLE AND EXCLUSIVE REMEDY AND ALL OTHER REMEDIES OR DAMAGES AT LAW OR IN EQUITY ARE WAIVED. NEITHER PARTY SHALL BE LIABLE FOR CONSEQUENTIAL, INCIDENTAL, PUNITIVE, EXEMPLARY OR INDIRECT DAMAGES, LOST PROFITS OR OTHER BUSINESS INTERRUPTION DAMAGES, BY STATUTE, IN TORT OR CONTRACT, UNDER ANY INDEMNITY PROVISION OR OTHERWISE.

8.5 **Procedure for Indemnification**.

(a) Other than with respect to any third party claim as provided in Section 8.5(b), Buyer or Seller, as applicable, on behalf of itself or another Buyer Indemnified Person or Seller Indemnified Person, as applicable (Buyer or Seller, in such capacity, an "**Indemnified Person**") shall give to the other Party (Seller or Buyer, in such capacity, an "**Indemnifying Party**") notice of any matter that such Indemnified Person has determined has given rise to a right of indemnification under this ARTICLE 8, as soon as reasonably practicable after making such determination but in any event within forty-five (45) days of such determination; *provided, however*, that the failure to provide such notice shall not release the Indemnifying Party from any of its obligations under this ARTICLE 8 except to the extent that the Indemnifying Party is materially prejudiced by such failure.

(b) If a claim by a third party is made against a Seller Indemnified Person or a Buyer Indemnified Person, as applicable, and if Buyer or Seller, in its capacity as the Indemnified Person, intends to seek indemnification with respect thereto hereunder, such Indemnified Person shall promptly furnish written notice to the Indemnifying Party of such claim. The failure of the Indemnified Person to deliver prompt written notice of a claim shall not affect the indemnity obligations of the Indemnifying Party hereunder except to the extent the Indemnifying Party was substantially disadvantaged by such delay in delivery of notice of such claim. The Indemnifying Party shall have thirty (30) days after receipt of such notice to elect to undertake, conduct and control (through counsel of its own choosing and at its own expense) the settlement or defense thereof, and the Indemnified Person shall cooperate with it in connection therewith, *provided* that the Indemnified Person may control such proceeding, if (i) the Indemnifying Party chooses counsel not reasonably acceptable to such Indemnified Person, (ii) the Indemnifying Party does not pursue with reasonable diligence such defense, negotiation or settlement, or (iii) in the reasonable opinion of such Indemnified Person and its counsel, such action, suit or proceeding involves the potential imposition of criminal liability upon such Indemnified Person or a conflict of interest between such Indemnified Person and the Indemnifying Party. The Indemnifying Party shall permit the Indemnified Person to participate in such settlement or defense through counsel chosen by such Indemnified Person (but the fees and expenses of such counsel shall be borne by such Indemnified Person). No compromise or settlement of any third party claim may be effected by the Indemnifying Party without the Indemnified Person's consent unless (*w*) there is no finding or admission of any violation of applicable Law or admission of wrongdoing, or misconduct, (*x*) such compromise or settlement does not involve the entry by the Indemnified Person of a consent order or similar agreement with any Governmental Authority that would encumber any of the assets of an Indemnified Person or impose a restriction on or otherwise materially adversely affect any Indemnified Person or the conduct of its business, (*y*) as a condition of any such compromise or settlement, the Indemnifying Party obtains a complete release of any Indemnified Person potentially affected by such third party claim, and (z) the sole relief provided is monetary damages that are paid in full by the Indemnifying Party. So long as the Indemnifying Party, at the Indemnifying Party's cost and expense, (1) has undertaken the defense of, and assumed full responsibility for, all indemnified Damages with respect to such claim; (2) is reasonably contesting such claim in good faith, by appropriate proceedings; and (3) has taken such action (including the posting of a bond, deposit, or other security) as may be necessary to prevent any action to foreclose a lien against or attachment of the property of Seller Indemnified Person for payment of such claim, the Indemnified Person shall not pay or settle any such claim. Notwithstanding compliance by the Indemnifying Party with the preceding sentence, the Indemnified Person shall have the right to pay or settle any such claim, but in such event it shall waive any right to indemnity by the Indemnifying Party for such claim. If the Indemnifying Party fails, within thirty (30) days after the receipt of the Indemnified Person's notice of a claim of indemnity hereunder, to notify the Indemnified Person that the Indemnifying Party elects (at the Indemnifying Party's cost and expense) to undertake the defense thereof and assume full responsibility for all indemnified Damages with respect thereto, or fails, at any time after having given such notice, to contest such claim in good faith or to prevent action to foreclose a lien against or attachment of the Indemnified Person's property as contemplated above, the Indemnified Person shall have the right to contest, settle, or compromise such claim and the Indemnified Person shall not thereby waive any right to indemnity for such claim under this Agreement, *provided* that the Indemnified Person shall not settle or compromise any such claim without the prior written consent of the Indemnifying Party.

(c) Each Indemnified Person shall take commercially reasonable steps to mitigate all Damages relating to a claim.

ARTICLE 9
DISPUTE RESOLUTION

In the event a dispute, controversy or claim arises hereunder, the aggrieved Party will, as soon as reasonably possible after acquiring knowledge thereof, deliver written notification of the dispute to the other Party. A meeting between the Parties will be held within twenty-one (21) days (as such number of days may be extended by mutual agreement of the Parties) of a Party's receipt of such notice attended by representatives of the Parties with decision-making authority regarding the dispute, to attempt in good faith to negotiate a resolution of the dispute. If the Parties are not successful in resolving the dispute, pursuant to the foregoing procedures, within twenty-one (21) days, the Parties will thereafter be entitled to pursue all such remedies as may be available to them hereunder.

ARTICLE 10
MISCELLANEOUS

10.1 **Notices.** Except as expressly set forth to the contrary in this Agreement, all notices, requests or consents provided for or required or permitted to be given under this Agreement must be in writing and must be delivered to the recipient in person, by a nationally recognized overnight courier or certified mail, postage prepaid, return receipt requested, or by facsimile or other electronic transmission. A notice, request or consent given under this Agreement is effective on receipt by the receiving Party, *provided* that a facsimile or other electronic transmission that is transmitted after the normal business hours of the recipient shall be deemed effective on the next business day and *provided further* that all facsimile and electronic notices transmitted hereunder shall be deemed effective on receipt by the sender of a specific acknowledgment by the recipient (automatic responses not being sufficient for acknowledgment). All notices and other communications must be given to a Party at its address as shown below, or to such other address as such Party may designate in writing from time to time to the other Party in accordance herewith.

If to Buyer: **Jack Chen**
General Energy Solutions USA, Inc.

If to Seller:
Montecito No. 38 Piso 28 Oficina 12

10.2 Further Assurances. From time to time, each Party agrees to (a) furnish upon request to the other Party such further information, (b) execute and deliver to the other Party such other documents, and (c) do such other acts and things, in each case as either Party may reasonably request for the purpose of more fully effectuating the transactions contemplated by this Agreement.

10.3 Entire Agreement. This Agreement, together with the Ancillary Documents and all other Contracts and documents expressly contemplated hereby to be executed by the Parties or their respective Affiliates in connection with the Acquisition supersede all prior discussions and agreements between the Parties with respect to the subject matter hereof and thereof, and any prior confidentiality agreements executed by the Parties in respect of the transactions contemplated by this Agreement, and contain the sole and entire agreement between the Parties with respect to the subject matter hereof and thereof, and there are no agreements, understandings, representations or warranties between the Parties other than those set forth herein or therein.

10.4 Governing Law.

(a) This Agreement shall be governed by and interpreted in accordance with the laws of the state of New York, U.S.A. without regard to its choice of law provisions. Except as otherwise provided in ARTICLE 9, each Party irrevocably and unconditionally submits to the exclusive jurisdiction of any state or federal court located in the state of New York, U.S.A. and any appellate court from any thereof, in any action or proceeding arising out of or relating to this Agreement or for recognition or enforcement of any judgment, and each of the Parties irrevocably and unconditionally agrees that all claims in respect of any such action or proceeding shall be heard and determined in such court. Each of the Parties agrees that a final judgment in any such action or proceeding shall be conclusive and may be enforced in other jurisdictions by suit on the judgment or in any other manner provided by law.

(b) Nothing in this Agreement shall modify any choice of law provision contained in any Material Contract. The law governing the Material Contracts shall be determined by the provisions of the Material Contracts.

10.5 **Venue.** Each Party irrevocably and unconditionally waives, to the fullest extent permitted by applicable law, any objection that it may now or hereafter have to the laying of venue of any action or proceeding arising out of or relating to this Agreement in any court referred to in Section 10.4. Each of the Parties hereby irrevocably waives, to the fullest extent permitted by applicable law, the defense of an inconvenient forum to the maintenance of such action or proceeding in any such court.

10.6 **WAIVER OF JURY TRIAL.** EACH PARTY HEREBY IRREVOCABLY WAIVES, TO THE FULLEST EXTENT PERMITTED BY APPLICABLE LAW, ANY RIGHT IT MAY HAVE TO A TRIAL BY JURY IN ANY LEGAL PROCEEDING DIRECTLY OR INDIRECTLY ARISING OUT OF OR RELATING TO THIS AGREEMENT OR THE TRANSACTIONS CONTEMPLATED HEREBY (WHETHER BASED ON CONTRACT, TORT OR ANY OTHER THEORY). EACH PARTY (A) CERTIFIES THAT NO REPRESENTATIVE, AGENT OR ATTORNEY OF ANY OTHER PERSON HAS REPRESENTED, EXPRESSLY OR OTHERWISE, THAT SUCH OTHER PERSON WOULD NOT, IN THE EVENT OF LITIGATION, SEEK TO ENFORCE THE FOREGOING WAIVER AND (B) ACKNOWLEDGES THAT IT AND THE OTHER PARTIES HAVE BEEN INDUCED TO ENTER INTO THIS AGREEMENT BY, AMONG OTHER THINGS, THE MUTUAL WAIVERS AND CERTIFICATIONS HEREIN.

10.7 **Severability.** In the event that any provision of this Agreement is determined by a court of law to be illegal or unenforceable, the other provisions shall nevertheless remain effective and shall remain enforceable (provided the substance of the agreement between the Parties is not thereby materially altered).

10.8 **Binding Effect; Assignment; Financing Parties.** This Agreement shall not be assignable by either Party without the prior written consent of the other Party, except that: (i) this Agreement may be assigned by Buyer to Financing Parties as collateral security to such Financing Parties, as more fully set forth in Section 10.9 below; and (ii) this Agreement may be assigned without consent to a Person acquiring all or a controlling interest in the business or assets of Buyer or to any Affiliate of Buyer; provided that any such assignment under clause (i) or (ii) above shall not relieve the assigning Party of any of its obligations under this Agreement. Except with respect to the assignment permitted under clause (i) of this Section 10.8, no assignment of this Agreement by either Party for any purpose whatsoever shall be valid until all obligations of the assignor hereunder shall have been assumed by the assignee by written agreement delivered to the other Party. This Agreement shall be binding upon and shall inure to the benefit of the respective successors and permitted assigns of the Parties. Any assignment which does not comply with the provisions of this Section 10.8 shall be null and void.

10.9 **Financing Party Requested Documents.** In connection with any collateral assignment by Buyer of this Agreement to Financing Parties as allowed under Section 10.8, Seller agrees to enter into an agreement in form and substance reasonably satisfactory to Seller directly with the Financing Parties and Buyer under which Seller shall consent to such assignment and will agree to other customary and reasonable provisions for the benefit of the Financing Parties, including reasonable provisions under which the Financing Parties or their designees (i) may assume or transfer the rights of Buyer under this Agreement, (ii) shall be entitled to receive from Seller copies of certain notices relating to defaults and other similar matters hereunder that Seller might provide to Buyer, (iii) obtain Seller's agreement, subject to any rights Seller may have hereunder, including any right of offset, to make all payments due to Buyer under this Agreement to an account designated by the Financing Parties or their designees, and (iv) shall be provided other customary or related benefits or protections as reasonably requested by the Financing Parties to support such financing, in each case reasonably acceptable to Seller and at no actual cost to Seller. In addition, Seller shall enter into such amendments to this Agreement as are reasonably requested by the Financing Parties in connection with the financing provided by such Financing Parties, *provided* that any such amendments (*x*) do not materially reduce the benefits or materially increase the risk of Seller hereunder, (*y*) are reasonably acceptable to Seller and (*z*) are at no actual cost to Seller.

10.10 <u>No Third Party Beneficiaries</u>. This Agreement is solely for the benefit of the Parties and their respective successors and permitted assigns and shall not, except as expressly stated otherwise herein, be deemed to confer upon or give to any other third party any right, claim, cause of action, or other interest herein.

10.11 <u>Confidentiality</u>.

(a) *<u>Confidential Information</u>*. Upon a Party (the "**Receiving Party**") receiving or learning of Confidential Information from or of the other Party (the "**Disclosing Party**"), the Receiving Party shall:

(i) keep such Confidential Information in strictest confidence and shall not disclose any such Confidential Information to any other Person, except as may be provided in this Agreement;

(ii) restrict access to such Confidential Information to employees (and others who agree to be bound by this Agreement) who have a need to know such Confidential Information for the purposes of this Agreement and who have been notified that such information is Confidential Information;

(iii) use such Confidential Information solely for the purposes of this Agreement; and

(iv) upon this Agreement's termination and at the request of the Disclosing Party, destroy or return any such Confidential Information in written or other tangible form and any copies thereof.

(v) "**Confidential Information**" shall include (A) any and all information prepared or delivered to a Party by the other Party or its Representatives (including information or data received by the other Party from a third party and as to which the other Party has confidentiality obligations) in relation to this Agreement, and (B) information that is known to a Party, or should be known to a reasonable person given the facts and circumstances of the disclosure, as being treated as confidential or proprietary by the other Party.

(vi) The terms of this Agreement, including any attachments, exhibits or annexes, shall also be considered Confidential Information.

(vii) Notwithstanding anything to the contrary set forth in this Section 10.11, the following information shall not be considered Confidential Information:

(A) information that at the time of disclosure or acquisition was publicly available or later became publicly available other than by breach of this Agreement or a confidentiality obligation owed to the Disclosing Party; or

(B) information that at the time of disclosure or acquisition was already known to the Receiving Party, except to the extent such information was disclosed to the Receiving Party pursuant to an agreement or understanding of confidentiality.

(viii) Except as otherwise expressly provided in this Agreement, neither Party shall, unless authorized in writing by the other Party to do so:

(A) distribute or disclose to any Person, firm, entity, or corporation (other than those otherwise authorized pursuant to this Section 10.11) any of the Confidential Information, or any related facts; or

(B) permit any third Person to have access to such Confidential Information.

(b) *Disclosure to Affiliates and Representatives*. Notwithstanding the foregoing, each Party shall have the right to disclose Confidential Information to such Party's Affiliates and any of such Party's or such Party's Affiliates' employees, officers, board members, consultants and attorneys and other Persons involved in assisting such Party or such Party's Affiliates in connection with this Agreement, provided that such Representatives are informed of the requirements of this Section 10.11 and agree to be bound in writing by the provisions of this Agreement. A Receiving Party shall be responsible for ensuring that all Persons to whom it discloses Confidential Information under this Agreement shall keep such information confidential and shall not disclose or divulge the same to any unauthorized Person pursuant to this Agreement's requirements.

(c) *Disclosure Pursuant to Applicable Law*. Notwithstanding anything to the contrary in this Section 10.11, in the event a Receiving Party is requested pursuant to applicable Law to disclose Confidential Information, such Receiving Party shall, to the extent permitted by applicable Law, give the Disclosing Party prompt notice of such request so that the Disclosing Party shall have the right to seek an appropriate protective order. If, in the absence of a protective order, the Receiving Party is nonetheless advised by counsel that disclosure of the Confidential Information is finally required (after, if advance notice to the Disclosing Party is permitted by applicable Law, exhausting any appeal requested by the

Disclosing Party at the Disclosing Party's expense), the Receiving Party shall have the right to disclose such Confidential Information.

(d) *Injunctive Relief*. Each of the Parties acknowledges and agrees that the other Party would be irreparably harmed if any Confidential Information of the Disclosing Party were to be disclosed to third Persons, or if any use were to be made of such Confidential Information other than that permitted under this Agreement, and further agrees that the Disclosing Party shall have the right to seek injunctive relief upon any violation or threatened violation of the terms of this Section 10.11, in addition to all other rights and remedies available at law or in equity, without having to post a bond or other security.

(e) *Survival of Confidentiality Provisions*. The terms and conditions set forth in this Agreement, including any attachments, exhibits or annexes shall be deemed to be Confidential Information subject to the confidentiality provisions of this Section 10.11. The Parties' obligations under this Section 10.11 shall remain in full force and effect for two (2) years following the termination of this Agreement.

(f) *Public Announcements*. Neither Party shall have the right to issue or make any public announcement, press release or statement regarding this Agreement unless the Parties jointly issue such public announcement, press release or statement or before the release of the public announcement, press release or statement, such Party furnishes the other Party with a copy of such announcement, press release or statement, and obtains the other Party's written approval, such approval not to be unreasonably withheld, conditioned or delayed; provided that, notwithstanding any failure to obtain such approval, no Party shall be prohibited from issuing or making any such public announcement, press release or statement if it is necessary to do so in order to comply with applicable Laws, legal proceedings or rules and regulations of any stock exchange having jurisdiction over such Party.

10.12 Amendments; Waiver. This Agreement may be amended only by written agreement executed by the Parties. Any term or condition of this Agreement may be waived at any time by the Party that is entitled to the benefit thereof, but no such waiver shall be effective unless set forth in writing duly executed by such Party. No waiver by any Party of any term or condition of this Agreement, in any one or more instances, shall be deemed to be or construed as a waiver of the same or any other term or condition of this Agreement on any future occasion.

10.13 Expenses. Except as otherwise expressly provided in this Agreement, each Party shall pay its own costs and expenses incurred in connection with the negotiation, execution and closing of this Agreement and the transactions contemplated hereby.

10.14 Counterparts. This Agreement may be executed in two or more counterparts, each of which shall be deemed an original, but all of which constitute but one agreement. Any counterpart may be delivered by facsimile transmission or by electronic communication in portable document format (.pdf) or tagged image (or similar) format (.tif), and the Parties agree that their electronically transmitted signatures shall have the same effect as manually transmitted signatures.

10.15 Drafting Interpretation. Preparation of this Agreement has been a joint effort of the Parties and the resulting document shall not be construed more severely against one of the Parties than against the other.

[*Signature page follows.*]

IN WITNESS WHEREOF, the Parties have executed this Agreement as of the Effective Date.

SELLER:

Consorcio Integrador Sonora 80M S.A. de C.V.

Name:
Title:

BUYER:

General Energy Solutions USA, Inc.

Name: Rongche Chen
Title: Managing Director

EXHIBIT A

Form of Assignment and Conveyance

###

ASSIGNMENT AND CONVEYANCE

THIS ASSIGNMENT AND CONVEYANCE (this "Assignment"), dated [__________], is made and entered into by and between [____] ("Assignor"), and [____] ("Assignee"). Assignor and Assignee are sometimes referred to herein individually, as "Party" and collectively, as the "Parties."

Recitals

A. Assignor and Assignee entered into that certain Shares Purchase Agreement, dated as of [____] (the "Purchase Agreement"), pursuant to which, among other things, Assignor has agreed to assign, convey, transfer and deliver to Assignee, and Assignee has agreed to accept and assume, all of Assignor's right, title and interest in and to the Equity Interests.

B. The Purchase Agreement requires that this Assignment be executed and delivered by the Parties.

C. Subject to the Purchase Agreement, the Parties desire to effect the assignment described above in accordance with the terms and conditions hereof.

Assignment

In consideration of the foregoing, the mutual promises contained herein and other good and valuable consideration, the receipt and sufficiency of which are hereby acknowledged, the Parties agree as follows:

1. ***Definitions.*** All capitalized terms used in this Assignment but not otherwise defined herein have the meanings set forth in the Purchase Agreement.

2. ***Assignment and Assumption.*** Assignor hereby assigns, conveys, transfers and delivers to Assignee, upon and effective from and after the date hereof, all of Assignor's right, title and interest in and to the Equity Interests. Assignee, upon and effective from and after the date hereof, and notwithstanding anything to the contrary in the Operating Agreement, shall be entitled to become a member of the Project Company and shall be entitled to exercise all rights and powers of a member of the Project Company and agrees to be bound by all provisions of the certificate of formation and Operating Agreement. Assignee hereby accepts all of Assignor's right, title and interest in and to the Equity Interests, and assumes all of Assignor's duties, obligations and liabilities arising with respect to the Equity Interests.

3. ***Effect of Agreement.*** This Assignment is executed and delivered pursuant to the Purchase Agreement and is subject to all of the terms, conditions and limitations therein. Nothing in this Assignment shall, or shall be deemed to, modify or otherwise affect any

81081928.2 0046936-00031

provisions of the Purchase Agreement or affect the rights of the Parties under the Purchase Agreement. In the event of any conflict or inconsistency between the terms of the Purchase Agreement and the terms hereof, the terms of the Purchase Agreement shall govern.

4. ***Further Assurances.*** Assignor and Assignee mutually agree to cooperate with respect to any of the matters described herein, and to execute such further deeds, assignments, assumptions, notifications, or other documents as may be legally requested or reasonably necessary for the purpose of giving effect to, evidencing, or giving notice of the transactions evidenced by this Assignment.

5. ***Successors and Assigns; Third Parties.*** This Assignment shall be binding upon and shall inure to the benefit of the Parties and their respective agents, successors and permitted assigns. This Assignment shall not confer any rights, benefits or remedies to any Person not a Party.

6. ***Governing Law.*** This Assignment shall be governed by and construed in accordance with the laws of the state of California without regard to its conflict of laws principles.

7. ***Titles and Captions.*** All section titles or captions in this Assignment are for convenience only, shall not be deemed part of this Assignment and in no way define, limit, extend or describe the scope or intent of any provision hereof.

8. ***Counterparts; Electronic Signatures.*** This Assignment may be executed in one or more counterparts, each of which shall be deemed an original, but all of which together shall constitute one assignment. Each Party hereby agrees that facsimile or electronic signatures (.pdf) shall be valid and binding on the Parties.

[*Signature page follows.*]

EXHIBIT B

Form of PPA Clarification Letter

###

[Insert date]

City Hall of ___________
[insert address]

Reference is made to that certain ________________________________ (the "**PPA**"), by and among Consorcio Integrador Sonora 80M S.A. de C.V., a Variable Capital Corporation with address on the street Montecito, number 38, floor 28, office 13, Residential Development Napoles, Delegation Benito Suarez, Mexico Federal District ("**Sonora 80M**"), and the City Hall of ________________ Sonora, with address on the street ______________________________ ("**City Hall**"). Capitalized terms used but not defined herein shall have the meaning ascribed to such terms in the PPA.

Reference is made to that certain Termination of Rights agreement between Sonora 80M and Munisol S.A.P.I., a Mexican corporation ("**Munisol**") dated ______________, whereby Sonora 80M assigned all its rights and delegated all its obligations under the PPA to Munisol, and Munisol accepted such assignment and delegation of rights ("**Assignment Agreement**").

Now therefore, in return for good and valuable consideration, the sufficiency of which is hereby acknowledged and agreed, the parties hereby agree to the following and amend the PPA as follows:

1. The City Hall hereby acknowledges the Assignment Agreement and accepts the assignment and delegation to Munisol of all rights and obligations under the PPA.

2. The City Hall and Munisol each represent and confirm that the PPA constitutes a legal, valid and binding obligation that is currently in effect and enforceable against it in accordance with its terms.

3. For purposes of Clause 3.8.2 and Exhibit F to the PPA, the term "Hours of normal operation" means the total number of hours in a year that the solar park delivers the quantity of electric energy specified in Exhibit A to the PPA.

4. Notwithstanding anything to the contrary in PPA, the City Hall hereby acknowledges and agrees that the definition of "Equipment" in the PPA means any Photovoltaic Generating Units as well as the designs, materials, components, and auxiliary equipment identified in a final design approved by the Federal Electricity Commission ("CFE") for construction of the solar park. Neither Sonora 80M nor the New Corporation will be in breach of any obligation of the PPA for installing, operating, or maintaining any Photovoltaic Generating Units or designs, materials, components, or auxiliary equipment identified in a final design approved by CFE for construction of the solar park.

81081928.2 0046936-00031

EXHIBIT B

Form of PPA Clarification Letter

###

[Insert date]

City Hall of ___________
[insert address]

Reference is made to that certain ______________________________ (the "**PPA**"), by and among Consorcio Integrador Sonora 80M S.A. de C.V., a Variable Capital Corporation with address on the street Montecito, number 38, floor 28, office 13, Residential Development Napoles, Delegation Benito Suarez, Mexico Federal District ("**Sonora 80M**"), and the City Hall of ________________ Sonora, with address on the street ______________________ ("**City Hall**"). Capitalized terms used but not defined herein shall have the meaning ascribed to such terms in the PPA.

Reference is made to that certain Termination of Rights agreement between Sonora 80M and Munisol S.A.P.I., a Mexican corporation ("**Munisol**") dated ____________, whereby Sonora 80M assigned all its rights and delegated all its obligations under the PPA to Munisol, and Munisol accepted such assignment and delegation of rights ("**Assignment Agreement**").

Now therefore, in return for good and valuable consideration, the sufficiency of which is hereby acknowledged and agreed, the parties hereby agree to the following and amend the PPA as follows:

1. The City Hall hereby acknowledges the Assignment Agreement and accepts the assignment and delegation to Munisol of all rights and obligations under the PPA.

2. The City Hall and Munisol each represent and confirm that the PPA constitutes a legal, valid and binding obligation that is currently in effect and enforceable against it in accordance with its terms.

3. For purposes of <u>Clause 3.8.2</u> and <u>Exhibit F</u> to the PPA, the term "Hours of normal operation" means the total number of hours in a year that the solar park delivers the quantity of electric energy specified in <u>Exhibit A</u> to the PPA.

4. Notwithstanding anything to the contrary in PPA, the City Hall hereby acknowledges and agrees that the definition of "Equipment" in the PPA means any Photovoltaic Generating Units as well as the designs, materials, components, and auxiliary equipment identified in a final design approved by the Federal Electricity Commission ("CFE") for construction of the solar park. Neither Sonora 80M nor the New Corporation will be in breach of any obligation of the PPA for installing, operating, or maintaining any Photovoltaic Generating Units or designs, materials, components, or auxiliary equipment identified in a final design approved by CFE for construction of the solar park.

81081928.2 0046936-00031

5. The City Hall hereby consents to the delegation of the guarantee obligations of Sonora 80M in Clause 19 of the PPA to General Energy Solutions USA, Inc., a Nevada corporation.

6. Notwithstanding anything to the contrary in the PPA, for purposes of Clause 19 and Exhibit G of the PPA, the City Hall hereby agrees to accept any form of guarantee suitable to General Energy Solutions USA, Inc., a Nevada corporation.

7. Clause 3.12.3 of the PPA is hereby replaced in its entirety by the below:

The parties agree that the power supply provided by SONORA 80M or the New Corporation to THE CITY HALL strictly depends on the availability and quality of the solar radiation, which is naturally not under the control of any of the parties. Due to the foregoing, any variation thereof that causes SONORA 80M or the New Corporation to fail to meet the obligations in Exhibit A or Exhibit B shall be considered a cause of Force Majeure for SONORA 80M or the New Corporation.

8. Clause 4.3 of the PPA is hereby replaced in its entirety by the below:

In case THE CITY HALL materially breaches any obligation of this Agreement, or terminates this Agreement during its term of validity for any reason other than an Event of Default, as defined by Clause 12.1, by Sonora 80M or the New Corporation, THE CITY HALL shall pay to SONORA 80M or the New Corporation a payment equal to 75% (seventy-five percent) of the net present value of the future cash flows that SONORA 80M or the New Corporation will no longer receive during the validity of this Agreement.

9. Clause 12.1(c) of the PPA is hereby replaced in its entirety by the below:

Omissions or failures on behalf of SONORA 80M to inform THE CITY HALL of any event or circumstance regarding the Equipment which implies an imminent threat to life, of which it has knowledge or should reasonably have knowledge, and that causes damages to the personnel or employees of THE CITY HALL or any third party.

10. Clause 12.3.1 of the PPA is hereby replaced in its entirety by the below:

Actions and effects of SONORA 80M. When SONORA 80M has the right to terminate this Agreement early under Clause 12.2, provided THE CITY HALL has not remedied the event of default within the period stipulated in Clause 13, it may:

a. Suspend the power supply with prior notice to THE CITY HALL to that effect at least thirty business days in advance.

b. Terminate this Agreement with prior notice to THE CITY HALL to that effect at least thirty business days in advance.

c. SONORA 80M shall not be responsible for damages caused to THE CITY HALL or any third party due to the discontinuation of the power supply or termination of

81081928.2 0046936-00031

the Agreement pursuant to this Clause 12.3.1, provided that both actions shall be performed with prior notice, in accordance with the foregoing Clauses 12.3.1(a) and (b).

d. In the event that SONORA 80M terminates this Agreement pursuant to Clause 12.3.1(b), THE CITY HALL shall pay to SONORA 80M or the New Corporation a payment equal to 75% (seventy-five percent) of the net present value of the future cash flows that SONORA 80M or the New Corporation will no longer receive during the validity of this Agreement.

e. Actions and effects of THE CITY HALL. When THE CITY HALL has the right to terminate this Agreement early under Clause 12.1, provided that SONORA 80M has not remedied the event of default within the period stipulated in Clause 13, it may:

f. Terminate this Agreement with prior notice to SONORA 80M to that effect at least thirty business days in advance.

g. In the event that THE CITY HALL terminates this Agreement pursuant to Clause 12.3.1(f), THE CITY HALL shall pay to SONORA 80M or the New Corporation a payment equal to the amount calculated pursuant to Exhibit "E."

11. Clause 29.1 of the PPA is hereby replaced in its entirety by the below:

In case the Service complies with the specifications set forth in EXHIBIT "A", SONORA 80M shall not be liable for any damage that in any way results from the use or any Service of THE CITY HALL in its property beyond the Point of Delivery. The total aggregate liability for SONORA 80M arising out of or relating to this Agreement shall not exceed the total amount of payments made to Sonora 80M under this Agreement, whether such liability is based on or claimed under contract, tort, or any other theory at law or in equity.

[remainder of page intentionally left blank]

81081928 2 0046936-00031

Each party represents and warrants that: (1) it has the requisite power and authority to enter into this letter agreement; (2) the execution, delivery, and performance of this agreement has been duly and validly authorized; and (3) this agreement constitutes a legal, valid, and binding obligation, enforceable in accordance with its terms.

This letter agreement may be executed in one or more counterparts for the convenience of the parties hereto, each of which shall be deemed an original and all of which together will constitute one and the same instrument.

Yours very truly,

MUNISOL S.A.P.I.

By: ______________________
Name:
Title:

AGREED AND ACCEPTED:

CITY HALL OF ______________

By: ______________________
Name:
Title:

This signature page is attached to the PPA Clarification Letter executed for the Power Purchase Agreement dated ____________, such PPA Clarification Letter entered by and between Munisol S.A.P.I., represented here by __________, and the City Hall of ____________, represented here by ____________, with the ratification of the Secretary of the City Hall __________, and by the Treasurer ____________, on _________ [*date*].

81081928.2 0046936-00031

DISCLOSURE SCHEDULES

The information disclosed in one Schedule will suffice, without repetition or cross reference, as a disclosure of such information in any other Schedule only to the extent to which its relevance is reasonably apparent on its face. Any capitalized terms used in any Schedule but not otherwise defined herein shall be defined as set forth in the Shares Purchase Agreement.

Schedule 1

Project Assets

1. All those tangible and intangible assets related to the Project, including without limitation all Environmental Attributes and incentives available in connection with the Project.
2. All Material Contracts.
3. The environmental impact authorization issued on March 14, 2013 by the Secretary of Environment and Natural Resources (SEMERNAT), Official No. DS-SG-UGA-IA-0244-13.
4. Letter from SEMERNAT, through Mtro. Hector Ulises Cristopulos Rios, to the Project Company, Oficio No. DFS/SGPA/UARRN/367/2014, dated March 31, 2014.
5. *Analisis Tecnico de Condiciones de Terreno de Agostadero ubicado en La Costa de Hermosillo, Sonora*, by Ing. Jose Antonio Meraz Valenzuela, March 2014.
6. The permit for an aerial crossing over the Hermosillo-Bahia Kino highway for interconnecting the Project to the national electrical system, issued on March 7, 2013 by the *Junta de Caminos del Estado de Sonora*, Official No. JCES-11-01-0173-2013.
7. The permit for construction of the Project, License No. DGDU/CU/EBR/4857/2014, issued by the General Coordination of Infrastructure, Urban Development and Ecology (CIDUE) of the municipality of Hermosillo on October 1, 2014.
8. Approval of CIDUE of the *Cedula de Operacion Anual, en materia de Impacto Ambiental*, Oficio CIDUE/IME/11473/2014, issued on August 18, 2014.
9. Approval of CIDUE of the *Cedula de Operacion Anual, en materia de Impacto Ambiental*, Oficio CIDUE/IME/IRGG/2199/2015, issued on December 15, 2015.
10. Resolution of the National Institute of Anthropology and History (*Instituto Nacional de Antropologia e Historia*), Oficio 401.F(4)77.2015/CIS-1002, issued on October 6, 2015.
11. The permit of self-supply of electrical energy, No. E/1017/AUT/2013, Resolution No. RES/325/2013, issued by the Energy Regulatory Commission (CRE) to the Project Company on August 29, 2013, as modified on March 5, 2015 by RES/126/2015.
12. The December 3, 2015 letter from *Centro Nacional de Control de Energia* (CENACE), through Ing. Sergio I. de la Toba Coronel, to the Project Company, including Annex One thereto.
13. Collective Work Agreement (*Contrato Colectivo de Trabajo*), between *Sindicato de Obreros, Industrial, del Comercio, de la Construccion, y Trabajadores en General del Estado de Sonora* and Sonora 80M.
14. *Dictamen de Seguridad Aprobatorio*, issued on September 4, 2014 by the *Unidad Municipial de Proteccion Civil* of the City of Hermosillo, Sonora, Mexico.
15. Construction permit, License No. DGDU/CU/EBR/4857/2014, issued on October 1, 2014 by CIDUE.

81081928.2 0046936-00031

16. *Aprobacion de Anteproyecto para Produccion de Energia Solar y Oficinas*, Oficio No. CIDUE/MENM/11539/14, issued on August 22, 2014 by CIDUE.
17. Land Use License (*Licencia de Uso de Suelo*), Oficio No. CIDUE/MENM/11538/14, issued on August 22, 2014 by CIDUE.
18. Information of Land Use (*Informacion de Uso de Suelo*), Oficio No. CIDUE/DGDU/EBR/4478/14, issued on August 7, 2014 by CIDUE.
19. *Certificacion de Acuerdo de Cabildo*, signed by C. Profr. Juan Manuel Torres Deras, Secretary of the City of Alamos, dated October 27, 2011.
20. *Certificacion de Acuerdo de Cabildo*, signed by C. Lic. Axel Omar Salas Hernandez, Secretary of the City of Alamos, dated November 9, 2012.
21. *Certificacion de Acuerdo*, signed by C. Ing. Francisco A Jiminez Rodriguez, Secretary of the City of Caborca, dated March 2, 2012.
22. *Certificacion*, signed by C. Dr. Jesus Octavio Sandoval Valenzuela, Secretary of the City of Etchojoa, dated November 28, 2011.
23. *Certificacion*, signed by C.P. Jesus Villalobos Garcia, Secretary of the City of Hermosillo, dated December 17, 2014.
24. All Permits from all Governmental Authorities relating to all *Ramo 28* Guarantees, including but not limited to, any such Permits contained in the following documents (the document names are the document names in the electronic versions of the documents disclosed to Buyer):
    a. **City of Caborca**
        i. 8 Boletin Oficial Caborca
        ii. 7 Carta de Ingreso de Caborca al Congreso del Estado
        iii. 5 Acta 8 Caborca Garantias Ramo 28
    b. **City of Empalme**
        i. 12 Ingreso a Registro Federal de Deuda
        ii. 11 Registro de Deuda Estatal Empalme
        iii. 10 Ingreso a registro de deuda Estatal Empalme
        iv. 9 Boletin Oficial Etchojoa y Empalme
        v. 8 Carta de Ingreso de Empalme al Congreso del Estado
        vi. 7 Acuerdo de Garantias Ramo 28 Empalme
        vii. 6 Acta de Cabildo Garantias ramo 28 Empalme
    c. **City of Etchojoa**
        i. 8 Boletin Oficial Etchojoa y Empalme
        ii. 7 Cartas de Ingreso Etchojoa al Congresso del Estado
        iii. 6 Certificacion Acuerdo de Garantias Etchojoa
    d. **City of Hermosillo**
        i. Registro de Deuda Municipal Hermosillo
        ii. Registro de Deuda Federal Hermosillo
        iii. Registro de Deuda Estatal Hermosillo
        iv. Fideicomiso Hermosillo Ramo 28
        v. Cuenta Mandatada
        vi. Convenio Modificatorio Hermosillo
        vii. 8 Boletin Oficial Hermosillo
25. *Carta de Ingreso de Caborca al Congreso del Estado* (Numero de Oficio 17'0894/2014) (Feb. 4, 2014)
26. *Acta de Cabildo No. Sesion Ordinaria Numero Ocho* (Jan. 14, 2013)

27. *Registro de Deuda Estatal Empalme* (DGCP-108/2015) (June 12, 2015)
28. *Estudio de Mecanica de Suelos para la Construccion de un Parque de Energia Solar, en Hermosillo, Sonora, Laboratorio, Estudios y Servicios Profesionales, de Ingenieria S.A. de C.V.* (July 29, 2011).
29. *Parque de Energia Solar Planimetrico A-2, Ingenieria y Construcciones Sabodepa S.A. de C.V.* (July 2011)
30. *Parque de Energia Solar General A-1, Ingenieria y Construcciones Sabodepa S.A. de C.V.* (July 2011)
31. *Parque de Energia Solar Altimetria A-3, Ingenieria y Construcciones Sabodepa S.A. de C.V.* (July 2011)
32. *Proyecto Topografico Parque de Energia Solar, Ingenieria y Construcciones Sabodepa S.A. de C.V.*
33. *Planos de Proyecto, Servicios Especializados en Montajes Industriales S.A. de C.V.*
34. *Especificaciones Tecnicas de Equipos y Materiales, Servicios Especializados en Montajes Industriales S.A. de C.V.*
35. *Documentacion Proyecto Sonora 80M, Servicios Especializados en Montajes Industriales S.A. de C.V.*, Martifer Solar (May 2, 2013).

81081928.2 0046936-00031

Schedule 3.8

Capitalization Table

Shareholders	*Shares*	*Series*	*Value*
	Series A	*Series B*	
Consorcio Integrador Sonora 80M S.A. de C.V.	*30,000*	*21*	*$3'002,100.00*
Alumbrado Público de Hermosillo	-	*1*	*$100.00*
Municipio de Santa Ana	-	*1*	*$100.00*
Municipio de Alamos	-	*1*	*$100.00*
Municipio de Caborca	-	*1*	*$100.00*
Municipio de Etchojoa	-	*1*	*$100.00*
Municipio de Empalme	-	*1*	*$100.00*
Municipio de Guaymas	-	*1*	*$100.00*
Municipio de Hermosillo	-	*1*	*$100.00*
Ford Motor Company, S.A. de C.V.	-	*1*	*$100.00*
Total	*30,000*	*30*	*$3'003,000.00*

81081928.2 0046936-00031

Schedule 3.8

Capitalization Table

Shareholders	*Shares*	*Series*	*Value*
	Series A	*Series B*	
Consorcio Integrador Sonora 80M S.A. de C.V.	*30,000*	*21*	*$3'002,100.00*
Alumbrado Público de Hermosillo	-	*1*	*$100.00*
Municipio de Santa Ana	-	*1*	*$100.00*
Municipio de Alamos	-	*1*	*$100.00*
Municipio de Caborca	-	*1*	*$100.00*
Municipio de Etchojoa	-	*1*	*$100.00*
Municipio de Empalme	-	*1*	*$100.00*
Municipio de Guaymas	-	*1*	*$100.00*
Municipio de Hermosillo	-	*1*	*$100.00*
Ford Motor Company, S.A. de C.V.	-	*1*	*$100.00*
Total	*30,000*	*30*	*$3'003,000.00*

81081928.2 0046936-00031

Schedule 3.7(b)

Real Property Interests

[Sonora 80M provides]

Schedule 3.10(a)

Material Contracts

1. All Power Purchase Agreements listed on Schedule 2 to this Agreement, including all amendments or modifications thereto.
2. *Contrato Promesa de Obra y Operacion y Mantenimiento Para Una Planta de Produccion de Energia Electrica Mediante Paneles Fotovoltaicos Para La Empresa de Autobastecimiento Munisol SAPI*, dated May 1, 2012, between Seller and MTS Solar Sistemas Solares, S.A. de C.V.
3. *Contrato de Cecion de Derechos*, between Seller and the Project Company, dated July 9, 2015.
4. *Contrato de Cecion de Derechos*, between Seller and the Project Company, dated November 9, 2015.
5. *Convenio de Instalaciones y Cesion*, dated December 7, 2015 between the Project Company and the *Comision Federal de Electricidad*.

81081928.2 0046936-00031

Schedule 3.15

Project Company Bank Accounts

	Consorcio Integrador
Account holder:	Sonora 80M S.A. de C.V.
Banco:	BBVA Bancomer
Sucursal:	3646 World Trade Center
Cta No.:	0196043704
Clabe:	0121 8000 1960 4370 44

81081928.2 0046936-00031

Exhibit 9

Corporate Organization Chart Consorcio Integrador Sonora 80M, Mexico

1. **CEO:** Mtro. Ing. [redacted]
The CEO gets direct [redacted] 3.1. [redacted]d 4.1.

2. Director of Technical Management and Human Resources:
Mtro. Ing. Pablo Mayo

2.1. Subdirector of Operations:
Ing. Alfonso Cruz

2.1.1. Civil works Manager:
Ing. Jose Hugo Barcelo

2.1.1.1. Facilities Coordinator:
Arq. Alejandro Jardines

2.1.2. Electrical Installations Manager:
Ing. J. Pedro Balcazar

2.1.3. O&M Manager:
Ing. Javier Barcelo

2.2. Subdirector of Human Resources and Outsourcing companies:
C.P. Roberto Garcia

3.1. Subdirector of Institutional Relations and Legal Department:
Lic. Rodrigo Gurza

3.1.1. Public Institucional Relations Manager:
Lic. Alejandro Soto

4.1. Subdirector of Financial and Fiscal area:
Lic. Raul Stanford

4.1.1. Financial Manager:
Lic. Nancy Reyes

4.1.2. Fiscal Manager:
Lic. Ersyla Alcaide

Exhibit 10

PAGE 180

PAGE 181

PAGE 183

PAGE 185

PAGE 185

PAGE 186

Exhibit 11

Secretary of State
Articles of Organization
Limited Liability Company (LLC)

LLC-1

201704910038

FILED
Secretary of State
State of California
FEB 08 2017

IMPORTANT — Read Instructions before completing this form.

Filing Fee - $70.00

Copy Fees - First plain copy free; Additional copies: First page $1.00 & .50 for each attachment page; Certification Fee - $5.00

Important! LLCs may have to pay an annual minimum $800 tax to the California Franchise Tax Board. For more information, go to https://www.ftb.ca.gov.

IPC This Space For Office Use Only

1. Limited Liability Company Name (See Instructions – Must contain an LLC ending such as LLC or L.L.C. "LLC" will be added, if not included.)

Consorcio Integrador Sonora 80M US, LLC

2. Business Addresses

a. Initial Street Address of Designated Office in California - Do not list a P.O. Box	City (no abbreviations)	State	Zip Code
520 Broadway	Santa Monica	CA	90401
b. Initial Mailing Address of LLC, if different than Item 2a	City (no abbreviations)	State	Zip Code

3. Agent for Service of Process

Item 3a and 3b: If naming an individual, the agent must reside in California and Item 3a and 3b must be completed with the agent's name and complete California street address.
Item 3c: If naming a California Registered Corporate Agent, a current agent registration certificate must be on file with the California Secretary of State and Item 3c must be completed (leave Item 3a-3b blank).

a. California Agent's First Name (if agent is not a corporation)	Middle Name	Last Name		Suffix
Nobel		Chang		
b. Street Address (if agent is not a corporation) - Do not list a P.O. Box	City (no abbreviations)	State	Zip Code	
35 N. Lake Avenue, Ste. 705	Pasadena	CA	91101	
c. California Registered Corporate Agent's Name (if agent is a corporation) – Do not complete Item 3a or 3b				

4. Management (Select only one box)

The LLC will be managed by:

☑ One Manager ☐ More than One Manager ☐ All LLC Member(s)

5. Purpose Statement (Do not alter Purpose Statement)

The purpose of the limited liability company is to engage in any lawful act or activity for which a limited liability company may be organized under the California Revised Uniform Limited Liability Company Act.

6. The Information contained herein, including in any attachments, is true and correct.

Organizer sign here

By: Cheyenne Moseley, Assistant Secretary, LegalZoom.com, Inc.
Print your name here

LLC-1 (REV 06/2016)

2016 California Secretary of State

Secretary of State
Business Programs Division
Business Entities, 1500 11th Street, 3rd Floor, Sacramento, CA 95814

Welcome to California

Congratulations on the registration of your limited liability company with the California Secretary of State. Please see below for important information.

Required Statement of Information

California law requires limited liability companies to keep their public record updated by filing a Statement of Information with the California Secretary of State.

Limited liability companies must file a complete Statement of Information (Form LLC-12) within the first 90 days of filing the Articles of Organization or Application to Register, and then every 2 years after that before the end of the month of the registration date.

Statements of Information for limited liability companies must be submitted on paper to the California Secretary of State, and can be mailed or delivered in person (drop off) to the Sacramento office. Additional information regarding Statements of Information, including forms, instructions and current fees is available at www.sos.ca.gov/business-programs/business-entities/statements.

Current processing times for Statements of Information may be found at www.sos.ca.gov/business-programs/business-entities/processing-times.

Other Business Information and Resources

All business entities are subject to state and federal tax laws. You may wish to contact the following agencies to assist you with these issues:

- Internal Revenue Service – www.irs.gov or call (800) 829-1040 for forms and issues concerning Federal tax, employer identification numbers, subchapter S elections
- Franchise Tax Board – www.ftb.ca.gov or call (800) 852-5711 for forms and issues concerning franchise tax and state income tax requirements
- State Board of Equalization – www.boe.ca.gov or call (800) 400-7115 for forms and issues concerning sales taxes or use taxes
- Employment Development Department – www.edd.ca.gov or call (800) 300-5616 for forms and issues concerning employment and payroll taxes

Please refer to www.sos.ca.gov/business-programs/business-entities/resources for a list of other agencies you may need to contact to ensure proper compliance with the laws of the State of California. Please be aware that the California Secretary of State does not license limited liability companies. For licensing requirements, please contact the California city and/or county where the principal place of business is located and/or the state agency, or board with jurisdiction over the activities of the limited liability company

Exhibit
12

Operating Agreement

Consorcio Integrador Sonora 80M US, LLC,
a California Limited Liability Company

THIS OPERATING AGREEMENT of Consorcio Integrador Sonora 80M US, LLC (the "Company") is entered into as of the date set forth on the signature page of this Agreement by each of the Members listed on Exhibit A of this Agreement.

A. The Members have formed the Company as a California limited liability company under the California Revised Uniform Limited Liability Company Act. The purpose of the Company is to conduct any lawful business for which limited liability companies may be organized under the laws of the state of California. The Members hereby adopt and approve the articles of organization of the Company filed with the California Secretary of State.

B. The Members enter into this Agreement to provide for the governance of the Company and the conduct of its business, and to specify their relative rights and obligations.

ARTICLE 1: DEFINITIONS

Capitalized terms used in this Agreement have the meanings specified in this Article 1 or elsewhere in this Agreement and if not so specified, have the meanings set forth in the California Revised Uniform Limited Liability Company Act.

"Agreement" means this Operating Agreement of the Company, as may be amended from time to time.

"Capital Account" means, with respect to any Member, an account consisting of such Member's Capital Contribution, (1) increased by such Member's allocated share of income and gain, (2) decreased by such Member's share of losses and deductions, (3) decreased by any distributions made by the Company to such Member, and (4) otherwise adjusted as required in accordance with applicable tax laws.

"Capital Contribution" means, with respect to any Member, the total value of (1) cash and the fair market value of property other than cash and (2) services that are contributed and/or agreed to be contributed to the Company by such Member, as listed on Exhibit A, as may be updated from time to time according to the terms of this Agreement.

"Exhibit" means a document attached to this Agreement labeled as "Exhibit A," "Exhibit B," and so forth, as such document may be amended, updated, or replaced from time to time according to the terms of this Agreement.

"Manager" means each Person who has authority to manage the business and affairs of the Company pursuant to this Agreement; such Persons are listed on Exhibit B, as may be updated from time to time according to the terms of this Agreement. A Manager may be, but is not required to be, a Member.

"Member" means each Person who acquires Membership Interest pursuant to this Agreement. The Members are listed on Exhibit A, as may be updated from time to time according to the terms of this Agreement. Each Member has the rights and obligations specified in this Agreement.

"Membership Interest" means the entire ownership interest of a Member in the Company at any particular time, including the right to any and all benefits to which a Member may be entitled as provided in this Agreement and under the California Revised Uniform Limited Liability Company Act, together with the obligations of the Member to comply with all of the terms and provisions of this Agreement.

"Ownership Interest" means the Percentage Interest or Units, as applicable, based on the manner in which relative ownership of the Company is divided.

"Percentage Interest" means the percentage of ownership in the Company that, with respect to each Member, entitles the Member to a Membership Interest and is expressed as either:

A. If ownership in the Company is expressed in terms of percentage, the percentage set forth opposite the name of each Member on Exhibit A, as may be adjusted from time to time pursuant to this Agreement; or

B. If ownership in the Company is expressed in Units, the ratio, expressed as a percentage, of:

(1) the number of Units owned by the Member (expressed as "MU" in the equation below) divided by

(2) the total number of Units owned by all of the Members of the Company (expressed as "TU" in the equation below).

$$\text{Percentage Interest} = \frac{MU}{TU}$$

"Person" means an individual (natural person), partnership, limited partnership, trust, estate, association, corporation, limited liability company, or other entity, whether domestic or foreign.

"Units" mean, if ownership in the Company is expressed in Units, units of ownership in the Company, that, with respect to each Member, entitles the Member to a Membership Interest which, if applicable, is expressed as the number of Units set forth opposite the name of each Member on Exhibit A, as may be adjusted from time to time pursuant to this Agreement.

ARTICLE 2: CAPITAL CONTRIBUTIONS, ADDITIONAL MEMBERS, CAPITAL ACCOUNTS AND LIMITED LIABILITY

2.1 **Initial Capital Contributions.** The names of all Members and each of their respective addresses, initial Capital Contributions, and Ownership Interests must be set forth on Exhibit A. Each Member has made or agrees to make the initial Capital Contribution set forth next to such Member's name on Exhibit A to become a Member of the Company.

2.2 **Subsequent Capital Contributions.** Members are not obligated to make additional Capital Contributions unless unanimously agreed by all the Members. If subsequent Capital Contributions are unanimously agreed by all the Members in a consent in writing, the Members may make such additional Capital Contributions on a pro rata basis in accordance with each Member's respective Percentage Interest or as otherwise unanimously agreed by the Members.

2.3 **Additional Members**.

A. With the exception of a transfer of interest (1) governed by Article 7 of this Agreement or (2) otherwise expressly authorized by this Agreement, additional Persons may become Members of the Company and be issued additional Ownership Interests only if approved by and on terms determined by a unanimous written agreement signed by all of the existing Members.

B. Before a Person may be admitted as a Member of the Company, that Person must sign and deliver to the Company the documents and instruments, in the form and containing the information required by the Company, that the Managers deem necessary or desirable. Membership Interests of new Members will be allocated according to the terms of this Agreement.

2.4 **Capital Accounts**. Individual Capital Accounts must be maintained for each Member, unless (a) there is only one Member of the Company and (b) the Company is exempt according to applicable tax laws. Capital Accounts must be maintained in accordance with all applicable tax laws.

2.5 **Interest**. No interest will be paid by the Company or otherwise on Capital Contributions or on the balance of a Member's Capital Account.

2.6 **Limited Liability; No Authority**. A Member will not be bound by, or be personally liable for, the expenses, liabilities, debts, contracts, or obligations of the Company, except as otherwise provided in this Agreement or as required by the California Revised Uniform Limited Liability Company Act. Unless expressly provided in this Agreement, no Member, acting alone, has any authority to undertake or assume any obligation, debt, or responsibility, or otherwise act on behalf of, the Company or any other Member.

ARTICLE 3: ALLOCATIONS AND DISTRIBUTIONS

3.1 **Allocations**. Unless otherwise agreed to by the unanimous consent of the Members any income, gain, loss, deduction, or credit of the Company will be allocated for accounting and tax purposes on a pro rata basis in proportion to the respective Percentage Interest held by each Member and in compliance with applicable tax laws.

3.2 **Distributions.** The Company will have the right to make distributions of cash and property to the Members on a pro rata basis in proportion to the respective Percentage Interest held by each Member. The timing and amount of distributions will be determined by the Managers in accordance with the California Revised Uniform Limited Liability Company Act.

3.3 **Limitations on Distributions.** The Company must not make a distribution to a Member if, after giving effect to the distribution:

A. The Company would be unable to pay its debts as they become due in the usual course of business; or

B. The fair value of the Company's total assets would be less than the sum of its total liabilities plus the amount that would be needed, if the Company were to be dissolved at the time of the distribution, to satisfy the preferential rights upon dissolution of Members, if any, whose preferential rights are superior to those of the Members receiving the distribution.

ARTICLE 4: MANAGEMENT

4.1 **Management.**

A. **Generally.** Subject to the terms of this Agreement and the California Revised Uniform Limited Liability Company Act, the business and affairs of the Company will be managed by the Board of Managers, as further described below. The Members initially nominate and elect the Person(s) set forth on Exhibit B to serve as the Manager(s) of the Company. The Managers will act under the direction of the Members and may be elected or removed at any time, for any reason or no reason, by the Members holding a majority of the Voting Interest of the Company. Exhibit B must be amended to reflect any changes in Managers.

B. **Approval and Action.** Unless greater or other authorization is required pursuant to this Agreement or under the California Revised Uniform Limited Liability Company Act for the Company to engage in an activity or transaction, all activities or transactions must be approved by a majority of Managers, to constitute the act of the Company or serve to bind the Company, but if the Managers cannot reach a majority vote, the dispute will be submitted to the Members to be resolved by the affirmative vote of the Members holding at least a majority of the Voting Interest of the Company. With such approval, the signature of any Managers authorized to sign on behalf of the Company is sufficient to bind the Company with respect to the matter or matters so approved. Without such approval, no Managers acting alone may bind the Company to any agreement with or obligation to any third party or represent or claim to have the ability to so bind the Company.

C. **Certain Decisions Requiring Greater Authorization.** Notwithstanding clause B above, the following matters require unanimous approval of the Members in a consent in writing to constitute an act of the Company:

(i) A material change in the purposes or the nature of the Company's business;

(ii) With the exception of a transfer of interest governed by Article 7 of this Agreement, the admission of a new Member or a change in any Member's Membership Interest, Ownership Interest, Percentage Interest, or Voting Interest in any manner other than in accordance with this Agreement;

(iii) A merger or conversion under the California Revised Uniform Limited Liability Company Act;

(iv) Any other act outside the ordinary course of the Company's activities;

(v) The sale, lease, exchange, or other disposition of all, or substantially all, of the Company's property, with or without goodwill, outside the ordinary course of the Company's activities; and

(vi) The amendment of this Agreement.

4.2 **Meetings of Managers.** Regular meetings of the Managers are not required but may be held at such time and place as the Managers deem necessary or desirable for the reasonable management of the Company. Meetings may take place in person, by conference call, or by any other means permitted under the California Revised Uniform Limited Liability Company Act. In addition, Company actions requiring a vote may be carried out without a meeting if all of the Managers consent in writing to approve the action.

4.3 **Officers.** The Managers are authorized to appoint one or more officers from time to time. The officers will have the titles, the authority, exercise the powers, and perform the duties that the Managers determine from time to time. Each officer will continue to perform and hold office until such time as (a) the officer's successor is chosen and appointed by the Managers; or (b) the officer is dismissed or terminated by the Managers, which termination will be subject to applicable law and, if an effective employment agreement exists between the officer and the Company, the employment agreement. Subject to applicable law and the employment agreement (if any), each officer will serve at the direction of Managers, and may be terminated, at any time and for any reason, by the Managers.

ARTICLE 5: ACCOUNTS AND ACCOUNTING

5.1 **Accounts**. The Company must maintain complete accounting records of the Company's business, including a full and accurate record of each Company transaction. The records must be kept at the Company's principal executive office and must be open to inspection and copying by Members during normal business hours upon reasonable notice by the Members wishing to inspect or copy the records or their authorized representatives, for purposes reasonably related to the Membership Interest of such Members. The costs of inspection and copying will be borne by the respective Member.

5.2 **Records**. The Managers will keep or cause the Company to keep the following business records.

(i) An up to date list of the Members, each of their respective full legal names, last known business or residence address, Capital Contributions, the amount and terms of any agreed upon future Capital Contributions, and Ownership Interests, and Voting Interests;

(ii) A copy of the Company's federal, state, and local tax information and income tax returns and reports, if any, for the six most recent taxable years;

(iii) A copy of the articles of organization of the Company, as may be amended from time to time ("Articles of Organization"); and

(iv) An original signed copy, which may include counterpart signatures, of this Agreement, and any amendments to this Agreement, signed by all then-current Members.

5.3 Income Tax Returns. Within 45 days after the end of each taxable year, the Company will use its best efforts to send each of the Members all information necessary for the Members to complete their federal and state tax information, returns, and reports and a copy of the Company's federal, state, and local tax information or income tax returns and reports for such year.

5.4 Subchapter S Election. The Company may, upon unanimous consent of the Members, elect to be treated for income tax purposes as an S Corporation. This designation may be changed as permitted under the Internal Revenue Code Section 1362(d) and applicable Regulations.

5.5 Tax Matters Member. Anytime the Company is required to designate or select a tax matters partner pursuant to Section 6231(a)(7) of the Internal Revenue Code and any regulations issued by the Internal Revenue Service, the Members must designate one of the Members as the tax matters partner of the Company and keep such designation in effect at all times.

5.6 Banking. All funds of the Company must be deposited in one or more bank accounts in the name of the Company with one or more recognized financial institutions. The Managers are authorized to establish such accounts and complete, sign, and deliver any banking resolutions reasonably required by the respective financial institutions in order to establish an account.

ARTICLE 6: MEMBERSHIP – VOTING AND MEETINGS

6.1 Members and Voting Rights. The Members have the right and power to vote on all matters with respect to which the Articles of Organization, this Agreement, or the California Revised Uniform Limited Liability Company Act requires or permits. Unless otherwise stated in this Agreement (for example, in Section 4.1(c)) or required under the California Revised Uniform Limited Liability Company Act, the vote of the Members holding at least a majority of the Voting Interest of the Company is required to approve or carry out an action.

6.2 Meetings of Members. Annual, regular, or special meetings of the Members are not required but may be held at such time and place as the Members deem necessary or desirable for the reasonable management of the Company. Meetings may be called by any Member or Members, holding 10% or more of the Percentage Interests, for the purpose of addressing any matters on which the Members may vote. A written notice setting forth the date, time, and location of a meeting must be sent at least ten (10) days but no more than sixty (60) days before the date of the meeting to each

Member entitled to vote at the meeting. A Member may waive notice of a meeting by sending a signed waiver to the Company's principal executive office or as otherwise provided in the California Revised Uniform Limited Liability Company Act. In any instance in which the approval of the Members is required under this Agreement, such approval may be obtained in any manner permitted by the California Revised Uniform Limited Liability Company Act, including by conference call or similar communications equipment. Any action that could be taken at a meeting may be approved by a consent in writing that describes the action to be taken and is signed by Members holding the minimum Voting Interest required to approve the action. If any action is taken without a meeting and without unanimous written consent of the Members, notice of such action must be sent to each Member that did not consent to the action.

ARTICLE 7: WITHDRAWAL AND TRANSFERS OF MEMBERSHIP INTERESTS

7.1 **Withdrawal.** Members may withdraw from the Company prior to the dissolution and winding up of the Company (a) by transferring or assigning all of their respective Membership Interests pursuant to Section 7.2 below, or (b) if all of the Members unanimously agree in a written consent. Subject to the provisions of Article 3, a Member that withdraws pursuant to this Section 7.1 will be entitled to a distribution from the Company in an amount equal to such Member's Capital Account, which must be paid by the Company to such Member within ninety (90) days of the withdrawal date unless otherwise agreed in writing.

7.2 **Restrictions on Transfer; Admission of Transferee.** A Member may transfer Membership Interests to any other Person without the consent of any other Member. A person may acquire Membership Interests directly from the Company upon the written consent of all Members. A Person that acquires Membership Interests in accordance with this Section 7.2 will be admitted as a Member of the Company only after the requirements of Section 2.3(b) are complied with in full.

ARTICLE 8: DISSOLUTION

8.1 **Dissolution.** The Company will be dissolved upon the first to occur of the following events:

(i) The vote of the Members holding at least a majority of the Voting Interest of the Company to dissolve the Company;

9.2 **Mandatory.** The Company must defend, indemnify and hold harmless a Company Agent in connection with a Proceeding in which such Company Agent is involved if, and to the extent, California law requires that a limited liability company indemnify a Company Agent in connection with a Proceeding.

9.3 **Expenses Paid by the Company Prior to Final Disposition**. Expenses of each Company Agent indemnified or held harmless under this Agreement that are actually and reasonably incurred in connection with the defense or settlement of a Proceeding may be paid by the Company in advance of the final disposition of a Proceeding if authorized by a vote of the Members that are not seeking indemnification holding a majority of the Voting Interests (excluding the Voting Interest of the Company Agent seeking indemnification) or a majority of the Managers that are not seeking indemnification, as the case may be. Before the Company makes any such payment of Expenses, the Company Agent seeking indemnification must deliver a written undertaking to the Company stating that such Company Agent will repay the applicable Expenses to the Company unless it is ultimately determined that the Company Agent is entitled or required to be indemnified and held harmless by the Company (as set forth in Sections 9.1 or 9.2 above or as otherwise required by applicable law).

ARTICLE 10: GENERAL PROVISIONS

10.1 **Notice**. (a) Any notices (including requests, demands, or other communications) to be sent by one party to another party in connection with this Agreement must be in writing and delivered personally, by reputable overnight courier, or by certified mail (or equivalent service offered by the postal service from time to time) to the following addresses or as otherwise notified in accordance with this Section: (i) if to the Company, notices must be sent to the Company's principal executive office; and (ii) if to a Member, notices must be sent to the Member's last known address for notice on record. (b) Any party to this Agreement may change its notice address by sending written notice of such change to the Company in the manner specified above. Notice will be deemed to have been duly given as follows: (i) upon delivery, if delivered personally or by reputable overnight carrier or (ii) five days after the date of posting if sent by certified mail.

10.2 **Entire Agreement; Amendment**. This Agreement along with the Articles of Organization (together, the "Organizational Documents"), constitute the entire agreement among the Members and replace and supersede all prior written and oral understandings and agreements with respect to the subject matter of this Agreement, except as otherwise required by the California Revised Uniform Limited Liability

9.2 **Mandatory.** The Company must defend, indemnify and hold harmless a Company Agent in connection with a Proceeding in which such Company Agent is involved if, and to the extent, California law requires that a limited liability company indemnify a Company Agent in connection with a Proceeding.

9.3 **Expenses Paid by the Company Prior to Final Disposition.** Expenses of each Company Agent indemnified or held harmless under this Agreement that are actually and reasonably incurred in connection with the defense or settlement of a Proceeding may be paid by the Company in advance of the final disposition of a Proceeding if authorized by a vote of the Members that are not seeking indemnification holding a majority of the Voting Interests (excluding the Voting Interest of the Company Agent seeking indemnification) or a majority of the Managers that are not seeking indemnification, as the case may be. Before the Company makes any such payment of Expenses, the Company Agent seeking indemnification must deliver a written undertaking to the Company stating that such Company Agent will repay the applicable Expenses to the Company unless it is ultimately determined that the Company Agent is entitled or required to be indemnified and held harmless by the Company (as set forth in Sections 9.1 or 9.2 above or as otherwise required by applicable law).

ARTICLE 10: GENERAL PROVISIONS

10.1 **Notice.** (a) Any notices (including requests, demands, or other communications) to be sent by one party to another party in connection with this Agreement must be in writing and delivered personally, by reputable overnight courier, or by certified mail (or equivalent service offered by the postal service from time to time) to the following addresses or as otherwise notified in accordance with this Section: (i) if to the Company, notices must be sent to the Company's principal executive office; and (ii) if to a Member, notices must be sent to the Member's last known address for notice on record. (b) Any party to this Agreement may change its notice address by sending written notice of such change to the Company in the manner specified above. Notice will be deemed to have been duly given as follows: (i) upon delivery, if delivered personally or by reputable overnight carrier or (ii) five days after the date of posting if sent by certified mail.

10.2 **Entire Agreement; Amendment.** This Agreement along with the Articles of Organization (together, the "Organizational Documents"), constitute the entire agreement among the Members and replace and supersede all prior written and oral understandings and agreements with respect to the subject matter of this Agreement, except as otherwise required by the California Revised Uniform Limited Liability

Company Act. There are no representations, agreements, arrangements, or undertakings, oral or written, between or among the Members relating to the subject matter of this Agreement that are not fully expressed in the Organizational Documents. This Agreement may not be modified or amended in any respect, except in a writing signed by all of the Members, except as otherwise required or permitted by the California Revised Uniform Limited Liability Company Act.

10.3 **Governing Law; Severability**. This Agreement will be construed and enforced in accordance with the laws of the state of California. If any provision of this Agreement is held to be unenforceable by a court of competent jurisdiction for any reason whatsoever, (i) the validity, legality, and enforceability of the remaining provisions of this Agreement (including without limitation, all portions of any provisions containing any such unenforceable provision that are not themselves unenforceable) will not in any way be affected or impaired thereby, and (ii) to the fullest extent possible, the unenforceable provision will be deemed modified and replaced by a provision that approximates the intent and economic effect of the unenforceable provision and the Agreement will be deemed amended accordingly.

10.4 **Further Action**. Each Member agrees to perform all further acts and execute, acknowledge, and deliver any documents which may be reasonably necessary, appropriate, or desirable to carry out the provisions of this Agreement.

10.5 **No Third Party Beneficiary**. This Agreement is made solely for the benefit of the parties to this Agreement and their respective permitted successors and assigns, and no other Person or entity will have or acquire any right by virtue of this Agreement. This Agreement will be binding on and inure to the benefit of the parties and their heirs, personal representatives, and permitted successors and assigns.

10.6 **Incorporation by Reference**. The recitals and each appendix, exhibit, schedule, and other document attached to or referred to in this Agreement are hereby incorporated into this Agreement by reference.

10.7 **Counterparts**. This Agreement may be executed in any number of counterparts with the same effect as if all of the Members signed the same copy. All counterparts will be construed together and will constitute one agreement.

[Remainder Intentionally Left Blank.]

IN WITNESS WHEREOF, the parties have executed or caused to be executed this Operating Agreement and do each hereby represent and warrant that their respective signatory, whose signature appears below, has been and is, on the date of this Agreement, duly authorized to execute this Agreement.

Dated: 12/04/2017

Signature of Consorcio Integrador Sonora 80M S.A. de C.V.

EXHIBIT A
MEMBERS

The Members of the Company and their respective addresses, Capital Contributions, and Ownership Interests are set forth below. The Members agree to keep this Exhibit A current and updated in accordance with the terms of this Agreement, including, but not limited to, Sections 2.1, 2.3, 2.4, 7.1, 7.2, and 10.1.

Members	Capital Contribution	Percentage Interest
Consorcio Integrador Sonora 80M S.A. de C.V. Address: Calle Montecito 38, Piso 28, Oficina 12-13 Colonia Naples, Delegación Benito Juarez 03810 Cuidad de Mexico, Mexico		100%

EXHIBIT B
MANAGERS

Manager(s) of the Company are set forth below.

Exhibit
13

NUMBER

[illegible]

[illegible]

Consorcio Integrador Sonora 80M US, LLC

MEMBERSHIP CERTIFICATE

This Certifies that CONSORCIO INTEGRADOR SONORA 80M S.A. DE C.V. *is the registered holder of* 100% *Membership Interest(s) of the above named Company, transferable only on the books of the Company by the holder hereof in person or by Attorney upon surrender of this Certificate properly endorsed and in accordance with the terms and conditions of the Articles of Organization and the Operating Agreement of the Company, as amended to the date of transfer, copies of which may be inspected and copied during normal business hours at the principal office of the Company.*

In Witness Whereof, *the said Company has caused this Certificate to be signed by its duly authorized Manager(s) or Officer(s) and its Seal to be hereunto affixed*

this 4 *day* *of* DECEMBER *A.D.* 2017

Exhibit 14

wework

MEMBERSHIP AGREEMENT

HI ████ MARTIN

Please review your Membership Details below.

If you have any questions or concerns, please don't hesitate to reach out to us at santamonica@wework.com

PRIMARY MEMBER INFORMATION

Consorcio Integrador Sonora 80M US, LLC

Primary member: ████ Martin
████martin@sonora80m.com
4242388249

JOINING

WeWork Santa Monica

3064G · 1 person desk — $600.00/mo
Start date: December 1, 2017
Commitment term: 6 months

Additional Fees

Setup Fee — $0.00

INCLUDED CREDIT ALLOTMENTS

Conference room credits
5 total credits per month starting on December 1, 2017.

Print credits
120 total black & white prints and 20 total color prints per month starting on December 1, 2017.

SERVICE RETAINER SUMMARY

Service retainer fees for WeWork Santa Monica — $1,500.00
2.5x monthly membership fee

Your service retainer balance will be charged with any other additional fees.

TERMS & CONDITIONS

By electronically signing the(se) membership agreement(s) below, your company is entering into legally binding agreement(s). Please download and read carefully prior to signing. Any Agreement(s), including the(se) Terms and Conditions and Membership Details form(s), and any applicable Service Package Addendum(s), will be effective when signed by both parties. In the event of any conflict between the(se) Terms and Conditions and the Membership Details form(s), the Membership Details form(s) shall prevail.

When signing this (these) Agreement(s) you must have the proper authority to execute this (these) Agreement(s) on behalf of the company listed above and incur the obligations described in this (these) Agreement(s) on behalf of such company.

Please be advised that if there are multiple links to separate Membership Agreements displayed below, then by signing you are entering into multiple agreements with the separate WeWork building entities indicated in the linked agreements.

☑ I agree to the(se) Terms & Conditions, Payment Authorization Terms, Membership Details Terms, and any applicable Service Package Addendum in this (these) Membership Agreement(s). I additionally agree that in the event I have any pre-existing Membership Agreement(s) the terms of such Agreement(s) which are not revised, amended or terminated herein remain unchanged.

Community Manager's signature	Electronic Signature
Shelby Hoefling	[redacted]
WW 520 Broadway LLC	Consorcio Integrador Sonora 80M US, LLC
	Signed on November 7, 2017

WeWork
WW 520 Broadway LLC
520 Broadway, Suite 200

(424) 228-8836

Exhibit 15

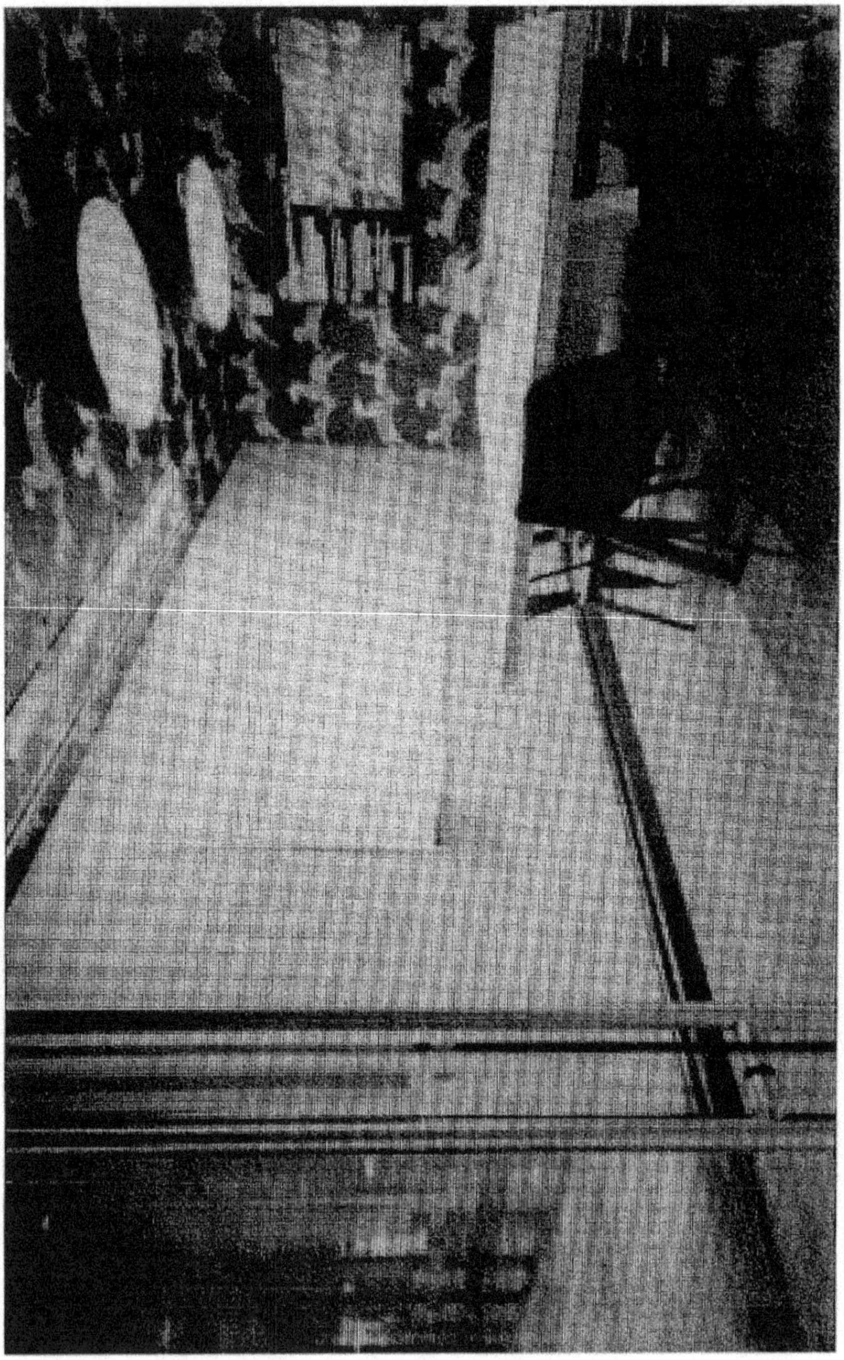

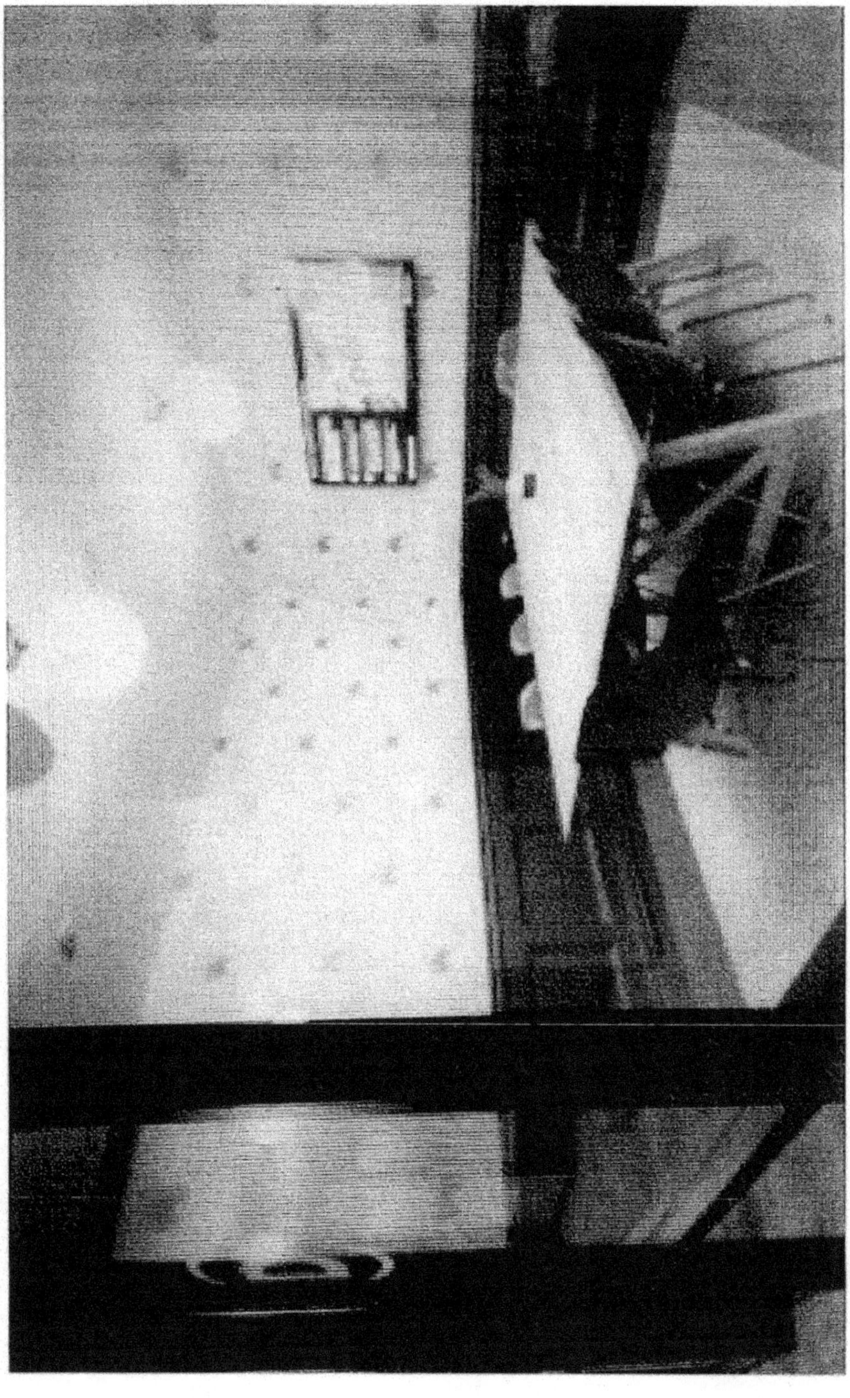

PAGE 215

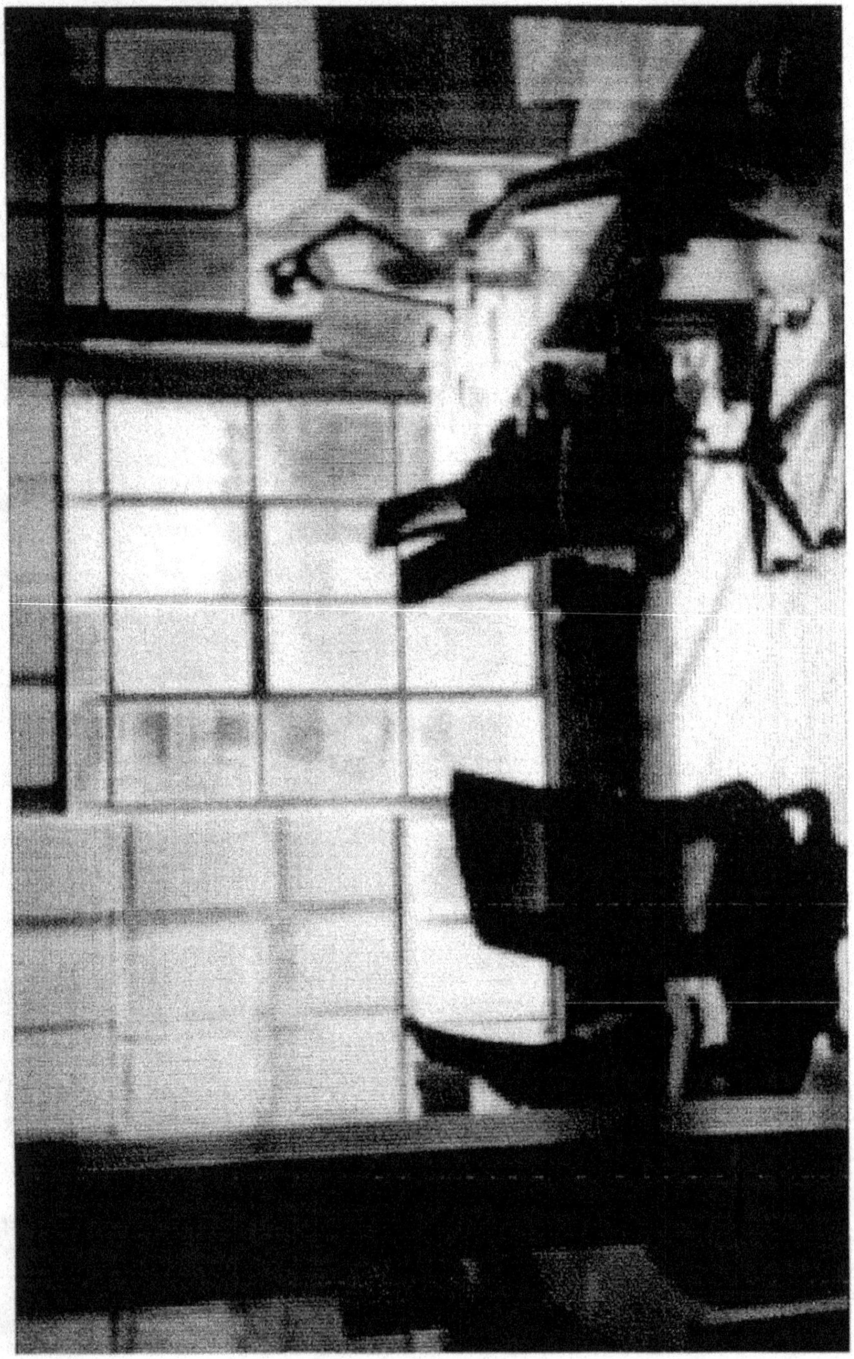

Exhibit 16

Corporate Organization Chart Consorcio Integrador Sonora 80M US, LLC

1. **CEO:**Mtro. Ing. ███ Martin Rodriguez
The CEO will get di███eports from 2. and 3.

2. Director of Technical Management and Sales:
Doc. Aida Huerta

2.1.1. Operations Manager (still vacant)

2.1.1.1. Facilities Coordinator (still vacant)

- **Four Solar panel installation and maintenance and Technicians** (still vacants)

2.1.2. Sales Manager (still vacant)

- **One sales executive** (still vacant)
- **One client service executive** (still vacant)
- **Two Consultants in international energy markets** (still vacants)

3. Director of Financial, Human Resources and Outsourcing companies:
Ing. Javier Rodriguez

3.1.1. Financial and Fiscal Manager (still vacant)

Exhibit 18

ESP
XDC571657 Y
18 08 2018
ESPAÑA
PASAPORTE
PASSPORT
REINO DE ESPAÑA
XDC571657
31 03 1976
18 08 2018
C.G.MEXICO
819341
P<ESPMARTIN<RODRIGUEZ<<CESAR<<<<<<<<<<<<<<<<
XDC5716573ESP7603318M1808188RE20150148332422

INSCRIPCIÓN COMO RESIDENTE
ARTÍCULO 23 DEL TRATADO DE FUNCIONAMIENTO DE LA UNIÓN EUROPEA
http://ec.europa.eu/consularprotection

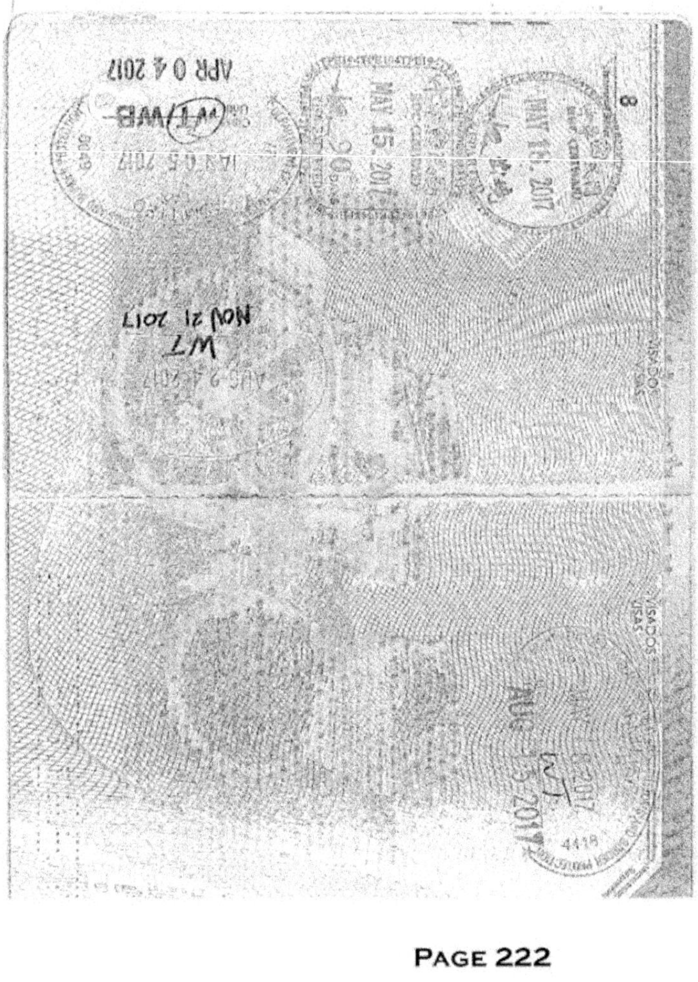
APR 0 4 2017
WT/WB
MAY 15 2017
WT
Nov 21 2017
VISADOS
VISAS

Exhibit 19

U.S. Customs and Border Protection
Securing America's Borders

Most Recent I-94

Admission (I-94) Record Number : 73068952085
Most Recent Date of Entry: 2017 November 23
Class of Admission : WT
Admit Until Date : 02/20/2018
Details provided on the I-94 Information form:

Last/Surname :	[redacted]
First (Given) Name :	[redacted]
Birth Date :	1976 March 31
Passport Number :	XDC571657
Country of Issuance :	Spain

Get Travel History

- Effective April 26, 2013, DHS began automating the admission process. An alien lawfully admitted or paroled into the U.S. is no longer required to be in possession of a preprinted Form I-94. A record of admission printed from the CBP website constitutes a lawful record of admission. See 8 CFR § 1.4(d).
- If an employer, local, state or federal agency requests admission information, present your admission (I-94) number along with any additional required documents requested by that employer or agency.
- Note: For security reasons, we recommend that you close your browser after you have finished retrieving your I-94 number.

For inquiries or questions regarding your I-94, please click here

Accessibility | Privacy Policy

	Date	Type	Location
1	2017-12-07	Arrival	OTM
2	2017-11-23	Arrival	OTM
3	2017-11-08	Arrival	OTM
4	2017-11-02	Arrival	SND
5	2017-10-19	Arrival	OTM
6	2017-10-05	Arrival	OTM
7	2017-09-20	Arrival	OTM
8	2017-09-06	Arrival	OTM
9	2017-08-24	Arrival	OTM
10	2017-08-10	Arrival	OTM
11	2017-07-25	Arrival	SYS
12	2017-07-05	Arrival	OTM
13	2017-06-20	Arrival	OTM
14	2017-05-31	Arrival	OTM
15	2017-05-20	Arrival	OTM
16	2017-05-18	Departure	Unavailable
17	2017-05-18	Arrival	SFR
18	2017-05-14	Departure	Unavailable
19	2017-05-14	Arrival	Unavailable

	Date	Type	Location
21	2017-04-13	Arrival	Unavailable.
22	2017-04-13	Arrival	Unavailable
23	2017-03-31	Arrival	Unavailable
24	2017-03-17	Arrival	Unavailable
25	2017-03-01	Arrival	Unavailable
26	2017-02-17	Arrival	OTM
27	2017-02-03	Arrival	OTM
28	2017-01-19	Arrival	OTM
29	2017-01-05	Arrival	LOS
30	2016-12-23	Departure	LOS
31	2016-12-21	Arrival	OTM
32	2016-11-24	Arrival	OTM
33	2016-10-26	Arrival	OTM
34	2016-10-13	Arrival	OTM
35	2016-10-05	Arrival	OTM
36	2016-09-28	Arrival	Unavailable
37	2016-09-22	Arrival	Unavailable
38	2016-09-14	Arrival	Unavailable.
39	2016-09-06	Arrival	Unavailable
40	2016-08-31	Arrival	Unavailable

	Date	Type	Location
41	2016-08-23	Arrival	Unavailable
42	2016-08-09	Arrival	OTM
43	2016-08-02	Arrival	Unavailable.
44	2016-08-02	Arrival	Unavailable
45	2016-07-19	Arrival	Unavailable
46	2016-07-06	Arrival	Unavailable
47	2016-06-29	Arrival	Unavailable
48	2016-06-21	Arrival	Unavailable
49	2016-06-15	Arrival	Unavailable
50	2016-06-08	Arrival	Unavailable
51	2016-06-01	Arrival	OTM
52	2016-05-26	Arrival	OTM
53	2016-05-19	Arrival	OTM
54	2016-05-12	Arrival	SYS
55	2016-05-04	Arrival	OTM
56	2016-04-27	Arrival	OTM
57	2016-04-20	Arrival	OTM
58	2016-04-07	Arrival	Unavailable
59	2016-03-30	Departure	Unavailable
60	2016-03-30	Arrival	Unavailable

	Date	Type	Location
61	2016-03-30	Arrival	OTM
62	2016-03-23	Arrival	SYS
63	2016-01-07	Arrival	LOS
64	2015-11-09	Departure	NYC
65	2015-11-06	Arrival	NYC
66	2015-09-16	Departure	LOS
67	2015-09-13	Arrival	LOS
68	2015-06-16	Departure	LOS
69	2015-06-13	Arrival	LOS
70	2015-04-04	Departure	DEN
71	2015-04-01	Arrival	DEN
72	2014-08-01	Arrival	HOU
73	2014-03-27	Departure	NYC
74	2014-03-24	Arrival	NYC
75	2013-12-26	Departure	DEN
76	2013-12-23	Arrival	HOU
77	2013-08-01	Departure	Unavailable
78	2013-08-01	Arrival	NOG
79	2013-05-12	Arrival	NOG
80	2013-03-02	Departure	LOS

	Date	Type	Location
81	2013-02-28	Arrival	LOS

Exhibit 20

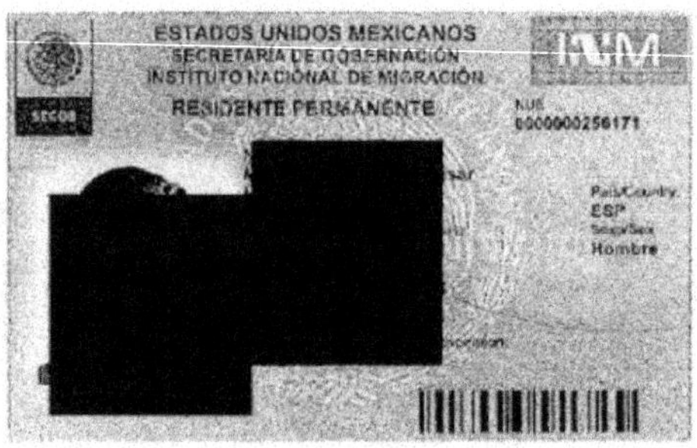
ESTADOS UNIDOS MEXICANOS
SECRETARÍA DE GOBERNACIÓN
INSTITUTO NACIONAL DE MIGRACIÓN
RESIDENTE PERMANENTE
NUE
0000000256171
País/Country
ESP
Sexo/Sex
Hombre

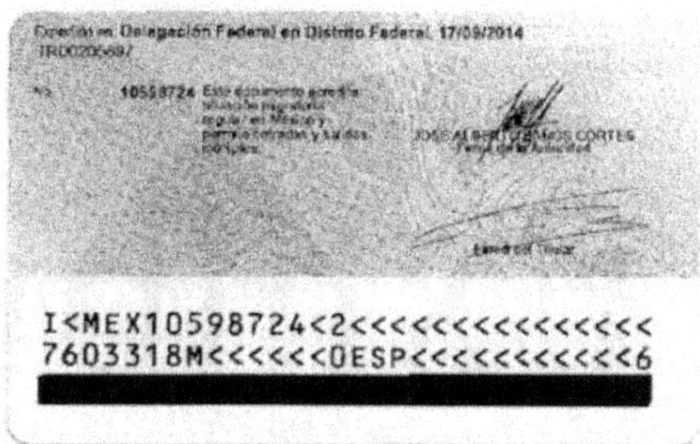
Delegación Federal en Distrito Federal. 17/09/2014
I<MEX10598724<2<<<<<<<<<<<<<<<
7603318M<<<<<<0ESP<<<<<<<<<<<6

Exhibit 21

CEO

Personal Information

Bithdate: March 31st, 1976

Borned in Madrid (Spain)

Phone number: +52 5536888088

E-mail: cesar.martin@sonora80m.com

Partner number of the COITT: 6439

Professional Experience

General Communications Secretary of Spain. SGC
Laboratory Technician

- From January 1st, 1999 to December 31st, 1999
- Functions: Analysis of radiant systems, communication equipments and power supplies, within the electromagnetic compatibility department of the SGC laboratory.

ALCATEL Spain (Central Quality Laboratory)
Analyst of Electromagnetic Compatibility

- From January 1st, 2000 to May 15th, 2000
- Functions: Evaluation and verification, according to national and international emission and electromagnetic immunity regulations, of telecommunications systems manufactured by Alcatel International.

Sociedad Española de Montajes Industriales SEMI S.A. – MAESSA of the ACS-DRAGADOS GROUP
Telecommunications Engineer

- From May 16th, 2000 to March 1st, 2004
- Functions:
    - Technical manager of OPGW fiber optic networks, auto-supported, channelized, in tunnels and special networks

MEXSEMI S.A. de C.V.

(Mexican Subsidiary of the Sociedad Española de Montajes Industriales SEMI S.A. – MAESSA of the ACS-DRAGADOS GROUP)

Project Manager of the Telecommunications Department

- From March 2th, 2004 to December 31st, 2006
- Functions:
    - General coordination of mobile phone networks
    - Technical direction of the radio communication facilities department

CEO of Mexico and Centroamérica

- From January 1st, 2007 to November 11th, 2009
- Functions:
    - Technical and administrative management of the subsidiary company, in the 5 different business areas of the main company (Communications, Electricity, Railways, Industrial and Petrochemical Installations)

CORPORATIVO CIE

CEO and Shareholder

- From November 12th, 2009 until today
- Functions:
    - Technical, administrative and strategic management of the corporation
- Group Companies:
    - Consultoria de Comercio Internacional de España S.A. de C.V. (Telecommunications)
    - Ultimate Orbis Telecomm S.A. de C.V. (OMV)
    - Proyectos Estratégicos Alce S.A. de C.V. (Energy Projects)
    - Profot del Noroeste S.A. de C.V. (Solar Projects)
    - Nitido Records S.A. de C.V. (Discography)
    - CABA Sport Club S.A. de C.V. (Sports Promotion)
    - Bodega Martin Yáñez (Wine Production)

CONSORCIO INTEGRADOR SONORA 80M S.A. de C.V.

CEO and Shareholder

- From April 1st, 2010 until today
- Functions:
    - CEO and Director of Strategic, Financial and Legal areas of the company of promotion, engineering, construction, commissioning and maintenance of the 80MW photovoltaic project in the state of Sonora, Mexico

Calle Montecito 38, piso 28, oficina 13. Colonia Nápoles. Delegación Benito Juárez.
CP. 03810, México D.F. Tel: + 52 5511070486
www.sonora80m.com

University Education

Polytechnic University of Madrid. EUITT
Telecommunication Engineer,
Telecommunications Systems Specialist

- Date of graduation: July 1999
- Graduated with Honor Matriculation

University Institute of Postgraduate, next to the Universities: Carlos III of Madrid, Autonomous University of Barcelona, Autonomous University of Alicante
MBA in Business Administration

- Date of graduation: December 2008
- Graduated with Outstanding

International Iberoamerican University
Doctorate in Projects

- Start date: November 2016

Additional Experience

- Speaker of the COITT Telecommunications College
- Technical Adviser for different governments and official organizations of Latin America
- Technical Advisor for the Secretary of Communications and Transportation in Mexico (SCT)
- Associate of the National Institute of Public Administration (INAP) of México

Calle Montecito 38, piso 28, oficina 13. Colonia Nápoles. Delegación Benito Juárez.
CP. 03810, México D.F. Tel: + 52 5511070486
www.sonora80m.com

SECTION 4
Business Plan

Consorcio Integrador Sonora 80M US, LLC
Business Plan
An International Solar Farms Development and Consulting Company

Written By: [redacted]

Table of Contents

Business Overview

Solar panel is rapidly gaining huge market acceptance all over the globe simply because of how effective and useful it has become to most people. Solar panel is simply a device that helps convert sunlight into electrical energy and stores it for use. There are loads of areas where you can use solar energy and that is the reason why a lot of inventions that is being powered by solar panel (energy) keep propping up.

You can use solar energy to power automobile, solar energy to power street lights; you can use solar energy to power your house (all of your electronics and electrical appliances inclusive), you can use solar energy to virtually power device that requires electrical energy to function et al. Using a solar farm is a cheaper option for people since they don't have to pay for the cost of installation of the panels, and the regular cost of maintenance for the panel, they just have to pay the annual fee to the solar farm company and enjoy electricity throughout the year. This is also a very much cheaper option than using electricity from power companies.

Basically, a solar farm is a large land area where multiple ground-mount solar tracking towers are installed. Usually it can be on a working farm or other open and mostly unimproved land. The Solar Farm Developers industry is made up of companies that mainly install and construct solar power grid systems, which is known as solar farms, on a utility scale. The work executed within the industry include new work, reconstruction, rehabilitation and repairs et al.

Statistics has it that an estimated 85% of U.S. residents can neither own nor lease solar panel systems because their roofs are physically unsuitable for solar or because they live in multi-family housing. At least

52 projects are under development in at least 17 states, and at least 10 states encourage their development through policy and programs.

The Solar Farm Developers industry has galloped ahead in recent years as a result of the rapid technological developments in our world, falling solar panel costs and favorable government policy. Going forward, the demand for solar panel installation is projected to continue to experience rapid growth.

With the ongoing government aid in the form of tax credits and rebates, along with technological advances in solar energy, as well as the rising popularity of solar power purchase agreements (SPPAs), the revenue generated in the industry is expected to grow sharply.

Statistics has it that The Solar Farm Developers industry in the United States of America, is worth $10bn, with an estimated growth rate of 46.5 percent. There are about 80 registered and licensed solar farm developer businesses in the United States and they are responsible for employing about 9,027 people. First solar is the leading player in this industry; they have the largest market share.

Most people who have stake in the industry will quite agree that the solar farms industry has come to stay and of course it is one industry that plays key roles not only in the business world and in our homes simply because it is one eco – friendly way of generating power.

Over and above, The Solar Farm Developers industry is very open to any investor who have the required start – up capital acquired the required trainings, skills and perhaps professional certifications to start his or her own solar farm business.

Consorcio Integrador Sonora 80M US, LLC.

Executive Summary

Consorcio Integrador Sonora 80M US, LLC is a U.S based and standard solar farm company. We have been able to secure a standard and well-positioned vast acres of land in the outskirt of California.

We are a solar farm group that is also into the solar panel installation, maintenance and consulting that is set to compete in the highly competitive.

The Solar Farm Developers industry not only in California, but also throughout the United States market.

Consorcio Integrador Sonora 80M US, LLC will offer services such as Thin-film solar power plant construction and CSP power plant construction and other related solar panel installation, maintenance and consulting services.

Our business goal is to become one of the leading solar farms America and we will make sure that we do all we can to compete favorably with leaders in the industry including companies that are into the production of eco-friendly energy.

Our team are going to be selected from a pool of certified and highly experienced solar panel / solar energy repair engineers and technicians in and around California and also from any part of the United States of America as the business grows.

We will make sure that we take all the members of our workforce through the required trainings that will position them to meet the expectation of the company and to compete with leading solar farms and solar panel installation and maintenance companies in the United States and throughout the globe.

At Consorcio Integrador Sonora 80M US, LLC, our client's best interest will always come first, and everything we do will be guided by our values and professional ethics. We will ensure that we hold ourselves accountable to the highest standards by meeting our client's needs precisely and completely. We will cultivate a working environment that provides a human, sustainable approach to earning a living, and living in our world, for all our partners, employees and for our clients.

Consorcio Integrador Sonora 80M US, LLC is founded by our CEO and Director of Strategic, Financial and Legal areas of the company of promotion, engineering, construction, commissioning and maintenance of the 80MW photovoltaic project in the state of Sonora, Mexico, Telecommunication Engineer, MBA in Business Administration, and actually studying the Doctorate in Projects, Mr. [redacted]

He combines the experience that can help build Consorcio Integrador Sonora 80M US, LLC to favorably compete with other leading solar farms in the United States of America.

Our Services

Consorcio Integrador Sonora 80M US, LLC was established with the aim of maximizing profits in The Solar Farm Developers industry.

We want to compete favorably with the leading solar farms and of course solar panel installation and maintenance companies in the United States which is why we have but in place a competent quality assurance team. We will work hard to ensure that Consorcio Integrador Sonora 80M US, LLC will not just accepted in California but also in other cities in the United States of America. Our products and services are listed below;

- Supply of solar energy
- Development of solar energy farms
- Engineering, procurement, construction, and financing of solar energy farms.
- Assert American companies that want to enter in the Latino America´s solar market, without the experience or the local knowledge

Our Vision Statement

Our vision is to establish a standard and world class solar farm and solar panel installation, maintenance and consulting company whose services and brand will not only be accepted in California but also in other cities in the United States of America.

Our Mission Statement

Our mission is to provide solar energy and professional solar panel installation and maintenance services and other related services that will assist businesses, individuals, households and non-profit organizations in ensuring that their solar panels are always in good shape to produce the required power output.

We want to build a solar farm and solar panel installation, maintenance and consulting company that can favorably compete with other leading brands in The Solar Farm Developers industry.

Our Business Structure

Consorcio Integrador Sonora 80M US, LLC is a solar farm and solar panel installation, maintenance and consulting company that intend starting small in California, as subsidiary of the main company in Mexico, Consorcio Integrador Sonora 80M S.A. de C.V., but hope to grow big in order to compete favorably with leading solar energy companies and solar panel installation, maintenance and consulting companies in the industry both in the United States and on a global stage.

We are aware of the importance of building a solid business structure that can support the picture of the kind of world class business we want to own. This is why we are committed to only hire the best hands within our area of operations.

At Consorcio Integrador Sonora 80M US, LLC, we will ensure that we hire people that are qualified, hardworking, creative, customer centric and are ready to work to help us build a prosperous business that will benefit all the stake holders (the owners, workforce, and customers).

As a matter of fact, profit-sharing arrangement will be made available to all our senior management staff and it will be based on their performance for a period of five years or more as agreed by the board of trustees of the company. In view of the above, we have decided to hire qualified and competent hands to occupy the following positions;

* Head, technical services
* Human resources
* Sales executives
* Accountant
* Solar panel installation and maintenance technicians
* Client service executive

* Consultants in international energy markets

Roles and Responsibilities

Chief Executive Officer – CEO (1):

1. Increases management's effectiveness by recruiting, selecting, orienting, training, coaching, counseling, and disciplining managers; communicating values, strategies, and objectives; assigning accountabilities; planning, monitoring, and appraising job results; developing incentives; developing a climate for offering information and opinions; providing educational opportunities.

2. Responsible for providing direction for the business.

3. Creates, communicates, and implements the organization's vision, mission, and overall direction – i.e. leading the development and implementation of the overall organization's strategy.

4. Responsible for signing checks and documents on behalf of the company.

5. Evaluates the success of the organization.

Head, Technical Services (3):

1. Serves as project manager of the organization; works directly with employees.

2. Develops strategic plan by studying technological and financial opportunities; presenting assumptions; recommending objectives.

3. Accomplishes subsidiary objectives by establishing plans, budgets, and results measurements; allocating resources; reviewing progress; making mid-course corrections.

4. Coordinates efforts by establishing procurement, production, marketing, field, and technical services policies and practices; coordinating actions with corporate staff.

5. Builds company image by collaborating with customers, government, community organizations, and employees; enforcing ethical business practices.

6. Maintains quality service by establishing and enforcing organization standards.

7. Maintains professional and technical knowledge by attending educational workshops; reviewing professional publications; establishing personal networks; benchmarking state-of-the-art practices; participating in professional societies.

8. Makes certain that the technical department perform efficiently, coordinate employee efforts, and facilitate communications between management and solar panel installation, repairs and maintenance engineers and technicians.

9. Ensures that the organization work in line with international best practices.

Human Resources (1)

1. Responsible for overseeing the smooth running of HR and administrative tasks for the organization.

2. Defines job positions for recruitment and managing interviewing process.

3. Carries out staff induction for new team members.

4. Responsible for training, evaluation and assessment of employees.

5. Responsible for arranging travel, meetings and appointments.

6. Oversees the smooth running of the daily office and factory activities.

Sales Executives (2)

1. Manages external research and coordinate all the internal sources of information to retain the organizations' best customers and attract new ones.

2. Models demographic information and analyze the volumes of transactional data generated by customer.

3. Identifies development opportunities; follows up on development leads and contacts; participates in the structuring and financing of projects; assures the completion of development projects.

4. Writes winning proposal documents, negotiate fees and rates

in line with organizations' policy.

5. Responsible for handling business research, market surveys and feasibility studies for clients.

6. Responsible for supervising implementation, advocate for the customer's needs, and communicate with clients.

7. Develops, executes and evaluates new plans for expanding increase sales.

8. Creates new markets cum businesses for the organization.

Accountant (1)

1. Responsible for preparing financial reports, budgets, and financial statements for the organization.

2. Provides managements with financial analyses, development budgets, and accounting reports; analyzes financial feasibility for the most complex proposed projects; conducts market research to forecast trends and business conditions.

3. Responsible for financial forecasting and risks analysis.

4. Performs cash management, general ledger accounting, and financial reporting for one or more properties.

5. Responsible for developing and managing financial systems and policies.

6. Responsible for administering payrolls.

7. Ensures compliance with taxation legislation.

8. Handles all financial transactions for Consorcio Integrador Sonora 80M US, LLC.

9. Serves as internal auditor for Clean Energy Technologies®, LLC.

Solar Panel Installation and Maintenance and Technicians (4)

1. Works with the team in projects such as crystalline silicon solar power plants construction, CSP trough power plants construction, CSP tower power plants, thin-film solar power plant construction, CSP power plant construction

2. Handles solar panel and accessories sales and supply for the organization, roof mounted panel installation, solar tracking panel installation, ground mounted panel installation, fixed rack panel installation, and monitoring services.

3. Handles other related solar panel installation and maintenance services.

Client Service Executive (1)

1. Welcomes clients and potential clients by greeting them in person or on the telephone; answering or directing inquiries.

2. Ensures that all contacts with clients (e-mail, walk-in center, SMS or phone) provides the client with a personalized customer service experience of the highest level.

3. Through interaction with clients on the phone, uses every

opportunity to build client's interest in the company's products and services.

4. Manages administrative duties assigned by the creative director in an effective and timely manner.

5. Consistently stays abreast of any new information on the organizations' products, promotional campaigns etc. to ensure accurate and helpful information is supplied to clients when they make enquiries.

Consultants in International Energy Markets (2)

1. Identification of business opportunities in multilateral institutions and public and private clients in Latino América.

2. Preparation of expressions of interest for business opportunities in multilateral institutions and public and private clients in Latino América.

3. Partial drafting of specialized technical content services for business opportunities in multilateral institutions and public and private clients in Latino América.

4. Identification and selection of solar power experts for international technical assistance projects.

5. Administrative, logistical and technical tasks for the implementation of international technical assistance solar projects

SWOT Analysis

Consorcio Integrador Sonora 80M US, LLC engaged the services of a core professional in the area of business consulting and structuring to assist our organization in building a well-structured solar farm and solar panel installation, maintenance and repair business that can favorably compete in the highly competitive Solar Farm Developers industry in the United States and the world at large.

Part of what the team of business consultant did was to work with the management of our organization in conducting a comprehensive SWOT analysis for Consorcio Integrador Sonora 80M US, LLC.

Strength

Our core strength lies in the power of our team; our workforce. We have a team highly trained and experience solar panel installation, maintenance and repair engineers and technicians, a team with excellent qualifications and experience in various niche areas in The Solar Farm Developers industry in America. Aside from the synergy that exists in our carefully selected workforce, our services will be guided by best practices in the industry.

Weakness

As a new solar farm and solar panel installation, maintenance and consulting company in California, it might take some time for our organization to break into the market and gain acceptance especially from top profile clients in the already saturated and highly competitive Solar Farm Developers industry; that is perhaps our major weakness. Another weakness is that we may not have the required cash to pump into promoting our business the way we would want to.

Opportunities

No doubt, the opportunities in the Solar Farm Developers industry is massive considering the support from the government and of course the number of individuals and corporate organizations who are now switching over to alternative energy such as solar energy. As a solar farm cum solar panel installation, maintenance and consulting company, we are ready to take advantage of any opportunity that is available in the industry.

Threat

Just like any other business, one of the major threats that we are likely going to face is economic downturn. It is a fact that economic downturn affects purchasing / spending power. Another threat that may likely confront us is the arrival of a new solar farm or solar panel installation, maintenance and consulting company in same location where our target market exist and who may want to adopt same business model like us.

Market Analysis

Market Trends

If you are keeping tabs of happenings in the Solar Farm Developers industry, you will agree that the demand for construction of utility-scale solar power projects has skyrocketed many thanks to substantial government support. So also, technological advancements in solar panel construction will definitely lead to a greater supply of low-cost panels, making solar panels more accessible for individual consumers, also lowering demand.

Another trend is that, The Solar Farm Developers industry has galloped ahead in recent years as a result of the rapid technological developments in our world, falling solar panel costs and favorable government policy. In the coming years, demand for solar panel installation is projected to continue growing.

Ongoing government aid in the form of tax credits and rebates, along with technological advances in solar energy, as well as the rising popularity of solar power purchase agreements (SPPAs), are expected to help revenue grow sharply going forward.

The demand for new solar farms has been backed primarily by government incentives, such as the Solar Investment Tax Credit (ITC), which encouraged private investment into solar technologies by offering tax credits. With these incentives, solar farms and other solar-power development projects have been built at accelerating rates over the past five years. Because solar technology is not yet cost-competitive with other types of energy used in electricity generation, such as coal and natural gas, government incentives have been the driving force behind industry growth.

Our Target Market

Before starting our solar farms cum solar panel installation, maintenance and consulting business in California, we conducted a market survey and feasibility studies and we are certain that there is a wide range of both corporate and individual clients who cannot successfully run their businesses without the services of solar panel installation, maintenance and repair companies.

In view of that, we have created strategies that will enable us reach out to various corporate organizations and households who we know can't afford to do without our services. Below is a list of the people and organizations that we have specifically market our products and services to;

- Banks, Insurance Companies and other related Financial Institutions
- Manufacturers and Distributors
- The Government (Public works department)
- Schools (High Schools, Colleges and Universities)
- Hotels
- Sport Facilities
- Television Stations

Our Competitive Advantage

Surviving in the business world as a solar farm cum solar panel installation, maintenance and consulting company requires more than, your expertise, knowing how to deliver standard repairs and maintenance jobs but also how to network with key people that matters; decision makers that can decide who will get a solar energy, solar panel supply, installation, repair and maintenance contract.

Without a shadow of doubt, there are loads of big time investors (Solar Panel Manufacturing Companies), that have a stake in The Solar Farm Developers industry; but one thing is certain, there is room big enough to accommodate the big solar panel installation, maintenance and consulting companies and the small solar panel installation, maintenance and consulting companies.

What smaller solar pan\el installation, maintenance and consulting companies need to do to survive in the industry is to concentrate on providing solar panel sales, maintenance and installation services to households, individuals, estates, communities, schools, hospitals and hotels et al before bidding for big solar panel supply, installation, and maintenance contracts from large corporations and government agencies (Public Works Department).

We are quite aware that to be highly competitive in the Solar Farm Developers industry / the solar panel installation and maintenance services industry means that you are not only expected to be able to deliver consistent and highly reliable solar panel supply, installation and maintenance jobs, but you must be able to meet set targets. No one would want to continue to hire your services if don't always meet up with the target date of completion of projects.

Our competitive advantage lies in the power and the knowledge of the energy markets our team; our workforce.

Sales Strategy

We are mindful of the fact that there is stiffer competition in the Solar Farm Developers industry / the solar panel installation, maintenance and consulting services industry; hence we have been able to hire some of the best marketing experts to handle our sales and marketing.

Our sales team will be recruited based on their vast experience in the solar panel installation, maintenance and consulting services industry and they will be trained on a regular basis so as to be well equipped to meet their targets and the overall business goal of Consorcio Integrador Sonora 80M US, LLC.

Our corporate goal is to grow Consorcio Integrador Sonora 80M US, LLC to become one of the top 30 solar farms / solar panel installation, maintenance and consulting services brands in the United States of America which is why we have mapped out strategy that will help us take advantage of the available market and grow to become a major force to reckon with not only in California but also in other cities in the United States of America.

Consorcio Integrador Sonora 80M US, LLC is set to make use of the following marketing and sales strategies to attract clients;

1. Introduce our solar energy company cum solar panel installation, maintenance and consulting Company by sending introductory letters

2. Promptness in bidding for solar panel supply, installation and maintenance contract from other cooperate organizations

3. Advertise our business in relevant business publications.

4. Attend relevant international and local expos, seminars, and business fairs.

5. Leverage on the internet to promote our business

Sources of Income

Consorcio Integrador Sonora 80M US, LLC is established with the aim of maximizing profits in The Solar Farm Developers industry and we are going to go all the way to ensure that we do all it takes to meet and surpass the expectations of all our clients.

Consorcio Integrador Sonora 80M US, LLC will generate income by offering the following solar panel installation, maintenance and consulting related services;

- Supply of solar energy
- Crystalline silicon solar power plant construction
- Thin-film solar power plant construction
- CSP power plant construction
- Ground mounted panel installation
- Fixed rack panel installation
- Monitoring services
- Assert American companies that want to enter in the Latino America´s solar market
- Other related solar panel installation and maintenance

Sales Forecast

One thing is certain, there would always be corporate organization, government agencies, households and individual who would need the services of solar panel installations, maintenance and consulting companies.

We are well positioned to take on the available market in The Solar Farm Developers industry and we are quite optimistic that we will meet our set target of generating enough income / profits from the first 24/36 month s of operations and grow our solar energy cum solar panel installation, maintenance and consulting company to enviable heights.

We have been able to critically examine the solar energy cum solar panel installation, maintenance and consulting market and we have analyzed our chances in the industry and we have been able to come up with the following sales forecast. The sales projection is based on information gathered on the field and some assumptions that are peculiar to similar startups in California.

Below is the sales projection for Consorcio Integrador Sonora 80M US, LLC, it is based on the location of our business and of course the wide range of our services and target market;

First Year-: $500,000
Second Year-: $1.0M
Third Year-: $2.0M
Fourth Year-: $3.0M
Fifth Year-: $5.0M

(This projection is done based on what is obtainable in the industry and with the assumption that there won't be any major economic meltdown and there won't be any major competitor offering same solar energy and solar panel installation, maintenance and consulting services as we do within same location. Please note that the above projection might be lower and at the same time it might be higher)

Generating Funding / Startup Capital

Consorcio Integrador Sonora 80M US, LLC is a business that will be managed by one of the owners, Mr. [redacted] and owned by the main company Consorcio Integrador Sonora 80M S.A. de C.V. as a subsidiary company of the group.

They are the sole financial of the business which is why they decided to restrict the sourcing of the start – up capital for the business to just two major sources.

These are the areas we intend generating our start – up capital;

1. Generate part of the start – up capital from Consorcio Integrador Sonora 80M S.A. de C.V. savings and sale of his stocks

2. Generate part of the start – up capital from personal savings from the owners of the company

(We have been able to generate about $1,000,000 (Consorcio Integrador Sonora 80M S.A. de C.V. $750,000 and personal savings $250,000) and we are at the process stages of obtaining a loan facility of $2,5 Million from our bank in Mexico)

Business Growth: Sustainability and Expansion Strategy

The future of a business lies in the numbers of loyal customers that they have the capacity and competence of the employees, their investment strategy and the business structure. If all of these factors are missing from a business (company), then it won't be too long before the business close shop.

One of our major goals of starting Consorcio Integrador Sonora 80M US, LLC is to build a business that will survive off its own cash flow without the need for injecting finance from external sources once the business is officially running. We know that one of the ways of gaining approval and winning customers over is to offer our solar panel installation, maintenance and consulting services a little bit cheaper than what is obtainable in the market and we are well prepared to survive on lower profit margin for a while.

Consorcio Integrador Sonora 80M US, LLC will make sure that the right foundation, structures and processes are put in place to ensure that our staff welfare are well taken of. Our company's corporate culture is designed to drive our business to greater heights and training and re-training of our workforce is at the top burner.

Check List / Milestone

1. Business Name Availability Check: **Completed**
2. Business Incorporation: **Completed**
3. Opening of Corporate Bank Accounts various banks in the United States: **In Progress**
4. Application and Obtaining Tax Payer's ID: **In Progress**
5. Application for business license and permit: **In Progress**
6. Purchase of All form of Insurance for the Business: **In Progress**
7. Conducting Feasibility Studies: **Completed**
8. Generating part of the start – up capital from the founders: **Completed**
9. Writing of Business Plan: **Completed**
10. Drafting of Employee's Handbook: **In Progress**
11. Drafting of Contract Documents: **In Progress**
12. Design of Logo for the business: **Completed**
13. Graphic Designs and Printing of Packaging Marketing / Promotional Materials: **Completed**

14. Recruitment of employees: **In Progress**

15. Purchase of the Needed furniture, office equipment, software applications, electronic appliances and facility facelift: **In Progress**

16. Creating Official Website for the business: **Completed**

17. Health and Safety and Fire Safety Arrangement: **In Progress**

18. Establishing business relationship with vendors and key players in various industries: **In Progress**

SECTION 5
Supporting Employer Applicant Declaration

November 29, 2017

U.S. Citizenship and Immigration Services
California Service Center
Attn: I-129 (L-1)
24000 Avila Road, 2nd Floor, Room 2312
Laguna Niguel, CA 92677

Re: ████ ████████

To Whom It May Concern:

Our company, on behalf of ███ ███, submits this letter in support of our L-1A visa petition.

Consorcio Integrador Sonora 80M S.A. de C.V., the parent company of Consorcio Integrador Sonora 80M US, LLC, was established in 2012 and is a successful solar farms development and consulting company located in Mexico City, Mexico. Including Mr. ███ Consorcio Integra███nora 80M S.A. de C.V. currently has 13 employees plus various independent contr███used for numerous projects.

███ has been employed as the Chief Executive Officer (CEO) of Consorcio Integrador Sonora 80M S.A. de C.V. since May 2012. Mr. Martin has demonstrated his abilities at Consorcio Integrador Sonora 80M S.A. de C.V. as shown by its tremendous growth and success.

Consorcio Integrador Sonora 80M S.A. de C.V. owns 100% of Consorcio Integrador Sonora 80M US, LLC and as its parent company, we are prepared to fully fund Consorcio Integrador Sonora 80M US, LLC, as necessary.

Given our success in Mexico, we expect our United States subsidiary to perform exceptionally as well. Consorcio Integrador Sonora 80M US, LLC, was established in the State of California on February 8, 2017 in an effort to establish our presence in North America. It is our intent to employ Mr. Martin as the Chief Executive Officer (CEO) of Consorcio Integrador Sonora 80M US, LLC, on a temporary basis to establish the operations of our United States subsidiary. Mr███ has been extremely valuable to Consorcio Integrador Sonora 80M S.A. de C.V. and we need him for our company to have success in the future. Without him, there is little chance of that happening.

Because of Mr. [redacted] expertise and knowledge, we have decided to offer him a position with our U.S. su[redacted] as our CEO for the yearly salary of $250,000 plus normal corporate benef[redacted]ven our success in Mexico, we are in a financial position to both remunerate Mr. [redacted] and commence doing business in the United States as soon as possible.

While focusing on our U.S. company, many of Mr. [redacted] roles and responsibilit[redacted] Mexico will be performed by Mr. Pablo Mayo Sanz [redacted]ver, the services of Mr. [redacted] in the United States will be used for a temporary period only. Once the operations of our company are fully established in the United [redacted] and the company has proven successful in the U.S. market, it is planned to have Mr. [redacted] return to our parent company in Mexico.

Based on the forgoing, we would ask for your kind consideration in approving our petition.

Sincerely,

Alfonso Avelino Cruz Suarez, Owner/Director
Consorcio Integrador Sonora 80M S.A. de C.V.

THIS PAGE IS INTENTIONALLY LEFT BLANK

www.ingramcontent.com/pod-product-compliance
Lightning Source LLC
Chambersburg PA
CBHW061354240926
51846CB00007B/1402